UNITED NATIONS JOURNAL

A Delegate's Odyssey

BY THE SAME AUTHOR

God and Man at Yale
McCarthy and His Enemies (with L. Brent Bozell)
Up from Liberalism
Rumbles Left and Right
The Unmaking of a Mayor
The Jeweler's Eye
The Governor Listeth
Cruising Speed
Inveighing We Will Go
Four Reforms

EDITOR

The Committee and Its Critics
Odyssey of a Friend: WHITTAKER CHAMBERS' LETTERS TO
WILLIAM F. BUCKLEY, JR.
Did You Ever See a Dream Walking?:
AMERICAN CONSERVATIVE THOUGHT IN THE
TWENTIETH CENTURY

CONTRIBUTOR

The Intellectual
Ocean Racing
What Is Conservatism?
Spectrum of Catholic Attitudes

William F. Buckley, Jr.

UNITED
NATIONS
JOURNAL

A Delegate's Odyssey

G. P. PUTNAM'S SONS
New York

FOR JAMES BURNHAM
With affection, gratitude, awe

Acknowledgments

As always, I am indebted to Agatha Schmidt Dowd for her help, though a little less so than before, now that I have to share her with her husband John, and her two little monsters, Christopher and John. Dino Pionzio I have acknowledged in the text of the book. James Manzi helped me hugely, and enthusiastically, with the research, and it only saddens me that I cannot give away the collection of papers he accumulated for a tax deduction. Robin Wu, of *National Review*'s research staff, was helpful and, as usual, all-knowing. Joseph Isola copyread the book with skill and devotion. And Frances Bronson, master coordinator and genial tyrant, stitched the whole together. I am grateful to my friends.

Contents

Introduction

In mid-June, on a weekday afternoon, I got word that John Scali had left word that I should telephone him. I knew Scali, though only slightly. We had traveled together—or more accurately, simultaneously—to China eighteen months earlier, I with the press corps covering Richard Nixon's trip, Scali as a special consultant to the President. He had been many years with the Associated Press, and then diplomatic reporter for ABC. Men of power are attracted to Scali. During the missile crisis, the Soviet Ambassador asked him to communicate privately with President Kennedy. This he did, and the formula he transmitted proved to be the key to the settlement. Now he and Nixon are personal friends, Nixon having asked him to quit journalism and join the White House staff. My memory of him was of a professional, of salty tongue and disposition, slightly balding with hard black hair, weather-beaten face, prominent nose, chain smoker, vigorous in manner and expression, yet with shy, and inquiring eyes. When, asked John Scali, could he and I talk? My schedule was bad, and I suggested the following week. "That's not soon enough." We settled on the next morning, breakfast at his suite; the suite of the Permanent Representative of the United States to the United Nations, to which august position Scali had been rather inconspicuously appointed soon after the Nixon landslide. The curiosity, at the time, had been provoked not so much by the arrival of John Scali as by the departure of George Bush. Bush was known as a Presidential favorite, of patrician cast, who had twice narrowly missed high elective office. When in 1970 he lost, in Texas, his race for the Senate, the President had named him to the UN, removing Charles Yost, a career diplomat whose continuation at the UN suggested less President Nixon's devotion to professionalism than his indifference to the United Nations. It isn't known what was the bargaining between Nixon and Bush, but it was felt that the designation of Bush suggested that Nixon continued to hold in some esteem the office of U.S. Representative to the UN, even if he didn't hold the UN in any great esteem. And, in any case, there were treacherous waters imminently to navigate. In a few months Nixon would be announcing his intention to travel to China. A few months after that, the annual attempt would be made by the bad guys to seat mainland China, and to eject the government-in-exile in Formosa. No doubt Nixon felt more comfortable giving instructions to Bush than to Yost, on how nicely to balance political and diplomatic considerations.

It crossed the mind fleetingly that Bush was being punished, rather belatedly in the last weeks of 1972, for having failed to achieve the desired result in the General Assembly in the fall of 1971 on the China debate. But there was a better explanation, and it was comforting to feel that Mr. Nixon's motives are sometimes altogether discernible. Bush was needed, as the clouds of Watergate began to gather, to head the Republican Party. His presence, prestige, his family connections (his father was Senator Prescott Bush of Connecticut), his genial and incorruptible air (Bush has about him something of the air of Elliot Richardson, leavened with the feeling that he is capable of pushing you into the swimming pool with your clothes on) made him greatly needed on the morale front. His replacement by John Scali, who had never run for political office, nor had training in government, nor had any personal constituency, suggested a great and urgent need either to reward John Scali, or to situate at USUN (as they call it) someone who would work most directly the will of the President.

John Scali, though he enjoys badinage and reminiscence, tends to come quickly to the point. He began by telling me, as he fingered a recent book of·mine, that the night before he had reread my dispatches from China, written when we had last seen each other, and that he thought they stood up very well. Since some of these were sulphuric in their criticism not so much of Richard Nixon's trip to China as of his behavior there, I was surprised, and of course pleased.

Now: he said, leaning back in his chair and swallowing coffee and cigarette smoke simultaneously—we're having a hell of a time over here at the UN. Do you know we have 150—*one hundred and fifty*—staff members down here? And enough generals and admirals to run the War Department? You know why? Because after the war they thought, those dumb bastards, that the UN would be the center of the disarmament talks, so they detailed a lot of military brass here, and they've been here ever since. You know, a few days after I got in here, one of the Ambassadors came to me complaining that the United Nations doesn't get any attention in the American press. I said to him: Jean, my boy, let me tell you something. I've been a journalist all my life, and I can tell you this: If I was the editor of a New York paper, I'd give the UN *exactly* as much space as it's currently getting. *Exactly* . . . Scali pauses, like Fulton Sheen, to let you enjoy, or meditate on, the operative word.

Then he told me that the UN was not very newsworthy, and not very important, but that it could be made more important, and more important to the United States and the West, and that people who had given up on it shouldn't give up on it, they should learn something more about it, and its uses—its strengths as well as its weaknesses. Meanwhile, he said, it needs a higher public visibility. Would I, he said suddenly, accept an appointment as a delegate to the 28th General Assembly? What he had in mind for me, he elaborated, was to be U.S. Representative on the Human Rights Committee. "You'd occupy the same chair Eleanor Roosevelt occupied," he smiled, "and Daniel Patrick Moynihan, two years ago."

I replied that I could not imagine a more improbable designation than me to the United Nations. Had he, I asked, read what I had written in the past about the United Nations? He waved his arm as if to say that that kind of thing simply doesn't matter—please don't bring it up.

What would I *do?* I asked. I would represent the United States on issues touching on human rights, at the Third Committee, which is what they call the committee that deals with human rights; and, as necessary, at the Plenary (which is what they call the General Assembly), and handle such other matters as were assigned to me, and were acceptable to me. How often would I need to be there? Well, he said, as often as you can, but we recognize that some people's schedules are more inflexible than others'. Pat Moynihan, he said, insisted that he had to continue to meet with his two seminars in Cambridge two days a week, so he came to New York only three days a week, during the three-month period between mid-September and mid-December that the Assembly meets. What about my twenty-five out-of-town lectures? I should cancel those I could, deliver those I could not. Any implicit inhibitions on anything I write in my syndicated column, or say on television? None—except that I must not give away state secrets. What is the composition of the United States delegation? It follows a pattern: The Permanent Representative is of course the head of the mission, except on such occasions as the Secretary of State is physically present. Then there are a couple of Ambassadors, subordinates of the Permanent Representative, who are attached to the permanent mission. Then there are two legislators, one, by tradition, Republican, the other Democratic. Then there is a public delegate—that would be me. Then there are five alternate delegates. He told me whom he had in mind.

I asked, (a) Have you cleared this with Nixon? and (b) What makes you so sure I could get confirmed by the Fulbright Committee? Well, he had not cleared it with "the old man," but he had cleared it with General Haig, who was "terribly enthusiastic." As regards the Fulbright Committee, hadn't the identical committee cleared me when I accepted a Presidential appointment in 1969 to serve on the United States Advisory Commission on Information? Yes, I said, but since then I have said a lot of unpleasant things about Senator Fulbright. True, said Scali, but since then you've also gotten yourself a brother elected to the Senate of the United States. Don't worry about Fulbright, he said.

Throughout the conversation I was privately resolved to turn the appointment down. I had pursued my questions both because I was curious about the answers he would give, and because I thought that courtesy required one not to laugh, stand up, and depart the room. I have always wondered at the general acceptance of the notion that that is the proper behavior when something preposterous is suggested to you. Senator Weicker was at just about that time publicly expressing his astonishment, across the committee table from John Mitchell, that Mitchell had not, upon being shown by Gordon Liddy his internal security program, kicked Liddy out of his office, the government, and the Attorney General's life. Things aren't done that way. If I were asked, civilly, by a civil man, would I take on the Directorship of the Gulag Archipelago, I would ask one or two questions, smile and say I'll sure think about it, leave quietly, and only then formulate my response, and my retaliation.

In the fifteen blocks between the Waldorf-Astoria and my office I changed my mind, and I do not think I concealed the reasoning even from myself. It was, I think, the only experience I ever had in pure, undiluted Walter Mittyism. I saw myself there, in the center of the great assembly at the UN (which I had never visited in my twenty years in New York), holding the delegates spellbound as I read to them from Solzhenitsyn, as I described the latest account of concentration camps in Mainland China, as I pleaded the case of the ballet dancer Panov. I would cajole, wheedle, parry, thrust, mesmerize, dismay, seduce, intimidate. The press of the world would rivet its attention on the case the

American delegate was making for human rights, repristinating the jaded vision of the international bureaucrats. It was a grand thought, and as I confided it to two or three of my colleagues, they caught my enthusiasm. After all, one of them—highly experienced in world affairs—pointed out, unless it's going to be in order to do that kind of thing, why would they want you? And if *you* say it, it's not the government saying it, because you are from private life. There was one possible explanation for it all, someone else suggested. "Nixon may want to make a public gesture, at about this time, to someone publicly identified with the right wing." Though I told them that Nixon had not yet been advised about the appointment, we agreed that that might be only the official version. Scali, after all, was close to Nixon, and neither of them had illusions about my feelings about détente. But, probing the hypothesis, we agreed that if Nixon desired to confer some sort of special recognition on a member of the right wing, it would hardly be an appointment to the United Nations. Such an appointment, widely publicized, would rather raise doubts about my discretion among American conservatives than inspire confidence in Nixon. (Irving Kupcinet would comment in the Chicago *Sun-Times*: "Is the President adopting a 'kill 'em with kindness' philosophy? He nominated one of his severest critics, William F. Buckley, Jr., to serve in the UN delegation under Ambassador John Scali. But then Buckley also has harsh words for the UN. . . .") No, it had to be that the man in command of the situation—Nixon himself; or Rogers, with Nixon's consent; or Scali, with Nixon's consent—had set out to redefine America's relationship to the United Nations. There was no other plausible explanation for making me a part of the enterprise, even for so short a period. I called Scali and said yes.

The summer wore on, and though the custom is for the President to announce his nominations at the end of July, nothing happened. This was Watergate Summer, and the

Executive Department was not functioning at peak efficiency. This was not true of the Federal Bureau of Investigation, whose agents telephoned everyone I knew, or had known: including the publisher of *National Review,* my day-to-day colleague, Mr. William Rusher. "But," he said wearily over the telephone to the agent, "you put Mr. Buckley through all of this in 1969, do we have to do it all over again?" "Yes sir. We need to know: Has Mr. Buckley done anything since 1969 that might embarrass the Nixon Administraion?" "No," Rusher mused. "But since 1969 the Nixon Administration has done a great deal that has embarrassed Mr. Buckley." The delegation, now formed, stood by.

1.

Washington Briefing

Ambassador Tapley Bennett of USUN telephoned to say that the delegates would need to spend the entire day on Friday at the State Department, to be briefed, in advance of the session which would begin the following Tuesday. I reminded him that our designation had been announced only that day, and would not be acted on by the Senate (or so I had been told) until after Friday. That apparently doesn't matter, though in such situations they keep these things quiet. If necessary, you are—pending your confirmation by the Senate—made a "consultant." There is a mysterious machine in Washington that causes things to get done just in time, like lifting the level of the national debt so as to be able to write out paychecks for civil servants. The only time this kind of thing doesn't work is if there is a targeted enemy. At a conspicuous level, a Carswell or a Haynsworth, with a big fight scheduled on the floor of the Senate. At a less conspicuous level, a Robert Strausz-Hupé appointed Ambassador to Morocco. Senator Fulbright dislikes him concentratedly, and just sits and sits and sits, and finally after many months a deal is worked out and the White House agrees to send him to Ceylon instead. Senator Fulbright has announced that he does not intend to schedule a hearing over the public delegates, and it is assumed therefore that we will be approved en masse. I sense a slight relief—the diplomat's relief—in John Scali's voice when he tells me this, coupled with just a trace of disappointment—the journalist's disap-

17

pointment—that it is not in store for him to witness an exchange between Senator Fulbright and myself. I told him that if a hearing were scheduled, I was quite prepared for it, having practiced docility the whole summer long. . . . It gave me high pleasure to reflect that, as a matter of courtesy, Senator Weicker would need to be present while I was being interrogated. This is the custom—a Senator from your home state, if possible the one who belongs to your own political party, is supposed to be physically present when the hearing begins. Polite committee chairmen customarily invite their visiting colleague to sit alongside the committee members. It is assumed that the regular members will feel inhibited in grilling someone in the presence of their colleague. I expect Senator Weicker, whom I had just made sport of in a column, would not have exerted himself to still Fulbright. But then there would also have been the benign presence of Senator Buckley, before whose phlegmatic charm razors are blunt, and arrows detumesce.

But indeed, Senator Fulbright a day or two later routinely passed the names along, and the Senate confirmed them. There was rather more attention given that day, than to our confirmation, to the confirmation of Mr. Henry Kissinger as Secretary of State. He, and we, would debut at the opening session of the General Assembly. He would speak, we would listen.

My official entry into the State Department was a little inglorious. I had flown in from New York, and composed my column on the airplane, telephoning it in from the airport: which meant I was saddled with my portable typewriter for the balance of the day. The taxi driver asked me which entrance to the State Department I desired. Apparently there are several. I asked for the closest, which turned out to be the most infra dig entrance, I discovered—the one the schoolchildren pass through to gawk. I gave my name to the guard, who asked me to spell it. He telephoned to the designated office, and much later a young lady appeared, having traveled the long diagonal length of the building.

Before letting me pass into her company, the guard told me that I should report forthwith to Room Such-and-such. There, he explained, they would give me a tag which I must affix to my typewriter. Otherwise, he explained, the guards would not permit me to leave the building with my typewriter, which would be wrested from me, as presumptive property of the State Department. I had read recently that the entire inventory of the cafeteria of the Pentagon needed replenishing every three and one half months, or whatever, and presumably now they were clamping down. It was never established, at the aborted trial in Los Angeles, whether the Pentagon's secrets are its, or the New York *Times's*. But the government's typewriters are indisputably its own, and the burden of proof is accordingly on the delegate—to prove that the typewriter is not stolen. (As postscript, the typewriter was in fact not tagged when I left, though to be sure I went out through the chic entrance, where I take it the burden of proof inexplicitly shifts in one's favor.)

The presiding officer was Mr. David Popper, who is Assistant Secretary of State in charge of International Organization Affairs. Portraits of his predecessors line the large conference room where soon we would begin our indoctrination, the five delegates, five alternate delegates and a staff of about ten or twelve others. I looked down the gallery and asked Mr. Popper where was the portrait of Alger Hiss? The post, he said—courtly and amused—had changed, since the days of Alger Hiss. He introduced me to my colleagues, most of whom I had never met. W. Tapley Bennett, Jr., was second-in-command after Scali. A tall Georgian, professional, spare but genial in manner, hugely courteous, who had served as Ambassador to the Dominican Republic and was there when Lyndon Johnson sent in the Marines in 1965—not, one gradually supposes on coming to know Tap Bennett, with the disapproval of his Ambassador. After that he had gone to Portugal as Ambassador until, in 1969, he was sent to the UN which he had had a taste of as a young man at the founding conference in San Francisco.

Next on the list, as it appeared in the printed brochure we were handed, was "The Honorable Robert N. C. Nix, United States House of Representatives." Mr. Nix, a portly black lawyer from Pennsylvania who was elected to Congress fourteen years ago, was to have the briefest exposure to the United Nations of any delegate, perhaps in history. On the opening day of the General Assembly, before his turn came to go to the rostrum to speak, Henry Kissinger occupied the principal seat at the UNITED STATES OF AMERICA desk. Now these desks run unbrokenly from aisle to aisle, so that the desk of the United States of America merges imperceptibly into the desk of the UNITED REPUBLIC OF TANZANIA (delegations are always seated alphabetically). There is room for only three chairs at desk level per country; and three seats directly behind, where senior staff members normally sit, whence to advise the delegates. At the second of the front chairs, Representative Nix sat down. There was an hour or so to kill before Kissinger's speech. Scheduled ahead of Kissinger was the Ambassador from Brazil. Before his speech, there was a lot of chitchat and a dozen photographers garlanding the brand-new Secretary of State. During the course of the hour and one half that Representative Nix sat cheek by jowl with Mr. Kissinger, Mr. Kissinger exchanged with him not one word, taking him—one supposes—to be the delegate of the United Republic of Tanzania, and suspecting—one gathers—that he spoke only Swahili. This experience of the United Nations by a senior black Representative in Congress was apparently conclusive. Congressman Nix joined us all at lunch later in the day, and then departed for his office in Washington, and was never seen again.

The next delegate listed was "The Honorable John H. Buchanan, Jr., United States House of Representatives." Buchanan, in his mid-forties, is a Southern Republican, in size and looks very much like a younger Muskie. He was ordained a Baptist minister before going into politics and

was a practicing pastor until his election to the House of
Representatives in 1964, and is quickly seen as a man of
diffident charm and rigorous mind.

The list of alternate delegates (there was, by the way, no
distinction drawn, other than in the official roster, between
"delegates" and "alternate delegates") began with Mrs.
Margaret Young. She is the widow of Whitney Young, the
Negro civil rights leader who died of a heart attack
swimming off Lagos in 1971. She is a woman of gentle
manner and speech, who has written several books on
prominent American blacks, and for the first time since her
husband's death was now resuming an active public role.
Halfway through the session she withdrew for reasons of
health, having meanwhile made several statements on the
general subject of minority rights.

Mark Evans, like Scali, is a personal friend of the
President. He is a Mormon, who conducted for many years a
radio and then a television program in Washington, and
went on to become public affairs director for Metromedia,
Inc., and also its vice-president. He looks like a middle-aged
Ingemar Johannson, is friendly, humorous, gloriously
conservative in his political convictions, and a fine orator
who won the National Oratorical Award in 1940. He is
determined to give his full attention to the UN job, has
suspended all his duties in Washington, and moved with his
wife to a suite in a New York hotel for the duration.

Richard Scammon is the Director of Elections Research
Center, a friend of Scali, vastly respected by the professional
psephologists, author (with Ben Wattenberg) of *The Real
Majority,* which was vaguely reassuring to Democrats coming
soon after Kevin Phillips' *The Emerging Republican Majority,*
which came along a few years before Watergate. Scammon is
built like Sidney Greenstreet, occupies most of any elevator,
is cheerful, sardonic, and terribly busy. His duties in
Washington kept him away from New York much of the
time.

William Schaufele has the rank of Ambassador, and is

permanently detailed, like Scali and Bennett, to the UN. He is a Yale graduate, a Midwesterner of German build and manner, a tough political analyst, who has served the State Department all over the world. In 1969 he was sent to Ouagadougou as our Ambassador to Upper Volta. There is no better training for the United Nations.

And, rounding off the list, Clarence Clyde Ferguson, Jr. He too is of Ambassadorial rank, having served as Ambassador in Uganda. He is a light-skinned Negro with a quick smile, great savoir faire, and though not yet fifty, enormously experienced. He was Dean of the School of Law at Howard University, and Professor of Law at Rutgers University before coming into the Kennedy Administration as General Counsel to the United States Commission on Civil Rights. He appeared to be in effective charge of policy in our dealings with the UN's critical Economic and Social Council, which in these parts they call ECOSOC.

David Popper told us that the United Nations is not nowadays held in very high repute in America, and he cited the three long critical articles that had appeared in the New York *Times* to coincide with the forthcoming General Assembly. I would learn that it is not possible, inside the UN, to refer to its shortcomings without going on to say: "however." . . . However, said Popper, we would soon discover the very considerable uses of the United Nations, concerning which he and the other members of the staff who would be addressing us that morning and afternoon, could not hope to do more than give us the lightest rundown. We had been given great packets of material. One brochure describing the United States Mission to the UN says coolly: "Virtually everything important that happens anywhere in the international scene is of concern both to the United States and to the United Nations." Verily is it so, said Popper. He then told us how very important was the role of the delegates to the General Assembly. Sure, most of us have had no diplomatic experience, but we would learn quickly. And, most important, the government would learn from *us!* He could not stress sufficiently how important and useful to the State

Department and to USUN were our views, which would be meticulously consulted. Besides, he said—no doubt duplicating the same expansive gesture made to the twenty-seven previous delegations by all the gentlemen whose portraits hung on the wall—"this delegation is surely the strongest we have ever had." I told Scammon later that I refused to believe he would prove to be a stronger delegate than Shirley Temple. It proved to be a typical male-chauvinist remark, because Miss Temple, who was a delegate two or three years ago, had scored very high in the esteem of the professionals.

We were reminded that the United States has a very special role in the UN. We are, for one thing, the most powerful nation in the world; the UN was pretty much formed at our instigation, for another. But most conspicuously, we are the host nation. Accordingly, we had to be especially attentive in many capacities. As regards our own, one of us had to be sitting at the U.S. desk *at all times. At no time* must that desk be empty, and if the speaker is a chief of state, or a Foreign Secretary, Scali himself would attempt to occupy the desk.

Now that meant from 10:30 A.M., with a break for lunch, on to 6, 7, or 8 P.M. It is perfectly all right to read while you are at the desk and, Scali told us, he sometimes even dictates quietly to his secretary, sitting behind him. You keep on your earphone, which suggests that you are listening to the speaker. But of course you can have the earpiece on upside down, and nobody is the wiser. There will be an aide actually listening to the speech to alert us in case the speaker should say something riveting; or in case he should insult the United States, in which event the delegate can ask for a Right of Reply. This must be granted, according to the rules. I was to learn that it is only in the course of exercising a Right of Reply that anything like extemporaneous commentary can issue from an American mouth.

Above all, we were warned, we must guard against falling asleep. Because, although there is very little publicity given to the United Nations, there are in fact a couple of on-duty television cameras embedded behind the cornices, the lenses roaming the floor of the Assembly in search of photogenic copy. It is thanks to these that we all got to see Khrushchev pounding his desk with his shoe a dozen years ago; and, this year, a few sentences from Kissinger's speech, and a near-brawl between the Cuban and Chilean representatives as they fought for the podium. But, as a rule, there is so little meat for these forlorn cameras they can be counted on unerringly to catch a United States delegate snoozing. So *don't snooze,* we are told, diplomatically. I whiled away my first hours at the chair reading the day's cables. Reading the cables is a terrible strain. Although they can be extraordinarily prolix, somewhere along the line the tradition developed that abbreviations should always be preferred where possible, and that the use of definite and indefinite articles is a form of conspicuous consumption. Thus you will be reading along and you will bump into AMPOLAD. I submit there is no reasonable man who can, from the internal evidence, deduce what the acronym stands for. It stands for—you discover on consulting a nineteen-page Glossary of Abbreviations—"American Political Adviser." Some people get used to it, I suppose. ASAP you finally accept instinctively as "as soon as possible." Some of them you would decline to memorize if it were your profession to to do so, e.g., BIRPI, which means United International Bureaux for the Protection of Intellectual Property—which itself means something I never discovered. In such a category is also, e.g., CAFRAD, for African Training and Research Center in Administration for Development. Some acronyms derive clearly from a language other than English—e.g., CERN for European Organization for Nuclear Research—but there is of course never any indication when this is about to happen. Some are used so infrequently as to cause one to wonder why they do not indulge in the use of the whole instead of the abbreviation; for instance, DLCOEA (Desert Locust Control Operations in East Africa). And every now and then you do have to use your native intelligence, as for instance when deciding whether IWC refers to the International Wheat Council, or to the

International Whaling Commission. It would seem to me an obvious improvement to use, as the lawyers do, the full title at the beginning of a telegram, then the useful and wholly literate: "hereinafter. . . ." As, The International Union for the Conservation of Nature and Natural Resources, hereinafter the IUCN. Very important, though, to retain the *the,* which is indispensable to the flow of the message. It is by the way incorrect to suppose that, as for plain citizens, every extra word costs the government more money. The wires are generally leased out on a full-time basis. And where there is a tiny cost for the incremental word, it might reasonably be offset by the reduced time and vexation at the other end of the part of the decipherer. Of course, it is possible that after half a lifetime, you get to read the stuff fluently. When that happens, more often than not, you get so you speak that way.

Soon after I began reading the cables at the General Assembly I saw one of our staff Ambassadors, spotting the telltale pink of my papers, turn pale with shock. The next day, at the weekly staff meeting attended by about fifty or sixty people, Ambassador Schaufele, looking neither to right nor to left, pronounced that *under no circumstances* were any of the cables, many of which contained highly classified material, to leave the building, within which security was airtight, and all the shelves have great big Security Labels, and there were guards posted at every floor.

We were told that at least one delegate was expected to be present at all diplomatic functions, and that a lady at USUN would coordinate these and, if necessary, would call and press one of us into service. Adlai Stevenson had told me ten years ago with great pathos that he found he had to go to an average of *three* per night during the Assembly. He was (a) top U.S. dog, at a time when (b) the top U.S. dog was also the top UN dog; and (c) a celebrity in his own right. It isn't quite as bad now, but by and large when a foreign country gives a reception, and the American isn't there, it feels slighted. A little less so now than before, I gather, which is why we could occasionally relieve Scali; but still, enough to justify our making it a point. And after all, there were nine of us not counting Scali, so the social burden would not prove too heinous. We could, moreover, call for a car and driver from the USUN pool to take us to any official function. And when we were acting as hosts, we could be reimbursed, up to a total figure of $200 over the course of the ninety-day session, for entertainment of foreigners. They call that "representation," as in the expression, "Representative Rooney is a skinflint where representation allowances are concerned." As delegates, we would be paid at the top permitted civil servant rate for every day we worked: $132, it comes to. If you worked every day, at that rate, you would earn a little over $38,000 per year, which is just under a Congressional salary, which is why that is the top salary.

We were soon done with the parietals and other housekeeping chores, and were reminded that the "astringent" criticism of the New York *Times* paid scant attention to the unpublicized worker of the UN—"the quieter side of the UN" was how Popper put it. Committees that deal with the environment, with national boundaries, meteorology, floods, agriculture, that kind of thing. We would not be seeing much of that in the hecticness of the General Assembly, but we would become gradually aware of these activities as we began to work our way through the huge agenda; and, in the individual committees, to come up against items proposed by these committees for action by the Plenary. Meanwhile, of course, there were some great political issues brewing, some of them of primary concern to the Security Council, where of course we have the veto power; others of concern to the General Assembly, where the session would begin, with 135 countries, 85 more than when the UN was founded: 75 of them Third World countries, which the United States no longer dominates. It used to be, Popper said, that the UN reflected cold war divisions, which were mostly East-West. But now—since about 1960—it has become rather a forum for North-South encounters. In those days the big issues were the Soviet Union and its myriad activities. Now the big subjects are colonialism, sovereignty over natural resources, and the evolution of the doctrine that the have-not nations, "as a matter of right," are entitled to economic help from the have-nations.

At a more concrete level, yesterday there had been a border incident, on the Syrian-Israeli line. Probably the matter would be brought up before the Security Council. A few days earlier there had been the coup against Allende, and Cuba, one of whose mischievous boats got mussed up, was threatening to raise the issue in some way. Popper advised me that the day before, at a meeting of the special Committee on Decolonization, Acosta, the Cuban representative, had referred to my appointment as delegate. With characteristic Communist flair for accuracy, he had spoken of "Senator William Buckley, one of the most reactionary and conservative legislators of the United States. . . ."

Joseph Sisco, Assistant Secretary for Mideast Affairs, was brought in to brief us on the Middle East. I regret to report that he was apparently unaware that a few weeks later there would be a major war in the Middle East, but then of course General Dayan, if it had been he speaking to us, would not have made that prediction either. Sisco told us that U.S. policy continued to be to stick with the Jarring Resolution of November 1967, which called for the return to the prewar frontiers of 1967. The endless wrangling over the super-exact meaing of the two or three critical phrases in that resolution, he said, reflected not a bit on any sloppiness in diplomatic craft. Rather it was a "constructive" ambiguity. He meant the sentence which the Israelis interpreted as calling for a return to the prewar boundaries after a political settlement, and which the Arabs interpreted as calling for a return before political negotiations began. Of course, a war, and the oil diplomacy, would soon change all.

Richard Sneider, concerned with East Asian and Pacific Affairs, followed. He told us that at the Non-Aligned Conference just concluded in Algeria, which had sponsored the usual declarations of the Third World, it had been resolved to ask the United Nations General Assembly to dissolve the United Nations Military Command, set up in 1950 when the North Koreans began their invasion. He explained why the United States is taking this move so seriously. What we have in the way of peace in Korea, he said, issues from an armistice agreement which whatever its shortcomings, has in fact succeeded over a period of twenty years in guarding a boundary that is accepted by North and South Koreans. Now if the commission were suddenly dissolved, there would be no official presence there which had been a party to the twenty-year-old armistice. This sudden disequilibrium could result in North Korea's renewing its aggression against South Korea, clinging to the line that it is after all One Country, and that the division between the so-called two Koreas is purely a matter of local concern, and none of the business of any foreign power, or of the United Nations. In the post-Vietnam climate, it would be very hard to do anything about a sudden return to Northern aggression. As things now stand, he said, the United States has 40,000 troops in South Korea, pursuant to a bilateral commitment with the UN, and no intentions of withdrawing them; under the circumstances, we must win that vote, or else run the risk of retroactively illegitimizing the entire UN venture in Korea. We have been trying, he said, to get some of the Communist states to recognize the sovereignty of South Korea, but so far we haven't succeeded. Meanwhile, we do have a hot line established between North and South, and both countries are sending observers to the United Nations. Moreover, neither Russia nor China has yet given any explicit support to the Algerian resolution. The last head count suggested we would win on the floor of the UN by a half dozen votes. But that is pretty hairy, and we must all work very hard on the subject.

On the African front, we were informed that there are three African preoccupations. The first is to complete decolonization. The second to end racial discrimination in South Africa. And the third, to get help for the poor states.

There would be any number of resolutions aimed in the specific direction of South Africa, and at Angola and Mozambique. There was a real possibility that the rebels in Portuguese Guinea would be recognized as sovereign, over the objections of Portugal; and even that a revolutionary government might be recognized as the rightful government of Angola. If this should happen, we were warned, chaos would ensue. Always the UN, if it recognizes a country at all, recognizes the de facto government. We, of course, take the orthodox position that Angola and Mozambique are provinces of Portugal, but we do not go out of our way to advertise this position.

Our biggest headache in Africa at this point, it was explained, is Rhodesia. What happened is that over a period of three sessions beginning just after Rhodesia broke away from Britain, the Security Council voted sanctions against Rhodesia. (This was done—I interpolate—over the most strenuous objections of such international lawyers and diplomats as Dean Acheson, who saw no justification in the Charter for voting these sanctions against a government that declared itself sovereign, and indeed exercised sovereign power.)

Having done so, we walked into one of those paradoxes of which the United Nations is surely the most fecund progenitor in history. The United States government found itself, in order to observe the sanction, buying chrome at a far higher price than Rhodesia sold it at—from the Soviet Union. Those who tried to coexist with the paradox pointed out that, after all, the UN was voting sanctions against Rhodesia, not against the Soviet Union, and the fact that there is no barbarity being committed within Rhodesia that isn't performed regularly in the Soviet Union on a Wagnerian scale has, well, nothing to do with it. But the majority of the Congress were crushed by the paradox, and simply voted a law, directing the government to purchase its chrome on the market at the lowest available price. This is the so-called Byrd Amendment.

The Byrd Amendment, we were told, has got us into most fearful problems with the UN. For one thing, it has made us unfaithful to the ideal of corporate action—an organizational transgression. For another, it has infuriated the black republics. John Scali told us that he had tried vainly to say to

Ambassadors from the African states that since only about 5 percent of Rhodesia's trade is taken by the United States, therefore the United States should take only "5 percent of the blame." But these nice, linear calculations do not work within the United Nations, a point to bear in mind; so Scali had just come from Congress where he begged it to repeal the Byrd Amendment. This he was able to do with some force by pointing out that suddenly the United States has found itself so glutted with chrome the Defense Department was actually selling some off. So that repealing the Byrd Amendment would not in fact result in our having to buy chrome from the Soviet Union. Senator McGee, Scali pointed out, is leading the fight in the Senate for repeal. And Senator McGee, he pointed out further, was a delegate to the 26th General Assembly. So it goes to show that involvement in UN affairs is something that affects your attitude toward the UN beyond the day when your commissions would expire. I see John Scali's point with greater clarity at this remove, as I write, even if I am not engaged in trying to repeal the Byrd Amendment. By the way, it *was* repealed, by the Senate, toward the end of the UN session. Until then, John Scali could only apologize for it, and explain, as he had to do day after day to the Russians in defense of the Jackson Amendment prohibiting Most Favored Nation Treatment for countries that interfered with the emigration of minorities, that the President does not control the Congress.

On South Africa, Scali reiterated the U.S. position. (1) We wholeheartedly oppose apartheid. (2) We have an arms embargo against South Africa. (3) We don't encourage American investment in South Africa—for instance we don't guarantee that investment as we do elsewhere, under certain conditions; but (4) neither do we forbid it. We cannot vote for sanctions against South Africa because we do not take the position that South Africa is a threat to world peace, and only in such circumstances can one properly invoke Chapter 7, never mind how come we vaulted these problems in voting against Rhodesia; and on the question of South-West Africa, we (5) side with the World Court in maintaining that the continued domination of South-West Africa is illegal. We would learn, in due course, about a shrewdly contrived plan to isolate South Africa by human rights machinations.

Coming up this year would be action against terrorists. The objective, as announced a year ago, is to discourage terrorism by getting every country to agree to return terrorists to the country whence they came, there to be punished. For a while, this idea apparently struck everyone at the UN as absolutely first-rate. For one thing, diplomats are far more often the targets of terrorism than, say, Israeli athletes. But at this point, the more militant Arab states, we were told, began lobbying among the Africans, hinting that the proposed antiterrorist resolutions would quash the liberation movements. . . .

The causes of everything bad, as seen in the United Nations, are (1) colonialism, (2) imperialism, (3) racial discrimination, and (4) economic inequality. So it was accepted that unless the resolution was quickly consummated, it would dissolve into a routine excoriation of Israel, Portugal, South Africa, and capitalism. At least we can hope to get out of it all something committing sanctions against people who shoot diplomats. It was assumed that that would meet with favor at the UN, as a sort of Diplomats' Protection Association.

We broke for lunch. I was seated next to Margaret Young. I reminisced about when last we met. It was at a dinner before the beginning of a remarkable tour. Her husband had organized a dozen journalists to take a trip through the black ghettos of the United States. I told her that a week after the trip began, at a function in Mississippi, a Southern matron I had known years ago when she roomed at Vassar with my wife, said to me, in her deeply accented voice, "Bill, dear, I tried to get you everywhere on the telephone two nights ago. Where were you?"

"I was at a brothel in San Francisco," I said—and before I could explain, someone interrupted us, and I never did get to see my old friend again. Mrs. Young looked mildly uncomfortable, and I rushed to remind her that Mr. Young had specified that we should all stay, at night, in black homes, or black-run motels, and that we had spent the night in question (chastely) at a motel in San Francisco which was primarily used as a brothel. She smiled, a little wanly; and I reflected that I haven't had much experience in diplomatic humor. I must ask Scali. . . .

Curtis Tarr, former president of Lawrence University, now with the State Department, served as our host. He gave us, after lunch, a soft-spoken talk about the great resources of the State Department, and how we were quite free to draw on them. Another official gave us a rundown on social and economic questions, pointing out that we were on the verge of getting an agreement to reduce to a flat 25 percent our share of the UN's bills, and that this will please Congress. Since its founding, we have sent over $10 billion to the UN, over half of this figure in voluntary contributions. Annually, our assessment is about $250 million. He pointed out some anomalies here and there, for instance the exclusion from ECOSOC of Israel in the Middle East—"a blatant violation of the UN Charter"; but we don't have the votes to take the issue before the International Court of Justice. We were told yet again that most countries are concerned with economic growth, not with peacekeeping, or the cold war, or whatever. And on the general subject of UN debate—"It is easy to grow tired of it because there is so much rhetoric tossed about." Little did we know; little does anyone know; it is not something one can describe, though one must try, and I shall; it must be experienced; you are never the same again; have you noticed that slightly distraught look when Shirley Temple smiles at you?

Upstairs, to meet the Under Secretary. Henry Kissinger has not quite yet been confirmed, and accordingly he continues to occupy his old desk in the White House, his office at State grandly vacant. Right across the hall is the Under Secretary, Kenneth Rush, in a splendid office full of flags and globes and big armchairs. He is Southern, a career man, informed to the fingertips.

Anything new on Chile? someone asks, and he informs us that, on landing in Mexico this morning, the widow Allende had changed her story. First she had said that her husband did indeed take his own life. Now she is saying that he was mowed down by the conquering fascists. Which version is correct? I ventured to ask. The first, he replied, as matter-of-factly as a professor indicating which was the correct answer on the paper, True or False. Moreover, he added, Allende had been boozing that morning. (Not a bad morning to drink, come to think of it.) Would there be any question about recognition? No, he said: the United States recognizes countries, not governments. We are taking the line that we still recognize Chile, and it is utterly an internal matter who is exercising authority in Chile. I reflected that that wasn't exactly the way we used to look at it in the good old days when President Kennedy was trying to democratize Latin America and, on one occasion, denied Peru an Ambassador for months because he didn't like the fresh set of colonels. Better this way, on the whole; though I was amused that Rush has a way of saying things as though it had *always* been so. ("Yes, sir," the lord mayor puffs on his pipe while applying his quill pen to paper, "in Salem we *always* burn our witches.") In the diplomatic world you don't get excited; it is part of the style. Scali gets excited. On the whole, getting excited is more exciting, though one mustn't get excited at what one hears in the UN, but for this you have to train.

The leavetaking was as inglorious as the arrival. It was raining and there were no taxis. Never mind, the State Department would provide a car. . . . Sorry, no cars; they're all out. The hell with it, I called a limousine service, and escorted Margaret Young to the airport, and we went back to New York.

2.

The First Day

I arrived early at my office. The receptionist at the lobby of the first floor is called Imogene, and she has been with the UN since Lake Success, and is beloved of everyone. Next to her is a Marine guard who, on receipt of a signal from Imogene not discernible to others, knows whether to salute when you enter. Ambassadors and delegates are saluted. Imogene, having memorized which floor your office is on, rushes to pre-push the button on the elevator, to spare you the trouble. She takes a shine right away to Rowley, my Cavalier King Charles spaniel, but then everyone does. They moon at each other for a while, and I go up. Dino Pionzio, who is already installed, introduces me to my secretary next door.

Dino is a blessing that hit me at Yale in my junior year. He is wearing beard and whiskers again, having briefly shaved them off last summer when we met and I asked him, in the flush of my excitement, to give me a hand. He had just finished winding up a career in government, had spent time with the CIA, and was headed now for a new career, in banking, in England. He speaks French, Spanish, and Italian, was at the top of our class at Yale, is infinitely engaging, utterly volatile in his emotions, but shrewd and purposeful in his handling of diplomats and bureaucrats, with whom he has mingled lo these many years. In him continues to shine that light which brought me here: the conviction that it is the unfortunate historical duty of the

34

United States to do something about the bad guys. Scali had told me I could have an aide, whom I would certainly require to keep track of things. It was agreed that if I would remunerate my own aide, I could go ahead and select him from outside the UN staff. I knew no one on the UN staff at that point, and in any case would have selected Pionzio even if Henry Kissinger had offered to be my aide.

A few days later, a senior staff member raised a point. Since Pionzio was known to have worked at one time for the CIA (for that matter, so did I for a few months after leaving college), not improbably one of the Communist delegates, most likely the vituperative Cuban, would denounce him as a CIA agent, and me as his puppet. I found the prospect more amusing than my superiors did, since I have always supposed that when the CIA wonders what it should order its agents to say, it picks up the latest issue of *National Review* to find out. Anyway, to make our liaison just a little less obvious when, crossing the street, we entered the UN, it was agreed that Pionzio, who usually sat at the visitors' gallery (there is not enough room for all staff members behind the delegates' chairs), would leave the chamber not with me, but a moment or two later, as if our movements were not concerted.

When this was proposed I thought it obvious that the little deception would merely draw attention to the dissimulation, should it indeed be the case that anyone was watching. Moreover, since the CIA and the State Department are known to be branches of the Executive, and since the rivalry between them is not of the kind that would get itself expressed through someone like me, whom (so the fantasy would require) the CIA gulled the State Department into appointing as a delegate for the purpose. . . . For the purpose of what? But I began to understand that Form becomes Substance, at the UN; and *to seek not to give offense* is *not to give offense*. So who knows, perhaps the little gesture defused the Castroites. And after all, the Bay of Pigs, which is the other approach, hadn't worked. And the days passed, and no one denounced Dino.

Dino gave me an urgent message. I should go instantly to the twelfth floor of our own building. There Ambassador Scali was engaging in a mini-debate with Soviet Ambassador Yakov Malik. I shot up the elevator, and there in the huge meeting room where the full staff of USUN met on Tuesday mornings, where an occasional cocktail party was given, where Henry Kissinger's two forthcoming lunches for the Arabs and the Africans would be given, was John Scali, halfway up the right leg of the U-shaped conference table, with a translator and two aides skirting him; and, opposite, Ambassador Malik, also with three in his company. Standing, by the head of the table, silent, were two or three Americans and Russians, listening to the exchange.

One wishes one could say about Malik that he is the last of the Stalinists, as one wishes one might say, looking up at a falling tree, that it was the last to suffer from the Dutch elm disease. Malik was very much around under Stalin, and like Gromyko—who won the closely disputed contest to succeed Molotov as Foreign Minister—is the kind of person Stalin had no trouble getting along with, else of course he'd be dead. He is about sixty-five, blondish hair and complexion, rawboned, not unlike the clean-shaven Russian soldier one saw in the posters, stepping across the Elbe to greet GI Joe, thirty years later. He has a deeply cultivated propensity for lying, and doesn't mind in the least doing it even in situations where he is sure to be caught in the act. A month later, at the height of the tension over the cease-fire and the composition of the United Nations Emergency Force that would monitor it, Malik finally agreed, phrase by phrase, to the text of the joint statement Russia and the United States would agree to. This was after hours of wrangling, day and night, and next door the Security Council was waiting patiently for the two critical negotiators to come out of one of the little anterooms, where the critical decisions are made. His approval having been given, a few moments later he was given the text to initial. To everyone's dismay he raised his hand, pointing to one provision, and said: *That is not satisfactory.* But you already approved of it, Scali exploded. "I have received fresh instructions," Malik replied. *From whom?* Scali shouted, not a body having entered or left the room in the past hour. "I have received fresh instructions," was all Malik would repeat. It happened that the proposed change was somewhere between meaningless and a slight improvement in the United States position, rendering the tergiversation inexplicable, and the exercise pointless. But such are their ways. Thus also the North Vietnamese, whose habit of similar, utterly pointless tergiversations Kissinger has described. (By contrast, Kissinger added, the Chinese, in his experience, never go back on their word.)

But on this occasion, Malik was expressing the Kremlin's deep annoyance at the number of Senators who were backing the Jackson Amendment. This was not in the spirit of détente, he complained, not rancorously—the audience was small, and entirely professional. Scali explained that the White House does not control the Congress, that the President had several times besought Congress not to pass the Jackson Amendment, that Secretary of State Kissinger had made a great point of his opposition to it during the Senate hearings, that he, Scali, opposed the Jackson Amendment, that he hoped Congress would reconsider —but what else was there to do? Malik listened to his own interpreter render the English, occasionally correcting him, and then rose and, as he is utterly adept at doing, became utterly affable, walking over and joining Scali at the end of the room, and putting his arm about him. I was about to suffer the greatest put-down of my professional career. "Mr. Ambassador," said Scali, "I want you to meet one of our new delegates, Mr. William F. Buckley, Jr." "Ah yes," said Malik, clasping my hand, and smiling broadly. "I know all about Mr. Buckley." Pause. "But let me tell you something, Mr. Buckley"—we all froze, as he paused, though the smile was still broad on his face—"I don't agree with you about *everything!*" In such terms might Julie Nixon address Tricia. Mortifying. The son of a bitch has wit, I thought. Although, not having seen any subsequent evidence of it, I like to think he stumbled into that castrating put-down.

We toured about the building meeting various helpful
staff members. The UN's location in New York City is a
source of constant vexation. Everyone attacks it from
different angles. We have at USUN a not inconsiderable
New York-minded staff, headed by a lawyer, whose job is to
run discreet interference for the delegates. Baroody of Saudi
Arabia is always complaining that the United States should
augment its contribution to the UN by returning the taxes
paid by delegates in rent, excise taxes, whatever. We are too
delicate to counter with the argument that this income to
New York is neutralized by the extra expense incurred in
looking after security requirements and whatever (though
researchers back in 1962 estimated that, net, the UN is an
economic asset to New York. So what? So are the Knicks.)
Probably if everyone had to do it again, the vote would be
against using New York as headquarters. But the obstacles to
moving are insuperable. Geneva has made it clear that,
thanks very much, but it has all the foreign diplomats
Geneva wants. Geneva and London, by contrast, tend to be
much more hard-boiled than the United States about such
matters as diplomatic license plates. There they are limited to
two per foreign country, no matter how large its legation.
Here in New York the Soviet Union alone has eighty-six
diplomatic license plates.

And then the problem of looking after the delegates in
New York is both taxing and delicate. You can actually lose
votes on account of it, I'm told. And sometimes you need to
be especially discreet. How, for instance, do you help a New
York hospital collect from Indonesia $8,000 for protracted
medical attention to an illegitimate child? . . . The other
day there was a street collision on Forty-second Street, which
had nothing whatever to do with U.S. diplomacy, but we
were called to settle it. . . . Algiers has just cabled us; they
want our help in getting a visa for a Mozambique Freedom
Fighter. . . . At the UN school, they want walkie-talkie
security for the kids. . . . There are 1,700 to 1,800
diplomatic cars, but only 450 parking spaces at the UN. In

the past ten days, the Soviet Union alone has picked up 350 traffic summonses. And get this: The Soviets took a stand a while ago that they don't believe in putting money into parking meters, because that way they will contribute to the Vietnam war. "Sometimes," our briefing officer sums up, "you get votes from people because you arranged to get champagne for them."

On the whole, things went pretty smoothly this year, though on one occasion the Egyptian Ambassador called in high dudgeon to say that there were demonstrators surrounding the Egyptian legation throwing stones, and that if the New York police didn't provide instant protection, he would instruct Egyptian security guards to shoot at the demonstrators. That got a pretty fast telephone call to City Hall, and a mini-war in New York City was avoided, which war the Arabs would have lost as decisively as the worst of their ill-starred military campaigns.

We were advised that the full delegation should be present to listen to the inaugural address of the new President.

The egalitarianism of the UN is so studied that every year seats are rearranged, to guard against the possibility that some nations, in virtue of later admission than others, or by alphabetical misfortune, should find themselves seated in less desirable places. Not that any two nations would likely agree on what the desirable or undesirable places are: There are advantages in sitting in the first row, but also disadvantages. It is more difficult, for instance, to snooze. Here in this chamber, luck of the draw, the front-row seats this year run from Rwanda to Luxembourg, in the second row from Botswana to Saudi Arabia, in the third from Kuwait to Brazil. Somewhere around one-quarter of the way along the second row the alphabet meets, consummating the equality of nations. The trouble with it all is obvious: Every time you want to find somebody, you must come either armed with a chart for that particular assembly room, or else you must edge up toward the front, mount a grave expression on your face, and move your eyes left to right, staggering up and down, like a Secret Service man when the President is speaking, until you find your mark.

The Temporary President, Mr. Trepczynski from Poland, pitched détente for a minute or two, then conducted the election for the Permanent President of the General Assembly. The vote is specified by the rules to be conducted by secret ballot, with the permanent members voting for an individual, not for a country. The ballots were ceremoniously distributed, and ceremoniously tabulated. The results were given from the chair:

> Number of ballot papers 130
> Invalid ballots 0
> Number of valid ballots 130
> Abstentions 0
> Number of members voting 130
> Required majority 66

Number of votes obtained:

> Mr. Benites (Ecuador) 129
> Mr. Amerasinghe (Sri Lanka) 1

It is not known who was playing little games in behalf of Mr. Amerasinghe, but of course it didn't matter. It was Latin America's turn, and it is agreed that other nations will accept the regional choice. In Mr. Benites they got a scholarly lawyer, a rather inept parliamentarian, a speaker of Spanish lovely to hear, who, however, is most fearfully long-winded, by Anglo-Saxon standards.

Benites touched every base. It must have been an oversight that he neglected to thank his parents for begetting him. He thanked everyone else.

Then a discreet tribute to Allende, who had addressed the UN at the previous session. *"It does not behoove me from this rostrum to pass a political judgment on his ideas or his political actions, but I must state that I have the deeply rooted personal conviction that he was a man who loved his people and defended his ideals with his blood and his life."* When you dismantle a statement like that, of course, you find that it applies as well to Hitler.

And then: *"May I also be allowed to express to the Government and people of Sweden my sincere condolences on the death of His Majesty King Gustav VI. During his noble existence and long years of reign he possessed the love of his people and the wisdom to lead them to a high level of social well-being and progress based on justice."*

I reflected that it is established UN doctrine that all countries should have gone to war against Hitler. In fact the good King Gustav kept his country out of that war, neutral. I reflected further on one of the marvelous anomalies on which the UN was founded. It was back in 1946, and routinely, along with everyone else, Sweden and Ireland and Switzerland were proposed for membership. Only to be blocked in the Security Council, which cited as the reason for doing so that Sweden, Ireland, and Switzerland were not "peace-loving nations." Sweden and Ireland and Switzerland were almost the only countries in Europe that hadn't gone to war, and were therefore, by one set of standards, the peace-lovingest of them all. Subsequently, of course, Sweden and Ireland were admitted; but Switzerland declined to enter, adopting the long European view that, as in the past, probably all serious negotiating business would be done on Swiss soil, and that therefore Switzerland was better off not getting entangled in any way with the international organization.

Fifty-five minutes later, President Benites concluded his address, and turned to the first business before the house.

In clerical detail, the UN is quite extraordinarily efficient. Transcripts are prompt, accurate, nicely printed in double-space typewriter font. Documents are distributed in all the official languages. Each of the committee rooms has, at one end, a Documents Office, where you pick up copies of current resolutions, letters to the committee from members, ukases from the Secretary-General, and Secretariat reports.

At the other end is a Conference Officers Desk. Here you find out who is scheduled to speak, you pick up advance copies of speeches and copies of recorded votes. They will deliver messages for you. The level of clerical competence is very high.

Occasionally there is a semantic frolic. There is a lot of money in the UN pension fund, and there is a Board of Auditors that does an Evaluation of the Fund. The Cubans protested against the "unsound" policies of the board, attacking it for having so much of its portfolio in dollars. We in turn referred approvingly to the "conservative" policies of the board. The rapporteur got confused and asked us which description of the fund was ours, which the Cubans', and one of our boys unsmilingly said that the Cubans were demanding "conservative" money policies, and so it is recorded. In Gulag Archipelago days, I suppose, we wouldn't have done it, as there would have been one less Cuban when the records were scanned in Havana, if records are scanned in Havana.

Pionzio suggested we stick around. The Plenary proceeded through administrative formalities. These concerned accreditation of new members and adoption of an agenda. It had been agreed, now that West Germany and East Germany had ratified the division of their own country, that both Germanys would be admitted to membership. A "decision" requiring action by the Security Council (which alone can authorize a new member) of the kind that sails through the General Assembly must pass several hurdles: (1) The United States and the Soviet Union must agree not to oppose. (2) China, France, and England—the three other veto-wielding powers—must agree. (3) Accepted spokesmen of the non-aligned powers must agree, say, Algeria, Nigeria, and Uruguay. And, of course, measures that do not go through the Security Council—and this is a growing number—cannot be stopped by any single veto-wielding power, because no single one of these powers—not even the Soviet Union—disposes nowadays of control over a majority. And in an emergency, which is whatever the General Assembly declares to be an emergency, if the Security Council is blocked by the exercise of a veto, the General Assembly can take over. This procedure, authorized in November 1950 for the purpose of frustrating Soviet efforts to frustrate us in Korea, is called "Uniting for Peace." It is surely the dumbest thing Dean Acheson ever contrived, and we have ever since been backing away from it, as France and the Soviet Union, who all along opposed Uniting for Peace, predicted we would.

And, in the opening minutes of the 28th General Assembly, one would quickly discern the emotional vectors.

Israel's Mr. Tekoah rose on a "procedural point." I was to learn that there is practically no enforcement of the parliamentary rules in the United Nations. Rules governing the length of speeches or the subjects speakers are supposed to restrict themselves to are simply ignored. I asked the parliamentarian at USUN why this was so, and he replied that the ruling of the President, if challenged, needs to be submitted to the Assembly, and the majority will not discipline one of their own. Israel is clearly not one of anybody's majority, but the slackness that provides cover for the non-aligned nations extends generally to indulgence, by the chair, of others. Mr. Tekoah, without quite explaining the procedural relevance of his point, described (at some length, and with characteristic eloquence) the delinquencies of East Germany in failing to assume its share of the blame for the Jewish holocaust. "It has compounded the gravity of that attitude by giving support and practical assistance to the campaign of violence and murder waged against Israel and the Jewish people by Arab terror organizations. Thus, the world stands today before the spectacle of one of the German States being once again associated with the denial to the Jewish people of its fundamental rights." Scali passed me a wry note: "When the Israelis stand up to object to East Germany's entry, please don't you stand up and second the motion."

The way it works is that a member of your staff goes over

to the clerk and brings back a list of the countries that have been "inscribed" to speak. It is usually pretty obvious what will be the burden of the statement made by a particular country. In the case of Israel, for instance, it was known that Tekoah would say something about reparations. Accordingly, after consulting with a regional leader, it is decided who will reply in behalf of the offended bloc. Of course, many can reply—as many as desire the floor: There is no limitation, save the chairman's right to keep the session going late into the night, disrupting the dinner plans of the diplomats' wives. But even then, a motion to adjourn has absolute priority and must be put to an immediate vote, and a majority can force the chairman to call that session to a conclusion.

Guinea took the floor. Incredibly, in denouncing Israel's denunciation of East Germany, she managed to bring Portugal into the act. The general device was to neutralize the criticism of East Germany by attacking West Germany and scoffing at the notion that West Germans had reformed. "We shall not dwell on the allegations which would have us believe that, as by a miracle, the wolves have become lambs, that German pilots who ceaselessly assist in the bombing of the citizens of Guinea-Bissau and Cape Verde, who have been inflicting sufferings on our brothers and our sisters, at the side of the Lisbon torturers, have suddenly become our friends and brothers. Very soon Portugal, deprived of its support, will be beaten by the valiant freedom fighters of Guinea-Bissau, Cape Verde, Mozambique and Angola. . . ."

This was not of course enough to satisfy the anti-Israel appetite, particularly inasmuch as Guinea spent herself primarily against Portugal. Mr. Abdel Meguid, Ambassador from Egypt, rose, and threw everything at Israel. ". . . I wonder on whose behalf Israel, in raising this procedural question, is speaking? In the name of victims, citizens of a third country at a time when Israel itself did not exist?" He spoke of Israel's "unsurpassed audacity." "Israel contends that a State has no right to join this Organization because of

alleged obligations owed to Israel, while at the same time
Israel itself, a member of this Organization, holds the record
for violated obligations. How many times has Israel rejected
United Nations resolutions? How many times has Israel
violated the Charter and the various conventions on human
rights? But the last straw is that while Israel speaks of
compensation, Israel itself is the only State that, ever since
1948, has constantly defied world public opinion, which, in
numerous resolutions of the United Nations, has charged
Israel with the duty of indemnifying the Arab people of
Palestine for their usurped homeland and the violation of
their fundamental rights. What a contradiction on the part
of Israel, what cruelty, what cynicism! . . ." There, already,
in a nutshell, the whole of the anti-Israel case, which would
be elaborated, in the following three months, a thousand
times, in every chamber, in every way.

Following the admission of new members, several sessions
were devoted to the approval of the agenda. This normally
goes through fairly smoothly, with here and there an
interpolation, usually wordy, always tendentious, for the
purpose of honing the polemical spirit. When Item 42 was
introduced—"Policies of Apartheid of the Government of
South Africa"—the South African representative rose to
deliver the most elegant demurral of the season: "I asked to
speak simply in order to record and to reaffirm our usual
reservation with regard to the inscription of Item 42 in the
agenda and to its eventual consideration. Our reasons for
this reservation have been explained at previous sessions of
the General Assembly"—and sat down. In other words: Why
say the same thing, year in year out? Of course, one reason
why the South African representative is driven to brevity is
that if he gives a speech, the Third World regularly walks
out, most ostentatiously. Notwithstanding that some of the
delegates are nimble, there simply isn't time to sprint out of
the room before a speaker has delivered three sentences.

I said that this was all the South African representative

said. Not quite. His first words were: "Sir, my Foreign Minister will be paying tribute to you on your election to the office of President when he addresses the General Assembly in the course of the general debate. May I, however, take this opportunity also to offer to you, on behalf of the South African delegation, our warm congratulations on your election?" They were congratulating the President on his election deep into the session, and the pause seemed all but imperceptible before they began congratulating him on the job he had done. It is a most cloying business, particularly since some countries believe that their congratulations are insipid unless delivered at very great length. There are 135 countries. Each representative prefaces a statement, as with South Africa, with a congratulation, and promising that the Foreign Minister will also deliver his congratulations. Not all Foreign Ministers arrive to speak, but many do. Potentially, we have here 270 congratulations on the President's nomination, followed by 270 congratulations on the job he has done. Meanwhile each of the eight working committees has a president. There are a hundred or so countries represented in each of the committees, each of whom delivers first a congratulation on the chairman's selection, then on the job he has done, though an effort is made to regionalize these congratulations. It is safe to say that there are more congratulations proffered during sessions of the General Assembly of the United Nations every day than at a royal wedding. A few of these are spare, and perfunctory; more are gooey; some approach sexual ardor.

The General Assembly agreed to consider a total of fifty-six items. The enumeration of these items, however, begins with No. 12 and ends with No. 110. In order not to confuse the genealogy, an item once numbered retains its number, even if shrinkage should, logically, reduce it. Some items get dropped; others are amalgamated. And with fifty-six items, most of them dispatched to committee for debate before being presented for action by the General Assembly, there is much to do that is important, and unimportant. The substantive items included (No. 107) the recognition of the exile government of Portuguese Guinea, various human rights items, world disarmament, peaceful uses of the seabed, to mention only a few; and perfunctory ones, as in (No. 28) "Appointment of members to the Peace Observation Commission" (this particular committee has met twice in twenty-three years, and has yet to issue a report).

On Monday, the agenda having been approved, the heads of state and Foreign Ministers would deliver their addresses. Kissinger was slated for noon.

John Scali invited the delegates and senior staff to a buffet dinner at his house. There is great resentment among these seniors because Senator Fulbright, seeking to make a querulous point, has, while approving the designation of the permanent members, denied them the status of Ambassador to which a few of them were, for whatever reason, entitled. There is talk about putting pressure on individual Senators in the Foreign Relations Committee to overrule Fulbright, and in due course this was successfully done. Senator Fulbright is overruled with reassuring frequency. On the whole, people who are Ambassadors, or have been Ambassadors, like to be referred to as "Mr. Ambassador." I find it terribly encumbering, though on the whole I was glad of it, as it spared us all, in numerous social situations, from the alternative, which was to give no name at all to the person we were addressing, since mastering the individual names of all the Ambassadors present at a session of the General Assembly is beyond the normal man's reach. Even Henry Kissinger would have been better off if he had referred to Representative Nix as Mr. Ambassador.

At drinks before dinner I proposed to Scali that a resolution be attempted on the floor of the General Assembly to invite Alexander Solzhenitsyn to address us. He was greatly taken by the idea, and called over to Tap Bennett to come discuss it with us. Bennett said that at the UN you just can't do things that directly. You have to invite not a particular man, but a classification of men, and not just as a one-shot deal, but as a program. Thus, Solzhenitsyn—but only as, say, the speaker for the 28th Session of the General Assembly; or, better, as the first of one or two speakers per session.

Scali beckoned John Howison, master UN parliamentarian and dominant voice in practical UN affairs, and tried out the idea on him. Who, besides Solzhenitsyn, is there of undisputed rank? they wondered. Well there was Pablo Neruda (until the next Sunday, when he died); there is Malraux. "Before long you'd soon be getting proletarian poets from China," Bennett warned. Someone suggested that perhaps the Nobel Committee could be persuaded to act as sponsors. Howison said the whole thing, if it could succeed at all, would take five years. Five years! I exclaimed. That would be fast, said Howison. But wouldn't we all profit from inviting Solzhenitsyn *anyway*, even if the invitation was shot down by the Soviet Union in some way or other? Wouldn't it embarrass the UN to vote *not* to invite someone so distinguished? What state could be got to proffer the invitation (obviously it could not appear to have originated with us)? Scali wondered whether Albania might be used. No, said Bennett. Albania is too much the same old thorn in Russia's side. How about Mexico? I asked. No, Mexico is hot on its resolution defining the obligations of rich states to poor states, and doesn't want to make any unnecessary enemies.

It dawned on me, and in due course this would become very clear, that the United States is the only superpower in the UN that has no functioning satellite. There is no state with which we have a sort of client relationship which we can use, lightly to detach ourselves from the sponsorship of any particular resolution. The Soviet Union, of course, has the entire Bloc, as, at the UN, they are given to calling Eastern Europe; and Cuba. China has Albania. Whatever Albania does, it is generally assumed that China is behind it. We are left with a clerical disadvantage of some significance. Because the United Nations decocts its own order of reality from the odd configurations of alliances—military, political, racial, and social—within it. And it matters not nearly so much as one would suppose that, for instance, Albania is there to do the bidding of China. There is a considerable symbolic—and therefore, in the UN, existential—difference between a proposal formally initiated by China and one formally initiated by Albania. It seemed to me that, anticipating the attrition of our influence within the UN, we might at least have exercised enough husbandry to hang on to one rigorously-reliable client state. Scali continued, throughout the evening, to allude to the desirability of devising a formula for inviting Solzhenitsyn; and the subject was never after raised again. There is talk about the big affair that will be given by Henry Kissinger to honor the delegates to the UN. It will be next week, at the Metropolitan Museum, about 500 people: everybody important (Rockefeller, Cronkite, that kind of thing), plus No. 1 UN delegates, plus those Foreign Ministers who were in New York. The invitations had already gone out, in the name of the U.S. Ambassador, but now word had come in from Washington that they were to be recalled; and reissued, in the name of Henry Kissinger. This struck some of us as a little bit like Napoleon wresting the crown from the Pope and placing it on his own head. But there was a silver lining. This way the bill would have to be paid by the State Department, not by USUN. Would you believe it, Scali said, the representation allowance for the entire United States mission is only $30,000? I didn't. That simply isn't much money for all those lunches, dinners, and cocktails. The Kissinger bash alone would cost $28,000. Scali said he wanted to see me the next afternoon "to talk about the committee assignments." I winced, having understood that there was nothing to talk about, that the decision on my committee assignment had been made last summer; and agreed to see him at three.

3.

Meeting with Scali

Scali's office was first occupied, the huge building having been just completed, by Henry Cabot Lodge. Then came James Wadsworth, Adlai Stevenson, Arthur Goldberg, George Ball, James Russell Wiggins, Charles Yost, and George Bush. It is functional-large, as distinguished from ostentatious-large. It has the requisite flags, and pictures of the Nixon family. But also memorabilia from other Presidents who involved Scali in various capacities, mostly as a journalist. There is the large desk, then four chairs around a table, where most of the meetings take place with one or two or three aides. I arrived in the middle of a social crisis.

Kissinger was hosting two lunches, on successive days—Monday and Tuesday. The first was for African representatives, the second for Arab representatives. The invitations had gone out. Now word came in that the tier of six North African countries resented being grouped with the Arab states, rather than with the African states. Our protocol official had sweetly replied that this had been done only because the countries in question were self-inscribed members of the Arab League. Their spokesman was unpacified. Very well then, USUN had countered: Come with the Africans on Monday, instead of with the Arabs on Tuesday. No. They wanted to be invited to come both Monday *and* Tuesday.

Now the normal man's reflex, when up against something like this, is to say directly: Come Monday. *Or* come Tuesday.

50

There is absolutely *no* question that that would have been Scali's reflex maybe even as recently as six months ago. It is another world, diplomacy. Scali and Bennett and Schaufele feared that unless the Arabs were given their way, they might boycott *both* meetings. And if they did that, Kissinger would be displeased. After all (they could hear him say), if USUN can't for God's sake administer two lunches without causing a great diplomatic disruption, what in the hell are all those people doing practicing diplomacy?

So we gave in. We invited them to *both*. (Four of them came to neither.) This is the diplomat's reflex. And Kissinger himself is very good at it. He went back and back and back to Paris to discuss cease-fire with Le Duc Tho, swallowing every kind of humiliation. Eventually he got his cease-fire. More properly, he got the necessary cover which permitted United States military withdrawal. It is a continuing question whether he got this as a reward for his patience, or in response to his impatience: the sudden carpet-bombing, as they call it. Perhaps the first has to precede the second; perhaps you must denominate them Arabs exactly insofar as they desire you to do so, and Africans the other times; and then hit them hard with the big ones. There were no big ones in the General Assembly, though one or two over in that direction. And you never can tell. A slight in the UN could mean, nowadays, a turn, clockwise, in the oil spigot.

There is an almost total African subservience to the Arab states. Murray Kempton has written that for all the talk about superpowers dominating postwar diplomacy, history will record that the postwar world was dominated by (a) Israel and (b) North Vietnam. In UN politics, the same historian will record that the United Nations, sometime in the early seventies, was dominated by—Algeria. In a sense, Algeria is shorthand for the Arab states. But Algeria itself combines a certain physical aloofness from combatant-Arab states that surround Israel; the prestige of having fought, successfully, a hard anti-colonial war against France; and the hard socialist-xenophobia that makes it a natural leader in bumptiousness. Its influence is over the Arab states, and their influence is over Africa. To know what Algeria will do is the easiest way of feeling the shape of any forthcoming vote, for the purposes of inquiring into what the African-Arab bloc will do. Not infrequently, the Africans will propose resolutions which are actually at the initiative of the Arabs. On one occasion one of these resolutions ran into a rough procedural tangle as the result of maladroit handling, and the Arabs had to pretend to be looking the other way. But when the difficulties appeared insuperable, they surfaced, and salvaged it.

We turned to the committee assignments. I asked why as a matter of curiosity my name had not yet been posted as delegate-in-charge of the Third Committee? I found the answers just a little evasive, and had my first premonition that Walter Mitty was dead, and would not rise again. Well, said Scali, there are a great many items, and some of them rather closely tailored to the interests and experience of other delegates. For instance, the one on racial discrimination. . . . Mrs. Young? I told him that Mrs. Young had told *me* that she hoped for once in her life to be able to participate in a discussion other than on racial discrimination. Well, yes. . . . And then both John Buchanan, an ordained minister, and Mark Evans, a very religious Mormon, are interested in the whole question of religious liberty. . . . I suggested that as many delegates as desired be assigned where desired to cover particular items, but that the whole of the operation should proceed under my leadership, so as to give the thing a little strategic direction. Scali agreed, though I could see that the designation was not to be consummated. Within a few days I would know the worst of it.

4.

Henry Kissinger

MONDAY

This was Henry Kissinger's week. He was in New York for the whole of it, and spent long hours conferring with every one of the Foreign Ministers who were present (this and the succeeding week are the ceremonial weeks for grand statements by heads of state and Foreign Ministers). At these meetings we delegates were not, of course, present. But we were there for his opening statement at the General Assembly; and for lunch that day for the African representatives; and on Tuesday for the Arabs; and on Friday for the Latin Americans; and Thursday night for the big banquet. And, Monday afternoon, he was with us when we all took our oath of office, and submitted to a photograph.

Kissinger is of course a superstar, and all attention was on him when he arrived at the Assembly Hall, about a half hour before the first speaker (Brazil), whom he would succeed. He had only just been confirmed, and indeed announced himself on mounting the podium as "probably" the juniormost Foreign Minister in the world, the "probably" no doubt an academic obeisance to the possibility that at least one coup had taken place during the fifty-five-minute speech by the Brazilian representative.

I had not seen Kissinger for about two months. I breakfasted with him at his office in the White House a week or two before he was named as Secretary of State. I did not, at that time, mention my own forthcoming appointment as a delegate. I reasoned that if he knew about it already and

53

desired to discuss it, he would do so; if he did not know about it, it might embarrass him that he didn't know about it, so better not to bring it up.

We have been friends for many years. We met in the mid-fifties, when he was at Harvard, and serving also as editor of *Confluence,* an academic quarterly. Brent Bozell and I had recently published a book on the McCarthy controversy, several chapters of which intensively studied the whole loyalty-security problem into which McCarthy had waded. Kissinger asked me to write an essay for his journal; I did; and it never appeared. A year or so later he asked me to go to Harvard to lecture to his international seminar. I did, once or twice, as did my colleague, the philosopher-strategist James Burnham. He repeated the invitation every year, and I began begging off, on the grounds that it was after all midsummer, and the round trip to Cambridge interfered seriously with my sailing. Often when he came to New York we would visit, usually at lunch. He was then closely associated with Nelson Rockefeller, and an advocate, always, of a realistic foreign policy, with minimum illusions about the intentions, or capabilities, of what in those days we used to call "the enemy."

In the spring of 1968 he told me that Nelson Rockefeller would like to meet me, because I had written in a column something about him which, Rockefeller and Kissinger agreed, mistook his background. The meeting took place late one afternoon. I had just flown in from St. Louis where I had had George Wallace on my television program, *Firing Line,* and they were both curious to know what he had said (nothing much), and how he had behaved (boorishly). Rockefeller then undertook, at rather exaggerated length, to recount to me his role at the founding of the United Nations. He was then Assistant Secretary of State for American Republic Affairs, and had observed at first hand some of the parliamentary devices by which the Communists had sought, at the Chapultepec Conference at Mexico City, to capture the organizational mechanisms of fledgling organizations.

He was fresh from his experience in Mexico when the UN convened in San Francisco, and arriving there he saw, to his horror, a prospective reenactment of what he had narrowly aborted in Mexico. He flew back in panic, to report to President Truman, but found him temporarily inaccessible. Accordingly he went to Senator Arthur Vandenberg, whom he persuaded of the urgency of his mission. Vandenberg got to Truman, Truman got to Stettinius, and the day was saved. The account was interesting, and one had the feeling it had been delivered before. Especially, one had the feeling that Kissinger had heard it before, though his attention was exemplary. Rockefeller rose, excusing himself that he had to attend a Republican dinner and couldn't think what to say. I teased him that he must have this difficulty at every Republican occasion; he laughed in polite recognition of a factional antagonism of long standing; and we all left, heading in three separate directions.

A few months later, during the Republican Convention in 1968, Kissinger was in close touch with me. He had a very simple, very direct mission. If Rockefeller was nominated, he could not possibly win the election if there were substantial defections from the right wing. Unquestionably there would be a call to defection, in the spirit of retaliation against Rockefeller's refusal convincingly to support Goldwater after Goldwater's nomination at the preceding convention. My responsibility, Kissinger urged, was to demonstrate to American conservatives that the country would be better off with Rockefeller as President, than with a Democratic President.

I twitted him that the question was entirely academic, inasmuch as Nixon was going to be nominated; I told him that if Nixon suddenly disappeared from the face of the earth, Reagan, not Rockefeller, would be nominated; and I told him, further, that Nixon had told me, accurately I believed, that even if he, Nixon, came out in favor of Rockefeller's nomination, the convention would not accept him, that only one man could effect such a nomination, and that was Goldwater; and Goldwater had no intention of doing that. And anyway, it was all sewn up for Nixon. Kissinger told me not-to-be-so-sure, but I knew that he didn't have any secret information he was husbanding, let us say to the effect that the majority of the delegates would prove to be on Rockefeller's payroll. Because Kissinger—and this is surely one of his most endearing habits—is implacably informative. If in fact he doesn't tell you everything he knows, he never leaves you thinking he hasn't. I knew at the time that his contingent operation, to woo a conservative to support Rockefeller's candidacy, was either formalistic or—more likely—evidence of his dogged ignorance of American politics, an observation I make without in the least intending to call into question the talents he disposes of as Secretary of State.

Then, during the summer, he asked to lunch with me. He had a few ideas he thought would be interesting to Nixon, in framing his foreign policy campaign speeches. But these ideas he must advance discreetly, as he would not wish it to appear, having just now left the dismantled Rockefeller staff, to be job-seeking. There was no question about the disinterestedness of the advice he sought to convey to Nixon, and I telephoned to Frank Shakespeare, who was working at Nixon headquarters. I recited Kissinger's qualifications, and Shakespeare went to Len Garment and John Mitchell, neither of whom had heard Kissinger's name before. They were impressed by his credentials, and said that they would introduce him to Nixon, except that Nixon was out of town campaigning. Kissinger's drafts were cordially received.

In late November I was lecturing in Los Angeles, and staying with friends in Pasadena. Kissinger reached me by phone. That day Secretary of Defense Clark Clifford had blasted Thieu for taking so adamant a stand on the requisite shape of the bargaining table in Paris. I still have the notes I took. "Nixon should be told," Kissinger said, "that it is probably an objective of Clifford to depose Thieu before Nixon is inaugurated. Word should be gotten to Nixon that if Thieu meets the same fate as Diem, the word will go out to the nations of the world that it may be dangerous to be America's enemy, but to be America's friend is fatal." I telephoned New York, a personal meeting was set up between Kissinger and the President-elect, and a week or so later my phone rang. "You will never be able to say again that you have no contact inside the White House."

I met with him perhaps a dozen times in the first four years. I remember the very first meeting. It was the spring of 1969, a Friday. Could I go down to see him? I told him it would have to be on Sunday, or not again for ten days as I was off on a lecture tour. "I will send a jet for you," he said. We discussed the details, and I told him I would take the ten o'clock shuttle back to New York. "No," he said, "the jet will take you back." He paused then over the telephone. "This," he said, "is going to ruin academic life." My escort officer, aboard the little White House jet, was an amiable, young-looking colonel—Alexander Haig.

I learned something of the exasperations Kissinger experienced. They were in part such exasperations as one would expect a man, so situated, so trained, to experience. But perhaps chief among them has been his experience with what he still calls—almost the last of the breed to do so—the American Establishment: its failure to understand what is important, and to give presumptive support when such support is clearly needed: but that is another story, and when I said to him, coming on him in the aisle of the General Assembly, surrounded by cameras and reporters and aides, "How is it going, Doc?" he turned and greeted me warmly, but a minute later the gavel banged down and I took my designated seat somewhere behind Kissinger. At one point, during the endless Brazilian overture, I leaned forward and whispered to him, pointing to the copy of his own speech which UN clerks were silently distributing, "Is it a good speech?" He leaned back and whispered: "No. It is a *necessary* speech."

I saw quickly what he meant. The chamber was unusually

attentive. Kissinger's (beautiful) mother and father, and his two children, sat just off to one side, and they were all rapt. Applause is extremely rare in the United Nations, but Kissinger received applause, when he went forward to speak, and after he had finished.

There was of course the congratulations for the new President.

After that comes (the formula is quite rigid) a compliment to the United Nations itself. It is acceptable to inject into that compliment just that little rhetorical detachment that gives the tribute fresh life. The device has an exact complement in all United Nations rhetoric concerning human rights. You always begin by saying: *"We have had enough of talk about human rights, we want now to advance human rights."* In the decade of the 1980's, no doubt we will have progressed to: "We have had enough talk about the talk about human rights, now we want human rights." As regards the UN, Kissinger's formulation was paradigmatic. "That President Nixon should ask me as my first official act to speak here for the United States reaffirms the importance that my country attaches to the values and the ideals of the United Nations." Bulletproof. Obviously our country attaches importance to the values and ideals of the United Nations. The question is whether the United Nations attaches any importance to the values and ideals of the United Nations. "It would be idle to deny that the American people, like many others, have sometimes been disappointed because this Organization has not been more successful in translating its architects' hopes for universal peace into concrete accomplishments." That is as far as one can go these days, speaking from the eminency of a foreign ministership. And note that the sentence is rhetorically dangled so as to all but require that the following sentence should begin with "But." "But, despite our disappointments, my country remains committed to the goal of a world community. We will continue to work in this Parliament of Man to make it a reality."

Then there followed, as so often is the case, a things-could-be-worse passage, leaving it to be understood that they would be worse save for the United Nations. "We . . . envisage a comprehensive, institutionalized peace encompassing all nations, large and small, a peace which this Organization is uniquely situated to foster and to anchor in the hearts of men. This will be the spirit of American foreign policy. This attitude will guide our work in this Organization." It is not clear to what "this attitude" refers. A vision is not, of course, an attitude. And Henry Kissinger no more believes that the United Nations is uniquely situated to foster peace than the United Mine Workers. As for the anchoring of our ideals in the hearts of man, United States policy is to forget the hearts of man, and concentrate on harmonizing United Nations policy with United States policy toward the Soviet Union. And that policy has nothing whatever to do with the hearts of man, but with the obviously desirable goal of peace.

And at a concrete level. "We start from a bedrock of solid progress. Many of the crises that haunted past sessions of the General Assembly have been put behind us. Agreement has been reached on Berlin; there is a cease-fire in the Middle East; the Vietnam war has been ended." These words were uttered four months before the East Germans raised a fresh challenge to the independence of Berlin, two weeks before Egypt, Syria, and Jordan launched a huge war in the Mideast, and in the same week when casualties from the Vietnam war were logging in at a level equal to the highest during the late, bloody, sixties. Kissinger could not have intended to convey that the Vietnam war was ended by the act of United States withdrawal, and that what was left was merely a civil war, which doesn't count: he could not have said that without gainsaying the entire analysis that justified the United States' intervention in the first instance. And, of course, the de jure arrangements involving Berlin were worked out between West Germany and the Soviet Union, without reference to the UN; and the cease-fire in the Middle East, about to end, had been the handiwork, substantially, of Secretary Rogers, and was unrelated to the work of the UN.

But UN speeches are not written to be analyzed. What

does one make of the following? "The United States deeply believes: that justice cannot be confined by national frontiers; that truth is universal, and not the peculiar possession of a single people or group or ideology. . . ." That is sheer diplomatic cant. We know that there is (rough) justice in West Germany, and injustice in East Germany. And the frontiers between them are as brazen as the Wall. The truth may very well be a universal, but the effective possession of it is most certainly that of a few people, and distinctly a part of an ideology of human rights and individualism. It would have been far more accurate to say: "The United States deeply believes: that justice should not be confined within national frontiers, though in fact it continues to be; that truth is universal, but even so, is not widely practiced."

But, as Kissinger said, it was a necessary speech. Concretely, he came out for separate representation for North and South Korea, for permanent membership in the Security Council for Japan, and for calling a World Food Conference. (This last, by the way, the 28th Assembly proceeded to do; and it is the kind of thing the UN can do, and should be encouraged to do.) And, at the end, a little more inaugural prose: "We can repeat old slogans or strive for new hope." Comment: We *will* repeat old slogans, and hope *will* continue to diminish. . . . It was over, and we went forthwith, across the street, to lunch.

On my right was the Ambassador from Gambia. I wish I had known that ahead of time, as I'd have looked up Gambia, and learned something about it. The gentleman was dressed in ceremonial African dress—which by the way is much rarer these days than in the immediate post-colonial period, when it was thought that emancipation is only expressed by fuzzy-wuzzy costuming. Christopher Dawson wrote a dozen years ago that the movement of world revolution was attested to by Khrushchev's wearing a fedora at the first summit conference. To be sure, Dawson wrote before Harold Macmillan went to Moscow wearing a shapka.

The Gambian was a charming gentleman, but gave me few conversational leads. I asked how was the weather in Gambia, and he replied that the weather in Gambia was always fine, and I replied of course Gambia is famous for its wonderful weather, and we beamed at each other. On my left was the Ethiopian Ambassador, distantly related to Haile Selassie, with whom in fact he had at one point fallen out. The emperor exiled him to Oxford, where he picked up some advanced degrees. I had vetted him because I had been asked to solicit his support for our stand on Korea.

It turned out that for a period before he went back into diplomacy he had served as chief of the Ethiopian airlines. During the period when he was the head of it, the Chinese had asked him to set up a route to China, as they wanted a commercial, African-run link into the continent. At the bargaining table, he told me, he had said to the Chinese that it would hardly be a profitable run considering the difficulty in getting visas to travel into China. At this point the Chinese astonished him, and he astonished me by telling me of it: the Chinese agreed that the Ethiopian airline could write out a fifteen-day visa to anyone—*anyone*—buying a ticket on the Ethiopian airline to China. I passed this news along to two or three of my frustrated friends who have been trying for years for a visa.

Kissinger always brings wit and self-deprecation to his toasts. "I don't know the international significance of my appointment as Secretary of State," he began, "but domestically my appointment represents the normalization of relations between the White House and the Department of State." That was probably lost on the thirty black Ambassadors, but was a cause of much hilarity among the thirty Americans, who had known of the tensions between Kissinger's office and Rogers' State Department. He went on ("I will not pretend to a competence in African affairs that I do not possess. . .") gracefully, without ever being obsequious. The response by the black delegates came in two waves. At once, by those who had been colonized under British rule;

after the translator had performed, by those who had been colonized under French rule.

At the UN, no matter how well it happens that they speak English, the French, the Chinese, and the Russians speak in their native tongue. Some of the Latin Americans will speak in English. The Arabs who speak English (most of them, except Algeria and Tunisia) speak an Oxford English of great precision, with here and there a little vernacular impurity of the kind that is taking'over Philippine and Indian English. . . .

The translator, seeking self-effacement, rendered Kissinger's prose in a slight sing-song that gave the thing the flavor of a ritual, like prayers said at the foot of the altar; and of course that is what it was. Speaking for his brothers, the Mauritanian delegate replied, "We are aware of your personal impact on the policy of détente. . . ." But, he explained, true détente was not possible for so long as people were subject to colonialism and racism. "We all know," he continued, "about your fight against Fascism and Nazism. We know we can count on you to help us in our similar fight." Henry was being conscripted to declare war on Rhodesia, Mozambique, Angola, and South Africa. The delegate expressed his bitter disappointment at Congressional approval of purchases of Rhodesian chrome. Henry looked grave, we all applauded, and lunch was over.

5.

BAROODY

After lunch Dino and I met in my office with the two staff members, senior and junior, who were detailed to the Human Rights Committee. There were others, but these two were, for us, most conspicuous. Guy Wiggins, a virtuoso Foreign Service officer with experience most recently in Panama, is the No. 1 staff official, early forties, blond, Grotonian in accent and attitude, University of California, Harvard MA, London School of Economics, shrewd, whimsical, cautious but attracted by spontaneity. Cameron Hume, late twenties, Princeton, Peace Corps, service in Italy, bright, laconic, drawlingly sarcastic, intensively learned in the minutiae of the Items we would be transacting within the Third Committee, and schooled in the consequences of them. He is on top of everything, and is studying at night, when he can, at the New York Law School. Wiggins-Hume work under the delegate in official charge of the individual Item. They are, of course, in minute-by-minute touch with the top staff, which is in constant touch with the State Department, whence the grand instructions flow. There isn't, at this particular meeting, any detailed briefing to go through, since the Third Committee, which is about to convene, is itself considering, as the Plenary was doing, the Items to be put on its agenda. We talk loosely, running our fingers lightly over the profile of some of the problems we could expect. The Soviet Union, during the last few months, and with quite extraordinary intensity in recent weeks, has been suffering from a very bad press for its refusal to grant exit visas to Russian Jews. That and the continuing internal campaign against Solzhenitsyn et al. have made the Kremlin the target of multifarious denunciations, so much so that in last Sunday's New York *Times* Russia almost rivaled Watergate. Accordingly the Soviet Union has tried one of its formalistic blitzkriegs. Having done nothing about the United Nations Declaration of Human Rights during the twenty-five years since it was formally adopted, now suddenly the Soviet Union has taken that Declaration and made out of it a Convention.

The terms are meaningless to the layman. I ceased to be a layman on that particular subject during my sophomore year at Yale when, as a member of the Yale Political Union's Conservative Party, I was assigned the job of speaking on the general subject, alongside other student speakers representing the Liberal and the Labor parties, at an evening meeting which would be addressed by Mrs. Eleanor Roosevelt, a United States delegate to the General Assembly and U.S. representative before the Human Rights Committee. The leadership of the Political Union had endeavored to persuade Mrs. Roosevelt to speak about the United Nations Declaration of Human Rights in general terms—to defend that Declaration, which was much criticized because of the rather preposterous lengths it went to. It seemed to the critics of such declarations, then as now, that the more luxuriantly expansive one gets in the enumeration of human rights, the more likely it is that the document will become a plaything of utopians and cynics. Thus the newly born Declaration of Human Rights, adopted in 1948, listed, for instance, the right of everyone to a "free choice of employment" and to "rest and leisure." But Mrs. Roosevelt insisted, in her undeniable way, on the resolution, "Resolved, The United Nations Declaration of Human Rights should be adopted as a Convention." This sent the undergraduate speakers to the political science books to discover the meaning of it all. Namely, that the adoption of said

Declaration by the United States government should be done in the form of a treaty—signed by the President, ratified by the Senate. From that moment on, that Declaration would become the Supreme Law of the Land, superior (and this was what the Bricker Amendment fight was all about) to the Constitution itself. This could mean that a plaintiff, suffering within the United States from a denial of any such right, could appeal to the United Nations for relief; that the World Court could assume jurisdiction; and that if the plaintiff was found to have a justified grievance, the government of the United States would be bound to grant relief and, presumably, damages.

It was my only meeting with that charming, befuddled lady, about whom James Burnham once wrote that she treated the entire world as her personal slum project. It was an instructive encounter at every level. At a reception before the debate we were chatting and she had a dry martini in hand. She looked up suddenly to notice a photographer about to snap her picture. Faster than Superman she twirled her cape in the way of the projected exposure, calmly perched her martini glass on a table, turned back empty-handed, and smiled at the photographer. I was terribly puzzled by the entire maneuver, but would see it again and again in the years to come, and a thousand times at the United Nations, where cocktail glasses are put aside when photographs are taken. Mrs. Roosevelt's side won the debate easily; indeed I was the only undergraduate speaker opposed. Reflecting on it since, I have come to a position less legalistic. The chances of the Declaration, once written into law as a treaty, actually getting in the way of American practice are probably less than the chances of the Declaration's getting in the way of Soviet practice. By which I mean that the potential inconvenience to us of lawsuits pleading extravagant protections is probably less worrisome than the inconvenience to the totalitarian states of laws of international standing which might serve as the basis for pleading elementary protections. Under the circumstances, on the whole I thought it a step in the right direction that the Soviet Union should have gone on to Convention.

But the Convention fever, our aides explained, has hit many of the member states of the United Nations for a single reason. As we would abundantly discover, the only human right concerning which there is anything like unanimity within the UN is the right against racial discrimination. This should probably be put more exactly. The right against discrimination by the white race against any other race: as witness, for instance, that the persecution of the Asians in Africa was never a cause in the United Nations. There the concern is exclusively to end white minority rule in South Africa, in Rhodesia, and in Mozambique and Angola.

Now, Hume explained, under a hypothetical construction of one of the anti-discrimination covenants which would probably come up before the Third Committee, the following could happen. If it were ruled that racial discrimination is a crime against humanity, and if the recognition of that crime were codified into the law of the signatory states via a United Nations declaration duly transformed into a covenant, an interpretation of that human right could make it a crime to do business with a business that also did business with: South Africa, say. Hypothetically a tourist in Damascus, presenting a Chase Manhattan Bank check at a travel office, could be seized and stuck in the pokey for consorting with a business which, doing business in South Africa, is therefore an accomplice in a continuing crime against humanity. The United States government, Wiggins and Hume told Dino and me, does not desire to precipitate such juridical nightmares.

Elected to serve as chairman of the Third Committee was Mr. Yahya Mahmassani, of Lebanon. He joined his government's Ministry of Foreign Affairs in 1962, and served several years in Nigeria before coming to the UN. He is considered a comer in the UN bureaucracy, a young, brilliant, patient—overpatient?—man of refined and precise manner, who presides in perfect English.

I occupied the United States desk for the first time when the Third Committee's session had already got under way. The chairman had proposed that all seventeen items referred to the Third Committee by the General Assembly should occupy equally the attention of the committee, and the English representative now suggested that they be taken up exactly in the same order in which they fell in the General Assembly's agenda. But everyone knows that items taken up for consideration early in the session are given more time than those left for the end: indeed, it is a preliminary parliamentary maneuver to push off toward the end those one wants least to discuss.

Inasmuch as the chairman had made it clear, and the sense of the entire proceeding made it equally clear, that the question now to be debated was *the order* in which the proposals were to be discussed, not their relative merits, I found myself getting restless at the quite extraordinary lengths to which a wizened delegate sitting thirty yards across from me in the circular committee room was going on and on in expressing his opposition to giving any attention at all to Item 57, which called for the creation of the post of United Nations High Commissioner for Human Rights. It happened that the United States position was in favor of a High Commissioner, which was one reason for resenting the speaker's attack upon it before the subject was upon us for substantive debate; another reason, it seemed to me, was that so obvious an ignorance of parliamentary punctilio should be exposed very early in the adventures of the Third Committee, before people got into bad habits. I leaned back to Guy Wiggins and asked him whether he agreed that the speaker was behaving improperly, and he said, yes, indeed he was behaving improperly, though as I thought back on it later, he seemed less surprised than I that people should behave improperly at United Nations committee meetings. Well, I whispered, why don't I interrupt, and ask the chairman to direct him to confine his remarks to the chronological question? Well, he said, sure, why not? Well—I continued in a whisper—what are the mechanics of an interruption? He told me that I should tap my pencil on the water glass in front of me: so I did. The chamber was visibly startled. A Point of Order, Mr. Chairman . . . and I made it, and managed to use twice the indispensable word in the United Nations—"distinguished." By the time I was through, three months later, I found myself referring, at a dinner party unrelated to the United Nations, to my distinguished cocker spaniel. The object of my pretty little demurral turned to me like the porridge-dispenser to Oliver Twist: a look of curiosity, graduating to indignation, and disdain, followed by a most copious reply, the point being that it is not possible to discuss the chronological priority without discussing substantive priority—all of it said with relish, leavened with paternalism, and with abundant references to the length of the experience of the speaker. I had, quite by chance, in my first encounter in the UN, run into: His Excellency Jamil Baroody, the Permanent Representative of Saudi Arabia.

Baroody is the most conspicuous figure in the United Nations, and it pays to ask oneself why. Inasmuch as the United Nations progressively interests fewer and fewer people, it is probably safe to say that Baroody's name is utterly unknown outside the UN, as indeed it was unknown to me at the time I accosted him. In fact, he has a following. It is a following he has picked up among those who follow televised United Nations debates, most of them in the Security Council, when there are grave issues of instant moment as when, three weeks later, the cease-fire in the Mideast would be discussed. Baroody is there speaking in front of the cameras, and he gets a lot of fan mail, generated by his polemical trenchancy, his delight in ad hominem arguments, his addiction to pop history, and the persuasive arrangement of his arguments. A speech by Baroody, over Channel 13, is quaint, theatrical, and in a strange way refreshing. A hundred speeches by Baroody is the ne plus ultra in UN-sadism I would estimate that between us, Dino Pionzio and I heard, in the hundred days of the General Assembly, one hundred speeches by Jamil Baroody. One day he spoke six times: at four different committees, and twice at the Plenary. The popular image of the United Nations as the densest collection of oratorical bores in the history of the world is owing as much to Baroody as to the next one hundred senior delegates who have served there. It is in part because he has served there forever (he was at San Francisco), and in part because he talks ten times more than the nearest competitor; in part because he never tires of repeating what he has said. Indeed, there is very little option for someone who speaks so much. If he had mastered the entire sum of human knowledge, he would still need, perforce, to repeat himself after a week or two.

It is a not widely observed phenomenon that nobody, but nobody, ever replies to Baroody. It is supposed, by him and a few sycophants, that this is because of his encyclopedic knowledge of the UN (there is no denying it), his facile use of historical analogy, his sarcasm, and his relentlessness. There is probably still another reason. Baroody is not afraid of anybody. That, of course, is true of few other delegates. But neither is he under any restraint. It is simply not conceivable that King Faisal would reproach him on account of anything he said. This means that he can get away, occasionally, with saying—in addition to the usual gallimaufry about Zionists and the causes of World War I and the suppression of the truth by the Associated Press—something that is true. And he would say it with the resolution of a man setting out from Southampton to sail around the world alone. At huge, uninhibited length. To do that would rupture the crystalliz- ing rubric of the UN. Suppose that something had got into Baroody causing him to take as much interest in, say, Solzhenitsyn, as now he takes in the oppression of the Palestinian Arabs. He would talk about Solzhenitsyn before the Special Political Committee, the First Committee, the Second Committee, the Third Committee, the Fourth

Committee, the Fifth Committee, the Sixth Committee, and the General Assembly, until the nervous membranes of the entire body would shatter with the pain of it. It would require someone like Baroody: nowhere to go up the diplomatic channels (he is not in line to succeed King Faisal); a carte blanche from his employer; a private income; comfortable old age; total self-assurance. That is the secret of the forbearance he is shown.

It is probably incorrect to generalize that no effective organization can put up with such protracted bores as Baroody. The Senate of the United States, for instance, has no choice but to put up with its bores, and under Senate rules, the bore can talk for as long as he likes, subject only to cloture. But what happens in the Senate is that the place empties when the bores hold forth. And since it is required that one be recognized by the presiding officer, it is less easy to get the floor than in the United Nations, where a Right of Reply, or a Point of Order, is almost never strictly interpreted. Moreover, in the Senate, the serious business is done, for the most part, at committee meetings, whose chairmen simply do not extend the privileges of the filibuster uniformly to their fellow Senators. If Baroody were a member of the Senate, exercising the rights he exercises in the United Nations, committee hearings would be held clandestinely in the cellars of the chairmen's homes to avoid Baroody-intrusions. In the UN there is a total fatalism about Baroody. It is born of a combination of restraints. The Americans know that in the past he has voted with us on important issues, and that his vote is influential with the Arab bloc. The Africans are generally subservient to the Arabs, from whom they accept leadership in the non-aligned bloc. The Soviet Union is afraid of him for the same reason the Americans are—his can be the swing influence. All the individual delegates are afraid of his sarcastic and relentless attacks. But most of all, in the current season, he is tolerated as the altogether uninhibited local revisionist who explains recent, and not so recent, history in terms of: the Zionists, and their influence on the United States.

Baroody is seventy years old, was born in Lebanon, a Christian with a Muslim wife, who received a doctorate in London before coming to the United States in 1939. His personal power issues from his lifelong friendship with King Faisal, who soon after the UN was founded appointed him (through his brother, King Ibn Saud) as Permanent Representative. Baroody supervised the education of a half dozen of Faisal's sons, and, it is said, supervises the investment of Faisal's portfolio in the United States. Discreet overtures to King Faisal, having as their objective the emancipation of the United Nations from Baroody, have been decisively and even angrily rejected.

Baroody will occupy a theatrical position without any reference to the strategic damage it will cause. In the tense debate on the question of expelling the Chinese Nationalists, which expulsion Baroody vigorously opposed, his failure to concert with others caused him to make a motion at a catastrophically maladroit point in the debate, and Ambassador George Bush to leave the floor in disgust, muttering something about Saudi Arabia's "unguided missile." When the Special Political Committee met to consider a budget for the Palestinian refugees, to be dispensed as usual by the United Nations Relief and Works Agency (UNRWA), Baroody calmly proposed that the United States should pay the whole of the budget, since (a) the United States is rich, (b) the displacement of the Palestinian refugees would not have happened except for United States aid to Israel, and (c) the United States' imperialistic wars in Korea and Vietnam cost many times as much money as was needed to care for the Palestinian refugees. This caused Delegate Mark Evans to rise sputtering in rage, recalling that the United States has contributed $23 million annually to UNRWA, for a total of 64 percent of the entire sums contributed since 1950. Baroody countered with the observation that the $500 million we have given for Palestinian refugees over twenty-three years hardly compares with the $2 billion we committed to Israel during a single day in the Yom Kippur War, and that our concern for the Palestinian refugees was exclusively political. He will unfailingly say that which causes the opposition to harden its resolve. "Finally, but as a last resort," he said in considering the question of Namibia (South-West Africa), "consideration should be given to the sending of troops by OAU [Organization for African Unity], which has an army at its disposal, to liberate Namibia. The United Nations sought peace and not bloodshed, but if there was no other solution, it would have to resort to arms."

His protracted performances before the Security Council—of which Saudi Arabia was not this year even a member—during the debate over the cease-fire was an investment of the whole Baroody, and a revealing exercise in the uses, within the UN, of an anti-Jewish, anti-Zionist rhetoric.

It is a source of great historical anguish, in the UN, that the dreaded and odious Israel was formed as the result of a United Nations resolution. Accordingly it has become necessary to establish that the United Nations was then under the domination of the United States, that the United States was under the domination of Harry Truman, and that Harry Truman was under the domination of American Jews. These points Baroody so relishes to make that the foreplay is endless. First he will warn that the kept, Zionist-controlled press in the United States will not report his words—they will go even to the length of using static over the airwaves, to keep the public from hearing Baroody (Baroody regularly refers to himself in the third person). Here is a typical paragraph: "We have an Arabic proverb which says: 'He who starts the evil bears the greatest responsibility.' But now suffice it to say that the present situation is only the latest link in a long chain of events; and here I would like to address myself to every one of you members of the Council and, if the mass media of information allow my voice to carry beyond this chamber, to the people of the United States—because I am not talking only to you; you receive instructions from your Governments, and many of you are in the straitjackets of instructions; and as if sometimes the straitjackets of instructions were not enough, many of you put on the tight pants of procedure and we engage in a lot of talk without any action. How do I know this? I participated umpteen times in the Assembly and in this Council where resolutions were passed which Israel did not heed. When it suited it, or rather its representatives, they wantonly said: 'The Arab States can always muster votes.' Muster votes? I must remind Mr. Tekoah [the Israeli representative]—who, I believe, was in Shanghai at the time, in 1947—I do not know where he was, but I was present in Lake Success. We, muster votes? What did the Zionists do at Lake Success? It is better to ask it in reverse: what did they not do to bring pressure to bear on the United Nations, which counted only 51 or 42 Members then?"

Analysis, conducted at that pace, freezes the nervous system. Here in the Security Council fifteen Ambassadors are convened even as people are shooting at each other in the Mideast, a concrete proposal before the house, it is getting into the evening.

". . . *the Zionist movement, as I have mentioned time and again, is not native to the Middle East: it is a political movement started in Central and Eastern Europe by people descended mostly from the Khazars, who came originally from the northern tier of Asia on the outskirts of the Caspian Sea, and who settled, in the first century, in what today is southern Russia. There was a confrontation in the eighth century. One of the things that helped [Zionism] at that time was the Dreyfus Affair in France, when Herzl completed his Zionist manifesto and put the last touches in the Rue Cambon behind the Ritz, in a small hotel. I walked there last summer to see if the plaque was still there. I think they are reconstructing the hotel. There will be a larger plaque to commemorate the Zionist manifesto of Herzl. . . . I did some research in the City of London about the Balfour Declaration. I must mention it—2 November is not too far. After the Zionists found out that Kaiser Wilhelm II, who made a trip to Istanbul in 1898, could not persuade Sultan Abdul Hamid, on the request of his Jewish friends, to give an enclave in Jerusalem to the Zionists, and when the Kaiser told the Zionists that he had not succeeded—of course the Kaiser went, not as an emissary for the Zionists; he went to negotiate the Berlin-Baghdad railroad. . . . I am glad to see that my good friend Mr. Scali is back here, because I have a great deal of respect for his sincerity—although sometimes he has to use words to express the policy of his Government. We are all servants of our Governments. But I am adducing the facts of history, and I am sure my good friend Mr. Bennett and Mr. Scali's other colleagues will convey what I have said about how the United States was railroaded into the First World War by the Zionists, and to a large extent also into the Second. . . . There are 6 million [Jews in America] I believe. I do not like round figures, unlike Mr. Tekoah, who talks about those who lost their lives—but 6 million more or less. What do they do? They own most of the mass media of information. I wish I had the list with me; I have looked but unfortunately I have not. . . . I was asked to address an audience in Town Hall in 1944. Do you know where it is? It is off Sixth Avenue, the Avenue of the Americas. I think they still have meetings there. . . ."*

No one who has not read the original speech will believe the enormity of the act of charity for which I am responsible by this truncation. But the lethal diplomatic dose was as yet unadministered. *"For 25 years, and even before, I warned the Council and I warned the United Nations that there will be no peace as long as this foreign element is among us, a festering wound that has caused the abscess and the high fever. And there will be no peace unless the pus is drained from the body politic and the body social of the Arab world."* This—to an Israel which the Arab states have been reassuring could, if it drew back to its 1967 borders, continue to survive as an independent nation. And, as the Security Council struggles to make the cease-fire stick, *"Even if the war ends tomorrow, it will be recommenced at a future date, either by Israel or by the Arab States, by the Arab people."* Here is all the world begging Israel to negotiate in confidence that the Arabs have had a change in heart concerning their original goal to destroy Israel. . . . *"Once our enemies stretch out their hands to live as human beings* without a flag, *we will accept them in our midst,* but not under a flag."

. . . THE PRESIDENT. I should like to make an appeal to my good friend Ambassador Baroody. We have had a rather long day—

MR. BAROODY. Why did you not appeal to the Soviet Union?

THE PRESIDENT. —and it is rather late in the evening.

MR. BAROODY. Yes, it is late. Never mind. What do you think we are doing here? Playing? We have to work.

THE PRESIDENT [he is, by the way, Sir Laurence McIntyre of Australia]. We admire—indeed greatly admire—the eloquence of the Ambassador of Saudi Arabia. I should like to remind him that he was the very first speaker I heard in the United Nations in 1950 and I have enjoyed his eloquence since then. But I would, if I may, appeal to him to wind up.

MR. BAROODY. Yes, I shall wind up to please you as a friend, Sir. I shall take the floor again tomorrow. There is "Tomorrow and tomorrow and tomorrow" as Shakespeare said in *Macbeth*. I shall wind up, Sir. I mean that. It will take me two or three minutes. . . .

Well, I had run into Baroody. And the question of course is: Were he and the United Nations made for each other? One Senator remarked, on learning in 1934 that Louisianans had sent Huey Long to the Senate, that Caligula had at least sent both ends of a horse to his senate.

I returned from the Third Committee to my office, discussed with Dino some thoughts that had been plaguing me, sat down and wrote out a memo to Scali, copy to Henry Kissinger.

6.

Staff/Kissinger Lunch/Memo to Scali

TUESDAY

    I attended the first full staff meeting, on the twelfth floor, Scali at the head of the table, Tapley Bennett on his right, at the short end of the long, rectangular table. I was placed next to Scali, at the beginning of the long leg on the left, then Mark Evans. Opposite me was Congressman Buchanan, then Margaret Young, and Richard Scammon. The legs trailed northward about fifteen places at either side and then joined, forty feet opposite Scali. Two rectangular arrangements of easy chairs, surrounding the table, were reserved for the staff. The new press officer was introduced. He is Courtney Sheldon, who has just come in, replacing Nicholas King, who stood by for a week or two of overlap. By most extraordinary coincidence, I was instantly at home with both of them. I knew King from his days in Paris as head of the United Press supervising a staff that included my sister Priscilla. Courtney Sheldon has had a long and illustrious career with the *Christian Science Monitor,* and was one of the dozen correspondents I had joined on the tour of the ghettos under the auspices of Whitney Young. He is hungry for publicity for the UN, it being his job to get publicity for it, and he is always open, obliging, resourceful. Scali followed the procedure of calling first on Bennett, then on Schaufele, occasionally on one or two section heads, then seriatim on the principal staff representatives of the eight committees. They would in turn brief the room on the problems that lay immediately ahead. The atmosphere was a little too formal, and, with sixty to seventy people attending, there was not much dialogue, though one could gather by the feel of a staff member's report what was the general importance attached to his activity. It is as natural in the United Nations as in any organization that the importance of the corporate task looms larger than in reality it is; and that the distortions apply equally within the subdivisions. It is extremely hard to engage oneself wholly in a fortnight's debate on Napalm and Other Incendiary Weapons and All Aspects of Their Possible Use (Item 34) without becoming extra-clinically involved. I was much struck by the quality of the briefings. To be sure, there are the locutions, accretions on every institutional body. The acronyms, obviously; though there is a conscious —even self-conscious—effort, in deference to the lay delegates, to draw these out. When this is done, the speaker, perhaps to convince his colleagues that he is performing thusly not out of any lack of familiarity for the lingo but in order to oblige the neophytes, draws out the words like a slow chord on an accordion. I am especially amused at the courtly compliments we pay each other. When a staff member recites the activities of the preceding week, he normally makes reference to a statement, or explanation, given by one of the delegates, in which case it is *always* characterized the same way: "The statement of . . . was very favorably received." It might have been the worst speech in the history of forensic literature. On the other hand, it might have been the best.

For the most part the reports were spare, well organized, pointed, and nicely phrased. It has been said for years and years that the countries of the world send their second-rate people to the United Nations, and much is made of this in Shirley Hazzard's (awful) book *Defeat of an Ideal,* though perhaps she is talking only about the Secretariat. The United States people appear to be absolutely first-rate; first-quality stuff, which I suppose means either that somebody Up There in the State Department wants our best foot forward in the UN, or else maybe people in the Foreign Service put in for USUN service, for a variety of reasons, none of them obvious.

This being the first meeting, most of the talk is general. Scali tells us that Kissinger feels *very* strongly about his World Food Conference, so we are to push it *very* hard, and make it one of our principal efforts during this Plenary. No one demurs, and the meeting is adjourned.

There is curiosity about how Gromyko will perform. He is to address the Plenary later this morning, before Kissinger's lunch for the Arabs. Détente is in very full swing these days, and we are all anxious to see what a lobotomized Gromyko sounds like.

As predicted, Gromyko's rhetoric was very low-key, and the name of no nation, excepting only the African white countries, passed wrathfully through his lips, though he did criticize the policies of some (unnamed) countries. "Détente," in Soviet usage, appears to have become something much larger than the word itself would suggest, even as the NEP and the Five-Year Plans soared over their fixed meanings. But the mellifluousness notwithstanding, no points are surrendered. Thus, cataloguing the fruits of détente, *"An end has been put to the war in Vietnam. The flames of one of the most dangerous hotbeds of war have been extinguished. The just cause of the Vietnamese people has won a major victory."* And, later, *"True to its convictions of internationalism, the Soviet Union will continue to render the necessary assistance and support to the Democratic Republic of Vietnam and to side with the patriotic forces of Indochina."*

One learns almost instantly in the United Nations—I mean, it took me, oh, three days—that the convention is very simply to ignore Soviet infractions against the stated ideals of the organization. Not merely against those ideals that are tucked away in the old idealisms of the venerable documents of the very early years. But to ignore those that are being hotly debated at that very moment. This becomes something in which everyone is automatically trained; even as, say, altogether spontaneous conversations deploring drunkenness will take place in households in which a principal is an alcoholic; after a while, nobody notices. Mr. Francis Plimpton, the aristocratic New York attorney who a half dozen years ago was a United States delegate, proclaimed it as an achievement of the United Nations that 98 percent of the world's colonialism had finally ended. I asked him how he arrived at that figure given the vast territorial subjugation by the Soviet Union of Eastern Europe, and do you know, he had never thought of it? He is a vastly educated man who could probably sit down and write, from memory, a competent history of Eastern Europe. But we are all trained to suspend our standards, and so confident are the Russians of their running immunity that they are palpably unembarrassed at inveighing passionately against such practices as they are themselves most proficient in.

"No Arab," Gromyko explained to the General Assembly, "can be persuaded that he should put up with the existing situation. The only wish of the Arab States who fell victim to imperialist aggression is to retrieve what was seized from them by force. And they are right." It would not have occurred to anyone there, notwithstanding the provocative formulation, put forward as a moral-geopolitical universal, to substitute "East European" for "Arab," or "the East European States" for "the Arab States."

He spoke—here were the sternest passages in his long address—about "the rigorous observance of the cardinal principle of international relations, non-interference in each other's internal affairs." He was of course much exercised, as Malik had been the week before, about the Jackson Amendment. "No one should yield to the temptation to teach others how to manage their internal affairs. It is no secret that there are some who would like to impose their own domestic practices upon others, but internal practices, internal laws, constitute the line on the threshold of each State at which others must stop. Were we to take the path of imposing our practice upon other countries, be it in the field of economic affairs or in the field of ideology, then those who are [now] trying to persuade us to adopt alien laws, morals or customs would probably object, and this is understandable and justifiable." The impudence boggles the mind. But even if one is disposed to say that East Europe is the permanent exception to all such injunctions concerning the privacy of internal policies, ten minutes later Gromyko was pronouncing upon "reservations of apartheid and racial discrimination, the wrathful condemnation they merit and the vigorous struggle necessary to bring about their complete elimination. The immediate duty of the United Nations is to contribute to an early and complete elimination of these shameful survivals of colonialism, wherever they still exist, be it Angola or Mozambique, Guinea-Bissau or Southern Rhodesia, or South or South-West Africa." A total acceptance of the double line is at the heart of the weakness of the General Assembly. It has eviscerated the organization's organizational idealism, though I would become convinced that there is a way around the dilemma.

Gromyko's principal ploy was a call for a 10 percent reduction in the amount of money spent by the great powers on armament, the money thus saved to be dispatched to the aid of the Less Developed Countries in Latin America, Africa, and Asia. It was hoary (the same thing had been proposed in 1958), non-serious (it is the incremental dollar that provides military security), and schematically cynical (how define the military budget in China and Russia?). USUN spent weeks maneuvering to show it up for what it was, which was done; and it was more or less tabled. It would have been fun, and very nice theater, if John Scali, accepting the Soviet argument that we spend $80 billion on arms while the Soviets spend only $40 billion, could have got up that afternoon and announced that Congress, acting faster than ever in its history, had segregated $8 billion and put them in escrow with a binding agreement to make them available for such uses as Gromyko had described, upon receipt from the Soviet Union of $4 billion of hard currency.

Beyond that, Gromyko, who though he probably did not then know the date of the forthcoming Arab offensive, almost surely knew it was in preparation, having contributed (or sold) if not 10 percent, at least 5 percent, of the Soviet military budget to Syria and Egypt, warned: "Again and again we have to go back to the situation in the Middle East and it must be said outright that the situation there is dangerous due to the continuing aggression of Israel. Can the fact that today the hotbed of war is smoldering there rather than blazing give any reason for complacency? There is a risk of the flames of war breaking out at any moment. And who can foretell the consequences of that?" The pitch to the Arab states was unmistakable.

And, *urbi et orbi*, from the papal throne of the religion of world revolution, the reiteration of the old dogmas, however muted. "Those who wage a struggle for their national liberation, for their inalienable human rights and dignity and against colonialism and racism enjoy the invariable support of the Soviet Union. It is beyond all doubt that the Soviet Union will go on doing its utmost for that struggle to end in complete success."

As I say, USUN was very pleased by the moderate tone of the address.

At the reception before we sat down for lunch, in the same room where the staff had met three hours earlier, I spotted Arnaud de Borchgrave, European foreign correspondent for *Newsweek,* and veteran scoop-maker on the Middle East. He told me he certainly hoped Kissinger would say something breathtaking, given the pains De Borchgrave had taken to attend the lunch. He had received, in Geneva, forwarded from New York, a telegraphed invitation from Kissinger to attend the lunch. He telephoned *Newsweek* editor Osborn Elliott and said, you surely don't want me to go to New York to attend one lunch, do you? Elliott, in behalf of *Newsweek's* stockholders, had said hell, no, he assumed the lunch would be crowded with journalists. But a little checking revealed that only two journalists had been invited: De Borchgrave—and Hedley Donovan, editor-in-chief of *Time*. Elliott groaned at the competitive disadvantage in the event of a hot story, and told De Borchgrave to come on over. He had arrived the night before, and would return to Geneva that afternoon. I told him that judging from the performance yesterday, Kissinger was not in a newsmaking mood.

We were called to our tables, and to my amazement I found I was seated next to—Baroody. My altercation with him the afternoon before had caused a light ripple at USUN, ranging from apprehension at the top level (would Baroody, who is vain, take offense, and be standoffish to the United States?), to underworld amusement, at the junior level, that, stooping to pick up my first daisy, I should have tweaked the local rattler. I have the vision of a little old man buried in the Protocol Section of the State Department who gives himself silent chuckles by seating people thusly. It cannot have been a coincidence that at President Nixon's banquet at Peking, I was seated between Felix Greene and Wilfred Burchett, the two most notorious fellow travelers in Asia. Baroody was most jovial, and proceeded, at our table composed of one U.S. delegate and five Arab Ambassadors, to speak non-stop through four courses, explaining his position on a High Commissioner, and other matters. How was I liking the UN? he finally asked. I told him it was too early to tell, though not too early to have preliminary impressions. The day before, I told him, a feature writer for the Washington *Post*, preparing a story on Watergater E. Howard Hunt, had telephoned to ask how long had I known Hunt. "Twenty-two years," I replied. "You keep pretty loose company, don't you?" the enterprising reporter commented. "Are you referring to my recent appointment to the United Nations?" I replied, and Baroody professed to be amused, and what I said reminded him of what he had said to somebody at Lake Success.

I suppose that Henry Kissinger is more aware of being Jewish than others are aware of his being Jewish. And one must suppose that that awareness was never more intense than at the first meeting by the first Jewish Secretary of State in American history with diplomatic leaders of the Arab world a fortnight before an Arab-Israeli war would begin. His introductory note was under the circumstances masterful. "You are all looking at me rather suspiciously," he said with the twinkle and light irony with which he handles most situations. "I am in the position of the police agent sent to penetrate a Communist cell. The police arrive and start beating everybody up. The agent says—'But I'm an anti-Communist!' The policeman, continuing the assault, replies, 'I don't care *what* kind of a Communist you are!'" Kissinger then said what one has to say in such circumstances, that he could not, so recently installed, make any major policy declaration; that he understood their concern, indeed, their anguish; that no permanent peace was possible in the existing situation. There was no translator today—all the Arabs understood English. I observed their faces, intent, swarthy, shrewd, inquisitive, with dark formless suits (I was to find the Arab diplomats on the whole the most engaging and intelligent of those from any single region). In short, said Kissinger, "though you come from a part of the world that has produced many miracles, you can't expect us to produce one." And he pledged the friendship of the United States. De Borchgrave would have to exercise all his resources, which as a matter of fact are abundant, to make *that* into a hot news story.

Speaking for the Arabs was the head of the Arab League, the Egyptian Mahmoud Riad. He spoke gravely, though not threateningly. He said he "hoped" to restore good relations, but that Palestinian rights "must" be respected. People differ on the meaning of passages in the Koran, he said. So it is with the meaning of Resolution 242 (that is how they refer, at the UN, to the Jarring Resolution). But, he sought to make it plain, the Israeli interpretation of it was nothing less than a perversion; a profanation, if you will. Glasses were raised, and the lunch ended; and Scali told me on the way out that he wanted to see me.

Scali was upset. First he was upset about my tangle with

Baroody. He was under the impression that I had been asked by the staff not to raise the Point of Order, which was of course incorrect. He gave me a little background on Baroody and his occasional usefulness. Then he was upset because he hadn't known Dino had once been in the CIA. I told him I had informed his two principal aides of the fact, had not informed him directly since he was in Europe when Dino and I made the deal; and what did it matter? He suggested the procedure Dino and I should follow when we left the Third Committee chamber. Mahmassani, he went on, has a high opinion of my work, and so I should seek him out, and perhaps arrange to lunch together. So much for the preliminary matters.

What he was most upset about was the memorandum I had written him the night before, which lay in front of him with red lines all over it. Now to begin with, he said, *don't send me any memorandums. Just come see me or call me. Secondly, don't ever send copies of your memorandums to Kissinger.* That was of course easy: Since I would no longer write him memorandums, there would be none to send copies of to Kissinger; or anyone else. He began reading out loud parts of the memo. I had written:

MEMO TO JOHN SCALI, CC: H. KISSINGER, GUY WIGGINS, CAMERON HUME, DINO PIONZIO
I have had a preliminary experience with the Commitee on Human Rights and accordingly wish to set down a few impressions, and to suggest the course of action I intend to follow, always on the understanding that you approve.

1. Although thus far the committee has dealt primarily with the agenda for the fall season, in fact (a) the discussions of the component parts of that agenda are colored by direct advocacy; and (b) acquiescence in the order in which the committee proposes to proceed is itself an act of acquiescence on the question of what is and what is not important.

2. The policy of détente with the Soviet Union and with

China governs the activity of the State Department, and the State Department obviously will move in ways consistent with that policy.

3. United States participation in the United Nations is in part a direct expression of United States foreign policy, in part it is an expression of the United States' contribution to strategic ideals of peace, justice, and freedom. It is not, in my opinion, inconsistent for the United States to express itself cordially to the representatives of the Soviet Union, in Washington and in Moscow and indeed in most engagements with its representatives at the United Nations, while at the same time representatives of the United States, in public debates on strategic questions having to do with human rights, maintain a dogged position seeking to reaffirm the ideals of the United Nations.

4. It is probably worth an entire paragraph to say what ideally would be taken for granted—namely, that the manner in which United States representatives express themselves, for instance, in the Committee on Human Rights, is important. They should speak diplomatically, amiably, and even, when the occasion calls for it, deferentially. But the substance of what they say must not be lost. That substance is to serve the paradigmatic point—namely, that human rights are at a very low ebb in this planet, in part because they are systematically violated by governments that seek to distract attention from these violations by pointing to violations of lesser countries.

5. I do not view the success of the United States mission as measurable alone in the body count at the General Assembly. Those votes there that we are likely to win, we are likely to win irrespective of any distracting adherence to our ideals as expressed at the Committee on Human Rights. Those that we will lose we are likely to lose anyway. It is of course possible that a delegate or two, taking direct offense at something said by the United States at the Committee on Human Rights, will penalize the United States by voting against us on the Korean resolution, say. But it is unlikely that the swing vote would be thus affected. And if it were, the tactical loss would need to be measured against strategic gains we would stand to make by an undisguised, and

undissimulated, constancy to ideals nominally promulgated by the United Nations.

6. The purpose of the extra-political agencies of the UN is ultimately diplomatic: When the committee talks about the necessity for freedom of information, it votes for improved communications, which in turn lead to the encouragement of democratic and libertarian impulses. When the committee talks about the right of emigration, or the right to practice one's religion, it argues for pressures upon totalitarian entities which lure them toward the open society which is the most reliable friend of stability and equilibrium.

7. The genius of the committees, and of the public-member conception, lies surely in the effort slightly to distinguish between the direct agents of the State Department and the slightly detached agents that constitute the delegation. These are American citizens, schooled primarily in their devotion not to parochial principles of human rights as chauvinistically enumerated in the United States Constitution, but in internationally accepted enumerations of said rights as written into the Declaration of which we are a signatory, along with the Soviet Union.

8. Accordingly, unless I am instructed to do otherwise, I plan, as the U.S. member in the Commiteee on Human Rights, to feel free to discuss human rights even if the inference can be drawn from what I say that I also believe in human rights within the Soviet Union. I shall do this most tactfully, and in such a way as to make it extremely difficult for the Soviet representative, or anyone else, to frame any objections to what I say in plausible language.

Now, said John. Détente is *it* right now. And all our diplomatic maneuvering within the United Nations *must* be done with reference to that overarching policy. Although almost certainly in due course I would be arguing human rights in the Human Rights Committee, and in language applicable to the Soviet Union and China, we must all get our bearings first, and plot our strategy involving the major issues that would be coming up before the Plenary. He said he does not want ever to have to disavow me. I interrupted to say that if for reasons of diplomatic exigency he should find it useful to disavow me, or something I had said, I would understand that completely. He said he thought the last paragraph of my memorandum well worded and correctly framed. But, he said, *all* speeches I make must be cleared with him. To be sure, sometimes it is necessary to speak extemporaneously, but in those circumstances I am to weigh carefully U.S. policy. He reiterated his intention to designate me formally as United States member on the Third Committee. He suggested that I stay in close touch with Bill Schaufele, who is very experienced, and he took me in and reintroduced me to him. He was clearly not in a mood to discuss the implications of some of the points I had raised in the memo. He is harassed by Kissinger's physical presence at headquarters, and by all the arranging necessary for the various meetings with the heads of state and Foreign Ministers; so I took my leave of him and Schaufele, and went down five flights to my office, to discuss everything with Dino, who offered to pack up if indeed his CIA record was going to embarrass me. I forced him to agree that that was preposterous, and left for my apartment, to study up for two *Firing Line* programs the next day, one of them with Sir Alec Douglas-Home, who is here for the UN and expressed through his staff a special interest in doing a *Firing Line* program. But first I put in a call to my brother Jim in Washington, and asked him to please have somebody from his staff go to the Legislative Reference Service of the Library of Congress and get me—real fast—some information.

7.

Home, Burnham, Journal

THURSDAY

Sir Alec arrived in New York with the reputation of the toughest man in town on the matter of human rights. He had addressed, last summer, the European Conference on Security and Cooperation at Helsinki. It was during the period of mounting publicity given to Soviet impositions on Jews who wanted to leave Russia, and on Soviet dissidents. The European Security Conference is about two things. It is desired by the Soviet Union because the Soviet Union wants de jure recognition of its hegemony over Eastern Europe. It is desired by the West in order to reduce armaments, leading to the desired European security. The day before, addressing the General Assembly as British Foreign Minister, Home said it again: that this time around there was going to be something more than mere talk about human freedom. There had to be a change of a practical kind in the nature of people's lives. This tied in very directly with my involvement with the Human Rights Committee. And, since Britain faces roughly the same problems we face, I thought it would be enlightening to see how he squared off to the dilemmas.

I had been tipped off that he freezes a little at the beginning of press conferences and television talks, but that if all goes moderately well, a thaw begins, and the shyness and aloofness tend to recede. It wasn't obvious whether I was being told to go easy on him. He arrived with rather more aides than we are used to accommodating at the *Firing Line* studios, but then of course he *was* the British Foreign Minister. I began by asking whether his speech at the United Nations, calling for concrete results, was in the spirit of the "détente we all seek"?

He did not retreat from the rhetorical formulation which, as I have already observed, is: We must not have rhetoric, but progress. "You know," he said, "we've had plenty of declarations of our intentions to live at peace with each other, but what we want now is some practical manifestation that this is something that means something to ordinary people. . . . We want to see not just pious declarations of a desire to live together happily, we want this translated into action."

WFB: "I would like to explore, if I may, the meaning of a sentence that you used in your address before the General Assembly, which I found very riveting. It was the one in which you said, 'I trust that the Communist countries will be able to prove that they are for the basic freedoms of people everywhere.' Now since this is conjoined to a passage in which you eschew pious declarations, obviously the kind of proof that you desire goes beyond merely rhetorical affirmations of their belief in freedom of all people. So what kind of proof would satisfy your test?"

Sir Alec said we had to be "realistic" and not "too ambitious." For instance, he said, families that are separated, one spouse living in the United Kingdom, the other in Russia, should be reunited, and it would be a good test of Russian intentions if they began permitting this. Also, he thought it would be good to have joint television programs, shown in Russia and in Britain, explaining life in each country. "It wouldn't be realistic to go, for example, for pulling down the Berlin Wall."

WFB: "At Helsinki you had said, 'If your conference is essentially about people and about trust, then it is essential that we should do something to remove the barriers which inhibit the movement of people, the exchange of information and ideas.' Now what did you mean by *we*, *'We'* should do something?"

He replied that "we want to begin to try to create for the Soviet Union that kind of confidence that allows free movement within the law—I must insist of course—always of the country concerned."

WFB: "At the press conference after your speech yesterday you were asked specifically [about] this point—this was in answer to Mr. Gromyko's having said that he would not tolerate any interference with his own system. You said, 'Mr. Gromyko need have no fear that we want to upset the internal laws of the Soviet Union. If those laws are so rigid as to prevent any of the things happening that I have suggested or may want to put forward, well, that is the Soviet Union's concern.' How does that reconcile with your statement that you should *do something*, again conjoined to your statement that this time around you will *not be satisfied* with pure rhetoric? How can you *do something* if you confess at the outset that all the Soviet Union has to do is say no and that's the end of the matter?"

He said we couldn't tell whether they would say no. "The answer *may* be no. If it is, then we go back to the kind of confrontation and frustration from which we in Western Europe want to get away."

WFB: "Well then, when you say, 'We should do something,' do you mean merely that you should importune the Soviet Union to make these modifications?"

HOME: "I think 'importune' is carrying on rather the language of the cold war, isn't it, which we want to get away from. We want to be able to say to the Soviet Union, 'Look, can you do this, this and this? If you can this will be fine because it will start to loosen up relations. . . .'"

WFB: "If, let's say, Senator Henry Jackson were sitting in your chair, and he had used the phrase, 'We should do something to remove the barriers,' and I were to say to him, 'What do you propose to do?' he would reply, 'Well, I propose to withhold certain trading privileges unless they do as Sir Alec has suggested.' So here he has a concrete non-rhetorical sanction that he is prepared to deploy. Question: (a) **Do** you have any sanctions that you are prepared to deploy or (b) if there are, must you for diplomatic reasons keep them under wraps?"

Sir Alec said he didn't think that "you want to talk in terms of sanctions. . . . I think you must use persuasion to the limit. If you can't persuade the other side . . . then we simply just revert, as I said, to a state of a passive sort of confrontation, which is very unsatisfactory."

WFB: "But then you *are* employing sanctions, because if you say, 'Otherwise we will revert to the status quo ante,' that means they don't get de jure recognition for the existing division of Europe; it means that they don't get Most Favored Nation by the West; it means that they don't get economic credits by the West. So in fact you *are* prepared to deploy sanctions, unless what you are saying is, 'We will ask them as a matter of goodwill to make it easier for Soviet citizens, but if they choose not to do so we will proceed anyway [with détente].'"

HOME: "I think if they refuse to make any progress, there is no alternative but to return to the status quo, but we don't want to do that. . . ."

I had got as far as you can take a Foreign Secretary. I started to move over to the military question, but Sir Alec was suddenly dissatisfied with how the other had been left, and went back to it:

HOME: "—just to finish off this part of it. I don't think one wants to talk in terms of increasing sanctions because we want a response from the Soviet Union, and if there is no response, it is not our fault. We have made the offer; we have made the suggestions. If they turn them down, well, that's their affair."

So much for the Flame of Helsinki.

The answer then—if it can be decocted from the above—is that the West would have evolved a new formula. Instead of settling for no concessions by the Soviet Union in the tender of human freedoms, our new formula would be to say that we would not settle merely for rhetorical calls for increased freedom, and then settle for them anyway.

After that, there was a little needling at targets of opportunity. I reminded him that his country had been quite prepared to use sanctions against Rhodesia. Well, Rhodesia wasn't a legitimately independent state when the sanctions were voted. But the Soviet Union is not legitimately in charge of Czechoslovakia. True, said Sir Alec, and then used language he would never have used within the halls of the United Nations, which suggests the strength of the taboo there. "The occupation of Czechoslovakia is repugnant and goes against all the trends of the modern world, which is decolonization." He went on more broadly. "We do not agree with the kind of relationship there is between the Soviet Union and the countries of Eastern Europe because they do impose their authority on these countries. Although they say the troops of the Soviet Union are in Czechoslovakia with the consent of the Czechoslovakian people, of course it isn't true, and therefore they are operating what I would call an imperialism which most of the rest of us would have discarded in favor of granting independence, real independence." But, said Sir Alec, he wanted to make it clear that he was against sanctions, that in fact it was under the socialist government that sanctions had been imposed against Rhodesia, and his own government was bound to them because the UN Security Council had now mandated sanctions.

And there we had it.

I left the studio and chatted with Dino in the car. We were disappointed, but not surprised, that Home had waffled on the practical points he had become celebrated for insisting upon. Dino told me Scali had called during the performance and wanted me to go directly when I was through to his suite at the Waldorf to discuss committee assignments. Three days earlier, at the General Assembly, I had scratched out a note to Scali: "Honorable John: At what point does Your

Excellency appoint me to Human Rights?" He wrote out in pencil, returning the note: "In the next few days when we parcel out assignments." We wondered whether finally he was about to issue the order assigning me as a delegate in charge of U.S. representation at the Third Committee.

Dino dropped me at the Waldorf, and I went up. Scali and Schaufele were in the living room putting together items from the UN agenda with proposed delegates. I was hot and hungry, and Denise Scali got me a sandwich and a beer as I looked over Scali's shoulder. He asked me if the proposed assignments were satisfactory. Would I take on Item 12, the Report of the Economic and Social Council—on which I would be fully briefed? Yes. And Item 24, Scientific Work on Peace Research? Yes (the above were the work of the Second Committee). And, before the Special Political Committee, would I handle the Report of the Special Committee to Investigate Israeli Practices Affecting the Human Rights of the Population of the Occupied Territories, Item 45? And, before the Third Committee, Observance of the 25th Anniversary of the Universal Declaration of Human Rights (Item 56), Creation of the Post of United Nations High Commissioner for Human Rights (Item 57), Freedom of Information (Item 64), Status of the International Covenant on Economic, Social and Cultural Rights, the International Covenant on Civil and Political Rights and the Optional Protocol to the International Covenant on Civil and Political Rights: Report of the Secretary-General, Item 65. And, finally, Measures to Be Taken Against Ideologies and Practices Based on Terror or on Incitement to Racial Discrimination or Any Other Form of Group Hatred (Item 66). I agreed.

There was a lot of very important work to be done there, but much of it far removed from the area of human rights. A lot that would take my attention away from the work of the Third Committee. Moreover, there was a clinical feel to the assignments, and once again, I could detect what by now was a palpable reluctance simply to designate me as the delegate to the Third Committee. I was going to tell Scali about Home, knowing he'd be interested. But I was as sure that Schaufele would not be interested, not because he is uninterested in anything interesting, but because he had work to do, and Home was by way of a digression. So I left.

I went to USUN, to my office, and spoke with Dino, always comforting. He told me my brother had called, so I called him back.

He read me from Public Law 357, 79th Congress, the United Nations Participation Act in the UN, 1945, Amended, Section 2c:

"The President may appoint from time to time to attend a designated session or designated sessions of the General Assembly to the United Nations not to exceed five representatives of the United States, one of whom shall be designated as the senior representative." . . . Well, no laws broken yet. And Section 3: "The representatives provided for in Section 2 hereof, when representing the U.S. in the respective organs and agencies of the UN, shall, at all times, act in accordance with the instructions of the President transmitted by the Secretary of State unless other means of transmission is directed by the President, and such representatives shall, in accordance with such instructions, cast any and all votes under the Charter of the UN."

Jim said he had more—namely, a report from the Foreign Relations Committee, presumably an exegesis on the United Nations Participation Act. "Section 3 adds to what is implicit in Section 2—namely, that the representatives of the United States to the various organs and the agencies of the UN shall at all times act in accordance with instructions from the President. Thus, it is again made clear that the representatives to the Security Council, the General Assembly and the other organs are not autonomous but act under the authority of the President."

"In a nutshell, Bill, you are not a free agent," the junior Senator from the state of New York summed it up. I had typed out the law as Jim read it out, and now I showed it to Dino, who was not surprised: on the other hand nothing surprises him, particularly if it is bad news.

On Saturday morning I thought about it all, and spoke on the telephone with James Burnham and Frank Shakespeare. My first impulse was to resign. My reasons would have been straightforward. That I had been permitted to believe that my appointment as delegate was for a purpose defined in some way as relevant to my experience and qualifications. I say "permitted to believe" because to say "led to believe" would be unfair to Scali. True, he had permitted me to think lascivious thoughts about the work that might be done within the Human Rights Committee. But there is no reason why Scali should be held responsible for my shocking failure to research Sections 2 and 3 of the United Nations Public Participation Act. Even now I do not understand the purpose of the layman-delegate. As I reflected on the history of the statute, and the lapidary limitations on the freedom of movement of the U.S. delegates, I can only assume that the 79th Congress, under the subtle direction of President Harry Truman, fleshed out Presidential concerns in a sort of bill of attainder for the benefit of Mrs. Franklin Delano Roosevelt. She was, of course, the most conspicuous figure (a) in the United States, in 1945, after the President; and (b) certainly in the United Nations, after nobody. She was a very strong-willed woman with her own constituency, and her appointment to the United Nations was something in the order of a national imperative. It is plausible to assume that Mr. Truman told somebody to tell somebody to make it goddamn well clear that old Boca Grande would be taking orders from *him.* These instructions are of course framed in categorical, generic language, and they reached out and ventriloquized me, occupying Mrs. Roosevelt's seat, a generation later. I had, to excuse me, only this, that I remembered two years ago press notices having been given to a superb speech by U.S. Delegate Daniel Patrick

Moynihan, in which he tore asunder one of those preposter-ous reports by one of those UN study groups, assigning the major share of the social blame for everything to the United States. It had been widely reported, and I read it at the time, and wrote about it, and assumed that Moynihan was exercising the freedom of the typical delegate. True, two or three days after Scali asked me to take the job, I spotted in a news story that Moynihan was in New York, accompanying Madame Nehru on a brief trip here. I cornered him over the telephone at the Harvard Club, and we spoke for very nearly an hour, during which he urged me to take the appointment. We touched on, but did not probe technically, the question of the latitude given to a U.S. delegate. He seemed to say that extemporaneous speeches, or speeches written in such a hurry that they could not reasonably be submitted for clearance, could be delivered without atomizing the chain of command. But of course. . . . Moynihan's period at the UN was pre-détente. And Moynihan, as a UN-loving liberal Democrat, would be granted a little more presumptive license than I as a curmudgeonly Republican conservative.

The principal argument against resignation was decorum. I set a considerable store by decorum, which is the piety shown toward the human relationships that insulate us against the ravages of impetuosity. I maintained nothing but affection and respect for Scali, and doubted that he had intentionally gulled me into taking a time-consuming job with the requirement that I should put in cold storage whatever useful skills I have developed. Moreover, to resign would be fatuous in a highly uncomplimentary way. Détente dated to before I agreed to serve. And the law robbing me of any personal autonomy was passed before my twenty-first birthday. What would I now be resigning in protest against? My failure to probe the job I had accepted?

The arguments against resigning, except for the sake of an instant's personal gratification, were overwhelming. More-over, looking at it the other way, the iron control of the White House over the deeds and words of the delegates to the General Assembly saved me from the embarrassment of personal association with positions taken by USUN with which I disagreed. And—to add to it all—I could not at this point find anything at all to justify the suspicion of last July that Nixon was appeasing the right wing by naming me as delegate. It had always seemed to me implausible. And anyway, very little attention had been given, publicly, to my appointment: the briefest notices in the newspapers, not even an editorial (that I knew of) remarking the anomaly. I fear that such is the situation that if Nixon had appointed his Irish setter as delegate, the managing editors of the Republic would not have noticed, unless it was suspected that he was being put beyond the reach of the Watergate grand jury.

On the other hand, I must not waste time—cardinal sin. It was then that I resolved to write a journal, and publish it, and see if I could come up with something useful. Perhaps a delegate's experience in the United Nations—and here it would indeed be important that he should be not a member of the Foreign Service, inured to the ways of diplomacy, or a longtime member of the USUN, trained in the perspectives of the United Nations—could say things, from a personal experience, that might be useful (might, as they would put it, in Washington, "furnish some inputs") in bringing about a better understanding of the United Nations. If this proved true, I found myself saying to James Burnham, then I would not, after all, emerge the screwee.

8.

General Assembly Foretaste/Chile

MONDAY

Meanwhile, at the General Assembly, Yugoslavia delivered its address, hard-line solidarity with the non-aligned, the Poles gave a non-provocative address about this and that, Colombia, having just purchased twenty-five Mirage jets, denounced the waste of arms purchases, and the Albanians, ever the servants of China, began circulating a letter from Prince Sihanouk to the Secretary-General making the case for ejecting the present representatives of Khmer (Cambodia) and accepting those of the petitioner Sihanouk, a warm-up for one of the issues USUN would take most seriously. And over at the Third Committee, Mauritania delivered a bitter attack against Portugal and NATO, and Romania called for censoring those nations that refused to impose sanctions against South Africa. And, at the Fifth Committee, Cuba inveighed against the "unstable capitalist monetary system," suggesting the adoption of a new, more stable currency unit which would be immune to inflation—a terrific idea, by the way.

It was with trepidation, never having lobbied before, that I met, by appointment, at the plushy, monochromatic lounge —Pullman, Premier Cru—just outside the General Assembly with Gabre-Sellassie, the Ethiopian Ambassador whose vote we courted on the Korean issue. Dino was with me, and Sally Werner, a pert, pretty, and extremely intelligent specialist on the Korean issue. Lobbying, at this level, is a ritual. But precisely because Gabre-Sellassie is a civilized man one cannot dispense with the ritual. In an economical universe,

I'd have said to him: Look, pal, you know the arguments for voting on our side. Are you going to do so or not? And if you are leaning against us, is there anything we can offer your government that might make you change your mind?

Instead, I went through my paces. I reminded him that the Ethiopians had actually sent troops to fight with us in South Korea, and that it was hardly a tribute to their memory, or to the integrity of the action, retroactively to illegalize it. He listened carefully as I repeated everything he already knew. Then he told us that he had not received final instructions on the matter from Addis Ababa, that in fact at the Algerian Conference of the Non-Aligned where the resolution to illegitimize the United Nations Force in South Korea was carried, Ethiopia had not been consulted ahead of time—leaving us to think that he was emotionally on our side. As a matter of fact, we knew this anyway. But we also knew the strength of racial and regional ties, and he confessed that the most we could reasonably hope for was an abstention. Invocations of regional and racial solidarity tend increasingly to prevail over a genuine, thoughtful national independence. And Ethiopia, already under a cloud for its Christian, dynastic, pro-Western tradition, is under great pressure not to break with the African monolith. In any event, he promised—he could do no less—he would definitely take my arguments into consideration, and we shook hands and separated. I filed a detailed report to Washington and, highly compressed, it went out in a report to American embassies all over the world along with other items of interest from that day's proceedings, as follows: GABRE-SEL-LASSIE (ETHIOPIAN) MADE PLAIN TO BUCKLEY IF HE HAD OWN WAY HE WOULD VOTE WITH US ON KOREAN ISSUE BUT STATED LIKELIHOOD WAS "BEST" WE COULD HOPE FOR IS ETHIOPIAN ABSTENTION. HE EXPLAINED ETHIOPIAN POSITION AFFECTED BY NON-ALIGNED CONFERENCE KOREAN RESOLUTION, POINTED OUT IMPERATIVES OF AFRICAN SOLIDARITY, AND ADDED HIS FONMIN [foreign minister] WILL MAKE FINAL DECISION. I had added in my memorandum, *pour m'amuser*, that I had not reminded the Ambassador of all the past favors done for Ethiopia by the United States, for instance the exiling there, twenty years ago, of New York pimp Mickey Jelke, who, in the wisecrack of the season, had been sent to Ethiopia to help Haile Selassie. That sentence mysteriously disappeared from the memorandum as circulated.

In the General Assembly, China spoke, and made the expected points. China's rhetoric, by the way, is rather low-key, nothing like the searing Red Chinese stuff of an entire rhetorical generation. China complained of a U.S.-U.S.S.R. hegemony. She called for the expulsion from the UN of the Lon Nol government in Cambodia, and for UN withdrawal from Korea.

A spirited morning in the General Assembly, the following Thursday.

Sixty-two non-aligned nations sponsored a resolution in the Second Committee calling for a Special Session of the UN General Assembly for the purpose of discussing Economic Development exclusively. It is as we had been told in Washington: The principal non-political concern of the LDC's (as they call them—the Less Developed Countries) is to devise a means of stimulating international economic redistribution. Toward that end a number of countries, working in a number of ways, are engaged; and it isn't yet clear (to me) what they will come up with of a concrete shape. It presumably wouldn't work for the special session of the 30th General Assembly, which is now scheduled to consider Economic Development pursuant to this resolution, simply to assess, say, West Germany, Japan, France, the United States, and the Soviet Union a share of their worldly goods, for the benefit of others, like a committee of Congress sitting down to decide what shall be the progressive rate of income taxation. Such a move would not go down well in the chancelleries of West Germany, Japan, France, the United States, and the Soviet Union. It would need to be more complex, and the gleam we think we see in their eyes is no doubt stimulated by the SRO performance of the Arab oil states. By coincidence, I traveled back this afternoon from

Washington with Peter Peterson, formerly Secretary of Commerce, and before that, international economic adviser to Nixon, and he gave me to read a paper he had just finished delivering to one of Robert Hutchins' Pacem in Terris jamborees, wherein Peterson noted that the old terminology is manifestly anachronized. It used to be the poor and the rich nations, or—depending on the preferred euphemism—undeveloped, underdeveloped, or less developed countries. More realistic, says Peterson, is to distinguish between the rich-rich nations, the poor nations, and the poor-rich nations. These last are the undeveloped nations which, however, are rich in natural resources. The usefulness of these natural resources came to the UN as a sunburst. What the Arabs could perform with their oil embargo, *mutatis mutandis* the Congolese and Chileans can perform with their copper, the Bolivians with their tin, the Mexicans with their silver and lead. It takes a certain amount of imagination, but not too much, to project the economic situation if several nations with oligopolistic control of a critical commodity concert, and parlay their advantages to their benefit, either by holding out for highly inflated prices or by exacting preferential economic arrangements—discriminatory pricing. It is something to keep one's eyes on. There isn't a strategy of resistance yet formulated, as witness our incompetence in coping with the Arab boycott, and the fragmentation of the West when confronted by it. Bob Kitchen, our principal expert in these matters, is highly sympathetic to the economic demands of the LDC's, and devotedly committed to the proposition that foreign aid is the very best kind of investment for the United States. One to watch.

I note that the Special Committee has reported on the U.S. Virgin Islands. It was instructed to inquire into the Virgin Islands (among other territories, none of them under Communist control) by a resolution of the General Assembly of last year called Declaration on the Granting of Independence to Colonial Countries and Peoples. The Special Committee notes solemnly several things: (1) The Virgin

Islands should determine their own future. (2) Although the United States has indeed held a general election in the Virgin Islands and convened a Constitutional Convention, the Special Committee believes that "there is a lack of significant constitutional progress toward the full implementation of the provisions of General Assembly resolution 1514 (XV)." (3) Although the Constitutional Convention's proposals were endorsed by a significant majority of the electors (there are a total of about 15,000), the committee "considers that these proposals and the resolution do not fully reflect the views and wishes of the people in regard to their future status." I was particularly interested by the reply from the Venezuelan representative made to the American who said: You object that the separatists in the Virgin Islands lost by a narrow vote, and thus you demand, in effect, a fresh election. If the separatists had *won* by a narrow vote, would you also demand a fresh election? "That," the Venezuelan said, "would be different." Accordingly, it urges the administering power (us) not to prejudge and prejudice "the status question." (4) The Special Committee is displeased that the Virgin Islands delegate to the U.S. Congress did not elect to appear before the UN Committee. (5) The Special Committee wishes the United States were more prompt in filing its Behavior Report with it. (6) The Special Committee notes that there has been a downward trend in tourism to the Virgin Islands, does not note that this is because tourists have been shot while playing golf in the Virgin Islands, and believes that something should be done to broaden the economic base of the Virgin Islands, to which end it is "of the opinion that the advice of the specialized UN agencies accustomed to dealing with such a problem might prove valuable." (7) It believes that something should be done to reduce unemployment (membership in the UN?), and to improve labor relations and to strengthen law enforcement. And, finally, (8) it reproaches the United States for not welcoming into the Virgin Islands a UN mission "to enable the Committee to acquire first-hand information on the situation prevailing in the Territory and to ascertain the views and wishes of the people concerning their future." It has not occurred to the committee to send its members down there disguised as tourists, thereby simultaneously (a) improving the tourist trade, (b) stimulating a desire for self-government, and (c) having a nice, sun-drenched vacation.

Afghanistan, Australia, and Morocco have spoken, and now it is Portugal's turn. But just as Antonio Patricio rises, the Soviet Union's Malik claims the floor on an "urgent" matter. He advises the General Assembly that he has just heard over the radio that the Chileans intend that very afternoon at 4 P.M. to execute "one of the outstanding leaders of Chile, Senator Corvalán, General Secretary of the Communist Party of Chile."

"One can disagree, one can fight along ideological lines, one can have a difference of view," said Malik, speaking for a country in which one cannot disagree, cannot fight along ideological lines, and cannot have differences of view—"but to kill, to shoot and to execute for ideological reasons is not permissible in the second half of the twentieth century." It was certainly permissible in the first half of the twentieth century. "We wish to appeal to you, Mr. President, and to the Secretary-General, to adopt urgent measures so that the threat may be removed from Senator Corvalán of Chile."

At this point Mr. Patricio, waiting by the rostrum for Malik to finish, began his speech. But the chamber had all but emptied. It is the practice of the non-aligned states to clear the chamber as a gesture of contempt for speakers from Israel, Portugal, South Africa, and (at least during this session) Chile.

Patricio spoke calmly, and at some length. Primarily he was concerned about the subsidizing of terrorism in Angola and Mozambique. "How can we claim that certain general principles which are declared to be fundamental in some areas are not valid for the entire world? How can we explain that the interpretation of these principles varies according to the latitude, the continent, or the level of economic development of the areas in question? Certain governments that, on the one hand, defend the inviolability of European borders, that claim the right to crush any form of subversion within their countries, and that condemn the terrorism which victimizes their citizens, on the other hand, support subversive movements in Africa, finance terrorism, and assert the right to violate the boundaries of southern Africa."

Concerning the movement to recognize the revolutionary government of Portuguese Guinea—they write it down now, in UN documents, as "Guinea-Bissau," he said: "In an international society of States—a reality on which the Charter of the United Nations is based—there is no possible justification for the bestowal on groups lacking an international juridical identity, of rights more ample than those granted to States."

Then he said something so palpably true about the political evolution of the General Assembly during the last few years that it is accepted as axiomatic and therefore never mentioned. "The influence of the African states in the debates and resolutions of the General Assembly is held to be dominant. And in fact, it is. Their votes are decisive in the resolutions that are approved, not merely because of their numbers but also because of the influence they have upon other countries, which keep them company in an alignment whose roots, however, are unfortunately not to be found in a conviction of the justice of the causes defended, or in the merit or efficacy of the resolution approved, but in bare-faced opportunism and convenience. Votes which are cast with Africa, in order to please Africa, are votes [I think he meant to say 'are often votes'] against the real interests of Africa. It has been said here, with some truth, that should this tendency continue, the United Nations would soon turn into a mere branch of the Organization for African Unity." Later in that day, a motion to permit representatives of the black liberation movements to participate in the debates, at the Assembly and in committee, was carried, 80 in favor, 9 (including the United States) against.

Since self-determination is ostensibly the anchor of UN policy, as Malik had stressed the preceding week, concerted action against Portuguese Africa had been based on an eristic construction of the Charter which now Patricio mocked. "The gravest accusation leveled against us, and one which is linked in a special way to the acceptance of this Organization, is that we constitute a threat to the independence and to the integrity of the African countries. It is even asserted that we are a threat to international peace and security. That is a strange, not to say astounding, accusation, which has repeatedly been made against us. But I ask you: Where are the African countries that have been invaded and conquered by Portugal? Where are the territories of African states annexed by Portugal? Which part of any African country has at any time been claimed by Portugal? Which frontiers in Africa do we seek to alter in our favor?"

Patricio went on at some length in order to attempt to document that political freedom in the territories was available without any reference at all to color, that the level of educational and economic activity had risen in Portuguese Africa above that in the rest of Africa, etc. etc. It is surprising that the Portuguese do not realize (no more do the South Africans) that evidence of concrete progress is least pleasing to the ideological critics of their regime, inasmuch as said figures are invidious, pointing to the relative lack of progress, economic and political, in the all-black countries. If by the end of the decade every twenty-five-year-old African living in Mozambique and Angola was a doctor, a lawyer, or a professor, earning $25,000 per year, and registering approval of ties with Portugal by 99 percent of the vote, the bitterness against Portugal in the United Nations would increase, not decrease. Still, the absence of Portugal's critics from the chamber stressed the huge frailty of the General Assembly, the overarching paradox. While as a legislative body it is useless, and while as a debating body it is invaluable, it does a great deal of legislating, and absolutely no debating.

Raúl Bazán, the Chilean representative jetted to New York by the generals after the coup, could not wait for Patricio to finish, to get his hands on the microphone in order to denounce Malik's accusation as "a monstrous example of cynicism and falsity, and a shameful means of using the General Assembly for the most shameful political purposes. . . ."

But Malik quickly interrupted Bazán, on the grounds that he was not speaking on a Point of Order. Benites (the President, presiding) eased Bazán off the podium. Baroody got into the act, seeking, as he put it, to avoid "pandemonium" and said a great many things, trying to pour oil on the water, and suggested that purely as a humanitarian gesture a telegram should be sent to Chile pleading for Corvalán's life. There followed a UN ritual seldom executed quite so brazenly. Delegates rose to denounce Chile and plead for Corvalán's life. Bazán had insisted that unless he was permitted to speak, it would all be a waste of time, but the President ruled that Chile was not appealing to a Point of Order, and Bazán was too inexperienced to know how to handle it. Accordingly, Bulgaria spoke about the "further monstrous crime" contemplated by the "fascist junta." And Poland rose, to say as much. Then Czechoslovakia, to say that it had been forced to break off diplomatic relations with the Chilean junta. Then Hungary. Then Mongolia. Then the German Democratic Republic. Then the Ukrainian Soviet Socialist Republic. Finally it was Bazán's turn.

He said he was glad, in retrospect, that he had not been permitted to speak earlier, because it had been so instructive to listen "to the six or seven speakers who preceded me, [to see] how hastily the satellite socialist delegations echoed the words of the Soviet Union." Then he really let the Soviet Union have it—the only time the Soviet Union got it in the General Assembly during the entire session. Just a few sentences, not more. "Of course I do not believe that there is any humanitarian concern on the part of the representative of the Soviet Union. Human life has never been respected in the life of the Soviet Union, where examples of not single but of massive executions abound, executions determined by the desire to eliminate anyone who dissents from the views of the lords of the Kremlin. Respect for human life among Soviet representatives is but a farce. Even now they are preaching to all the world that they have ratified the pacts and conventions on human rights, but take great care not to say that those conventions were rendered useless by the interventions of the representatives of the Soviet Union here since 1956 [the reference is to a tangle of technicalities by which the Soviet Union sought to slow down the whole Human Rights machinery] and that those pacts and conventions will go into force only in two or three generations as a result of their action. Now they do not feel bound by them. All that they are doing here is to speak untruths."

As to the factual matter under consideration, said Bazán, Corvalán was *not* going to be shot that afternoon; in fact, he was not even under sentence of death. He *was* in prison, charged with breaking laws that were in effect under the Allende regime, and can hardly be described as ex post facto laws of the junta. He would have a trial, and adequate defense, and there would be witnesses at the proceedings. (Six months later, Corvalán was still alive.)

One would think, on receipt of these reassuring factual data, that that would have ended that. But the momentum of the UN is not so easily checked. Cuba rose to denounce Chile. And Yugoslavia's speaker didn't even bother to adjust the sentence to conform to the news Bazán had just now given us: "And now we have the most disturbing information that the junta is preparing to execute in a matter of hours Senator Corvalán. . . ." At least, to give evidence that he was not a zombie, he might have said, "And now we have the most disturbing information—unconvincingly denied by the Chilean delegate—that the junta is preparing to execute in a matter of hours Senator Corvalán. . . ." Then Malik again, this time to talk about all the corpses in Chile following the coup. In the course of his long supplementary attack on Bazán, he acknowledged a little parliamentary maladroitness. His petition, that the General Assembly cable Chile to spare Corvalán, "was supported [he remarked] by a whole series of delegations. Unfortunately, the circumstances developed in such a way that the representative of fascist Portugal had been speaking and therefore our African friends had demonstratively left the room." But clearly that didn't sound quite right, because it suggested that he might have been critical of the Africans for leaving the chamber when there was duty to be done in behalf of Corvalán in Chile. So Malik, an old hand, said that *he too* had been absent. "We, as a mark of solidarity, followed their example and left the meeting hall. We did not choose to listen to the racist who was denying and ignoring the numerous decisions of the General Assembly and the Security Council designed to rid southern Africa of the last remnants of colonialism—and the most heinous and shameful kind—Portuguese colonialism. That is why we and our brothers and friends from Africa and Asia were absent; it was in protest against the fact that a Portuguese racist was speaking from this rostrum, the representative of a Government which is oppressing millions and millions of Africans." (That is Bolshevik pointillism. A few sentences later, Malik said: "All the partisans of Allende are being destroyed and killed by the junta." That would be in the order of 2 million people.)

It was left only for the representatives of the Byelorussian Soviet Socialist Republic, and of Romania, to make their statements denouncing Chile's scheduled execution.

Crowded into a single session of the General Assembly, one had everything one gets in the General Assembly.

9.

Waldheim Lunch/South African Credentials

I was invited, along with other members of the U.S. delegation, to lunch with the Secretary-General. By arriving exactly on time, I arrived early, and was ushered through an imposing number of corridors and security guards and aides, who were very pleasant. In due course Kurt Waldheim came. I had met him socially a year ago, and we chatted, Bloody Marys in hand. I had asked him a routine question about staff and found him explosively communicative on the subject. He terribly needed, he said, a deputy of his own choosing. There was the pause that requires the listener to ask the obvious question, which in this case was: "Well, why don't you get one?" Because, he said, he needed someone he had previously worked with and knew well, and that meant a West European, and how could "I, a European, possibly explain my choice?" Such, he said, were the pressures for symmetrical regional representation, all the way up the huge Secretariat, that he, a West European, could not possibly ask for, as deputy, another West European. He repeated —"What reason could I give?" I suggested that he try saying that he was an eccentric. He laughed. I asked him whether the genesis of the exact day set for the first meeting of the United Nations in San Francisco was widely known. He said not only was it not widely known, but he didn't know it himself. Well, I said, I read it in *Time* magazine years ago,

109

and was greatly struck by it. What happened was that at the Dumbarton Oaks Conference, where the preliminary meeting was held among the principals who would launch the United Nations, there was a very early deadlock, with the Russians holding out adamantly for some day in early May, and the Americans holding out adamantly for mid-April. The deadlock lasted for hours and hours, and suddenly a drawly British voice was heard, from deep within the lower echelons of the British delegation. It was a youngish Foreign Service officer, Gladwyn Jebb. "Why not April 25?" he proposed. The chairman of the meeting turned icily in the direction of the bumptious underling and said, "Why April 25?" "Because," said Jebb, "that's my birthday." Waldheim liked that, but I doubt he took it as serious precedent for a new approach to staffing the Secretariat.

Tap Bennett came in, and they reminisced—Waldheim who had been Austrian Ambassador to Canada and Austrian Foreign Minister, knew Bennett from way back. Bennett always chews the rag with wonderful relish, and the least conversations are puffed up with estrogen by his diffident, and comradely, enthusiasm. We sat down in the SYG's dining room ("SYG" is how Secretary-General appears in all the cables) and had a typical four-course meal. Came the toasts. I imagine that Waldheim has such a lunch every day, each time for a different delegation, though perhaps he might be permitted, discreetly, to put one or two countries' delegations together, since there were less than 135 lunches between mid-September and mid-December. He toasted the United States delegation, and devoted five or six minutes to the importance of the United Nations. John Scali replied. He is awfully good at that kind of thing. His rhetoric has that no-nonsense ring to it, which is a deadly necessity when you are toasting the United Nations, because only it can vault the skepticism that inevitably affects initiates. I listen carefully to after-dinner toasts, have heard a great many of them, have done a few of them myself almost uniformly awful, and I marvel at the skill of such as John Scali. The massage is indeed the message in these situations, because here one is, thirty-eight floors above the level of the East River, after a Bloody Mary, a white wine, a red wine, and a champagne, and perforce one must get into the spirit of the thing. I knew of a man, a graduate of Yale University who had played hard and successfully on the football team as an undergraduate, and never quite got over it, who during the thirties and forties would never miss a game, and such was his devotion that always he was asked by the coach to address the Yale players during half-time of the Harvard game. At that point he would say, with dread seriousness, that nothing those young players would ever accomplish, never mind if they lived to be eighty years old, would equal the importance of beating Harvard that afternoon. The point of it is that they left the half-time room believing it, and charged out onto the football field spiritually, intellectually, and physically disposed to perform miracles. I found myself getting a real lift, but of course it was not obvious what, descending the elevator, I could charge forth to do, though I think if I had run into Baroody in the lobby I might have rushed up and embraced him. As it happened, I had to go to Norfolk, Virginia, to give one of the speeches I hadn't been able to cancel. At 27,000 feet, I cooled off, though my admiration for Scali as half-time speaker did not diminish.

It had been a full day. In the morning, the black African states decided to pursue a parliamentary line against South Africa which made not only USUN but the entire Establishment within the UN extremely nervous. The non-aligned are flirting with the idea of taking away, by simple vote of the General Assembly, effective representational rights from any country against which grievances of substantive character had been lodged. The South African representative was poised to address the Assembly. Whereupon Mauritius, on a point of order, took the floor, and acting on behalf of the African states, whose spokesman Mauritius was during the month of October, pursued the following line of reasoning. South African apartheid is an effective denial of the vote of the black majority in South Africa. That had been pointed out and condemned over several General Assemblies. "We hardly see any logic in the attitude of the General Assembly in adopting resolutions according to which the representatives of the white minority regime of South Africa cannot speak for the entire population of South Africa, while permitting them year after year to take the floor in this Assembly and its Main Committees." Who says A must say B. The representative of Senegal, recognizing that the President would need to rule on Mauritius's point, rose to throw back his words at him. "It is obvious," he said referring to the congeries of resolutions on apartheid and related matters, "that [these] resolutions are binding, and Article 25 of the Charter reaffirms that binding character." Then he quoted from Benites' inaugural address. . . .

"I believe [Benites had said] that the legal basis for the binding nature of resolutions and declarations of the General Assembly lies in the fact that since the Charter of the United Nations is a multilateral treaty binding upon the parties to it, binding force is conferred on resolutions and declarations by the very provisions of the Charter on which they are based."

"Those are not my words," said Senegal triumphantly. "They were spoken by the President of the General Assembly during his opening statement this year. They are now more than ever of direct relevance. . . . [Accordingly] my delegation considers that it is morally, if not legally, impossible to permit the representative of the racist Vorster Government to address our Assembly in the present state of affairs."

Benites did not want a showdown, and hugged the rules to his bosom with great passion. He said that as a procedural matter, what it came down to was whether the South African representative had been approved by the Credentials Committee as representing the government of South Africa, and if that was what Senegal and Tanzania wanted a vote on—that the meeting should be suspended until the Credentials Committee could file its report—then they must make a motion exactly to that effect.

Baroody, who knows an impasse when he sees one, got up. As he knows very well how to do, he extruded a great deal of ooze, before coming to the hard parliamentary point, which he introduced with uncharacteristic tentativeness. "As far as I know—and I stand to be corrected by you or by any representative of this Assembly—the Credentials Committee has the authority only to verify whether the signatures on the letters of accreditation are authentic: that they emanate from a responsible official of the Government of the Member State."

He reminded them that what they were talking about was de facto expulsion. "But if South Africa is to be expelled from this Organization, as is the goal of a good majority of the United Nations, that can be done only by the Security Council. Admission and expulsion are the prerogatives of the Security Council." If the Assembly wanted to recommend to the Security Council that it expel South Africa, why that was something else. But, he said, you can't ask the Credentials Committee in effect to expel the South African representative, because "juridically the Credentials Committee has no power. It takes someone like me to draw your attention to this fact because I am sure my African and Asian brothers have faith in me."

He pointed out that Israel was still a member of the UN, even though it had been condemned, for one thing or another, twenty-five times.

And then, with little-cat-feet, and with not inconsiderable skill, on to the detonating point: "*I want also to draw the attention of my colleagues, regardless of whether they come from Africa, Asia or from anywhere else, to another point. Unfortunately, there are many governments that are not representative of their people. In every-day jargon we call them dictatorships. I am not going to mention names—God help me if I were to. I* believe there are about three or four dozen of them." (Of the 135 members of the United Nations 20 are governed by parliamentary representation.) "And these governments, regardless of ideology—mind you, I am not talking of an ideology, and to do so might get me in trouble—do not represent their people. This has nothing to do with color. Also human worth and dignity is not only a question of color but of the human person, regardless of his color, creed, belief or what have you. If we in this Assembly find that the credentials of South Africa are not valid, what will prevent me, or for that matter anyone else, from bringing before the General Assembly the necessity of expelling States X, Y, and Z on similar grounds? Let us be frank and courageous and not act merely by solidarity." Indeed. When last did King Faisal get carried to his palace on the shoulders of the citizens of Saudi Arabia after a free and contested election?

Benites had arrived well briefed on the procedural argument, and quoted from past Presidents in an attempt to narrow the issue. And he quoted from himself when, as representative from Ecuador, he had said a few years ago that he would "never sacrifice a legal principle for a political maneuver."

Senegal shot back with a shrewd legal-moral point. He was not asking for expulsion, he said, "as our doyen, Ambassador Baroody, has [suggested]." His point was that, it being grounded in the General Assembly's debates and resolutions that though there are 16 million people in South Africa only 3 or 4 million people vote for the government in power, then the representative of South Africa, whatever the Credentials Committee says, is not in fact authorized to act in behalf of South Africa. "That is why we raised our Point of Order. The African Group has not taken its decision lightly. Our ministers met in order to take it." But even then he took a step back. ". . . we do not wish to force a confrontation on the problem between Africa and the President; but we would ask the Assembly to reflect upon the choice the President has just made between the position of Africa and the position of South Africa."

Benites was very aggrieved by this formulation, and insisted he had taken no position; he had merely recited the rules of procedure. Nor did he back away from his legal point that resolutions of the General Assembly were binding on the individual states, by way of the Charter (if Benites were correct here, incidentally, the United Nations would cease to exist immediately).

The African states wanted a show of power without inviting the impasse that would come from overruling the President (which a majority can do). Accordingly (and by pre-arrangement—we had been briefed at USUN that this would be the Africans' fallback position), Senegal introduced a motion to suspend "the debate at this stage before the representative of South Africa takes the floor." It carried. 80 to 26 (the United States included), with 13 abstentions.

The next day the compromise was enacted. Syria moved that the report of the Credentials Committee be rejected. A vote on the motion carried, 72 to 37, with 13 abstentions. Instantly, Benites interpreted the vote as a "grave rebuke" against South Africa, and Mauritius—again by pre-arrangement—did not rise to ask the General Assembly to overrule Benites, for the purpose of interpreting the vote as intending more: namely, the rejection of South Africa's representative. But he did suggest that "friends of Africa" would join the boycott of the speech. Two-thirds of the chamber rose to leave. The rest of us sat, rather self-consciously.

Parliamentary strategists, musing over the debate, seem to agree that the General Assembly had treated itself to a preliminary skirmish, the result of which could be the effective expulsion of South Africa without so much as a nod to the Security Council. The technique had been adumbrated. The General Assembly could simply overrule the President's acceptance of the Credentials Committee's certification. Under such circumstances, South Africa (read also Israel, Portugal, or—with a slightly different introductory argument—Cambodia, Laos, South Korea; and in due course Chile, Greece, Spain, and so on) would not have been expelled from the United Nations, but neither would they have a vote or a representative in the United Nations. The positions of the Security Council and the General Assembly would not even be mutually exclusive in rigorously logical terms. The Security Council would recognize "South Africa." And the General Assembly would say that the Credentials Committee's certification of this particular representative as the representative of South Africa was . . . improper. Accordingly, South Africa would be listed as a "member" of the United Nations, but South Africa could not speak there, nor vote there. In point of fact, one wonders what difference it would make to South Africa. It has made no difference to Taiwan. But of course it would make a difference to the United Nations, which is probably why, during this Assembly, they did not push South Africa quite over the ledge. Next time maybe.

10.

The Cuban Incident

There was action in the General Assembly this afternoon. It was late, and the Cuban Minister of Foreign Affairs, Raúl Roa, began a long speech. Even for the UN, the vitriol was unusual. And especially so in this season of détente. Since in the recent period the satellitehood of Cuba by the Soviet Union has pretty much consolidated, diplomats pondered the meaning of Roa's raucousness, which they assumed had been cleared with Malik. As a sample, Roa said he wished to distinguish himself—a "simple human being"—"from those here who represent the bestiary and the forest. The henchmen of colonial racism and of imperialist propaganda have tried to cast a curtain of pretenses, fallacies, calumnies, scurrility, adulterations and vile accusations to disguise their machinations, their felonies, their knavery, their infamy, their crime and their irresponsibility. That was also the clumsy intention behind the ridiculous, lying, petulant, cowardly and low so-called 'I accuse' of the . . . rented Vice-Admiral, who dishonors this Assembly, bearing the stigma of traitor on his brow and his bloody garments after the murder of thousands of Chileans. . . ."

Roa spoke thus about Chile, and not much less harshly about the United States of course; but spoke also in similar terms about a half dozen other Latin American countries.

Chile was the first nation to inscribe itself for a Right of Reply, and Bazán walked to the podium. "I must once again tear the mask from the face of the representative of the

117

tyrant, Fidel Castro, who has just burdened us with a statement that is a prodigy of falsehood and hypocrisy. The Castro regime is the most abject of all in American history. It is a minority regime. It is a cruel and despotic one that took power by sword and fire, that keeps in power because of weapons and by terror and has torn up declarations of all human rights. It is a regime that is a scandal to the free mind of man. How, therefore, can it have the audacity to speak to us here of democracy and of decorum? How can they dare to impute to others every one of the crimes and aberrations, all the abuses and arbitrary acts, that daily they commit in their own country? . . ."

And ten minutes later, after defending his own country, he returned to the subject of Cuba. . . . "There is another difference that should be stressed, and that is that in Chile, where we respect human life, there has never been civil strife, although we know that in Cuba, Fidel Castro himself had, as his daily pastime, the watching of the executions before the *paredón*, to which he even invited some diplomats—"

At this point the official transcript of the General Assembly reads as follows:

> The speaker was interrupted by the representative of Cuba, who attempted to reach the speakers' rostrum, which gave rise to strong protests from other representatives.
>
> THE PRESIDENT: I cannot tolerate a disorderly situation of this kind. I shall, therefore, suspend the meeting.
>
> The meeting was suspended briefly, and then resumed.

What this account bowdlerized was this. Foreign Minister Roa began to walk toward the speaker, followed by four Cuban bodyguards. Roa was screaming *"hijo de puta!"* (son of a whore), and *"maricón"* (fag)—two all-purpose but very high-velocity Spanish swear words. At this point miscellaneous Latin Americans rose to block Roa's way—and Roa's bodyguards were seen poised to raise their pistols. It is the judgment of those closest by that shooting was very narrowly avoided. There are in fact no laws in the United Nations against carrying pistols, and though the UN Guards, chasing into the scene, were ready to throw themselves at the bodyguards if in fact they had lifted their guns, the possibility of Death in the United Nations was as close as delegates ever came. By a masterstroke of irony, at that very moment, a few chambers away, the Sixth Committee was discussing a "Draft Convention on the Prevention and Punishment of Crimes Against Diplomatic Agents and Other Internationally Protected Persons." None of the speakers pointed out that the General Assembly of the United Nations was that afternoon apparently as dangerous a place as any for internationally protected persons. The next day (we learned) there was a flurry of applications to the New York police by various delegates for permission to carry guns in New York. It would be illuminating to know exactly how many pistols are in the General Assembly when all the representatives are at their seats. We have nowadays the technology to get the answer to that question, by a little discreet X-raying. Perhaps someone will suggest to one of those roaming cameras up in the newsrooms behind the cornices that they shoot out an X-ray and identify the configuration of handguns among those gathered in New York to guard the peace of the world.

President Benites was greatly upset. He made a ruling for a brief recess, and was humiliated that his ruling had been overturned (though there is confusion as to the motive of those who voted nay). At that point Benites, all but in tears, informed his delegation in chambers, and the Secretariat, that he was going to resign: that he could not take it, particularly having had his ruling reversed. Scali was called in, and Brad Morse, the Under Secretary for Political and General Assembly Affairs, and everyone implored him not to do it, pointing out that resignation under such circumstances would bring great disrespect to the United Nations, which had been the intention of Roa; so, bravely, Benites returned to the presiding officer's chair and gaveled the General Assembly back to order. The Latin Americans were loaded for bear: They are a naturally eloquent race, and in no time at all they can produce a polished and lethal speech, long or short, preferably long. The limit was ten minutes per speaker. Brazil spoke of Roa's statement as using terms that "are perhaps common to his political vocabulary and which no doubt it is customary for him to employ as a compulsive syndrome of his ideological rabies." Bolivia finished off its speech with a fine peroration: "If Castro and Che Guevara thought that in Bolivia, and then in Chile, they could create new Vietnams, their mistake has cost them dearly. Whereas one rests in peace, free of his sinister missions, the other walks around in his luminous island which for him, like a bloody Macbeth, is a dark prison of which he is at once both jailer and prisoner." Paraguay, which had been denounced by Roa as a Fascist dictatorship, said: "In our Parliament senators and deputies of four different parties coexist; three of them in legitimate opposition. In Paraguay there are courts of law. There is no single party. There is no wall for executions. There are no revolutionary tribunals composed of fanatics, servile lackeys of the dictatorship. There is no capital punishment. There is no brainwashing for poets who think otherwise. We have newspapers which oppose us. There is no directed public opinion as there is in those countries that live under a single party and under the dictatorship of a proletariat. Yet, all this is redundant when the Foreign Minister of Castro has called representative democracy the [instrument] of the bourgeoisie and when he has irrevocably rejected it. We are, therefore, speaking two different languages. We believe in representative democracy and in multiple parties for the country as upholding ideological pluralism in the international field. As we say, he believes in the infallible dogma of Marxism-Leninism—the sole pontifex maximus urbi et orbi." Uruguay was the only country that alluded to the delegates' scandal of the bodyguards' firearms. "We are not afraid," he said, "of the representative of Cuba and his gunmen." John Scali said of Roa that "he once again has sunk to his usual level of gutter vulgarity as he speaks with the only language he can use—the outmoded vituperation of an earlier era. Time has passed him by." After clearing the record on the specific charge Roa had leveled against the United States, Scali said: "Castro's Foreign Minister speaks often of puppets. We can all agree there is no greater authority on puppets since his government is the original puppet on a string. We all know who pulls his strings, and how he dances!"

Exactly.

We all know it, and nobody says it. Not even in so high a pitch of general exasperation. Only one state—Uruguay—insinuated it. The American Ambassador would speak of the puppet, but not of the puppet master. Roa, exercising his Right of Reply to those who had replied to him, began by pointing out that Cervantes himself also swore on occasion, and then went on to say the usual things. He had been battered, but the taste of it, when it was all over, was that of the relish one takes in handling the little bully who walks into the room flaunting the manners of the big bully, thereby provoking his intimidated brothers to administer him a thorough thrashing—only to resume their seats, and pretend not to hear, when the big bullies return, storming into the room and saying, if a little less coarsely, much the same thing, out of that reasoned cosmopolitanism that comes from having been a successful bully for a very long time, and having atom bombs in one's lunch pail.

11.

Mobutu

THURSDAY

I got back in time to host a lunch at my apartment at Seventy-third Street for fellow delegate Buchanan, Foxy Carter, the Plenary officer who always knows what's going on, Admiral Harty, Henry Labouisse, who is the head of UNICEF, and Brad Morse, who physically intervened yesterday during the Chilean business to prevent physical combat between the Cuban and the Chilean representatives. Morse was a liberal Republican Congressman from Massachusetts before he left to take this job. His patience is legendary. He is always up there, sitting next to the President of the General Assembly, hour after hour. He claims to love the job fiercely, and is hard-bitten with UN fever. At lunch he suggested that "only the UN can provide solutions." I ventured to substitute the word "ventilate" for provide, and he agreed, amiable in all matters.

On to the Plenary. General Mobutu is to speak. He is a chief of state, and accordingly John Scali is seated at the delegate's chair. I am seated next to him, and on my left, Tap Bennett. Scali advises me in whispers that Mobutu has decided to expand on his prepared speech—by announcing that he will sever relations with Israel. Senator Humphrey got wind of this in the morning and phoned Scali to tell him to tell Mobutu that if he went through with it, that little piece of theater could cost Zaire (the Congo) exactly thirty million clams in American aid. Bennett relayed the message. (I wish I had been there. It would be interesting to know how *exactly* one says something of that sort. I am too embarrassed to ask

Bennett. It's like wanting, at age thirteen, to know *exactly* how the sex act is performed. . . . I shall have to ask Allen Drury.) Bennett leaned over and told me he doubted it would work, that Mobutu was riding the euphoria that hits people when they decide to do something dramatic at center stage. John Howison, flipping the pages of the prepared speech, noted the frequent use of the word "brother" by Mobutu, and recalled a line from Malamud's *The Tenants,* where the Jewish intellectual addresses the black novelist, "How're you doing, brother?"—only to be answered, "Who you calling brother, mother?" The allusion is to the fierce tribal hostilities in the Congo, and indeed throughout Africa, though at the UN they are all brothers. I whispered back to my colleagues my favorite Mobutu story, given to me as God's truth several years ago. Mobutu, it is generally accepted, bribed the Algerians to kidnap Tshombe. This they did, and proceeded to give him a truth drug to try to determine what were his secrets and where, if anywhere, did he have Congolese money stashed away, that kind of thing. So successful was the drug that the dazed Tshombe was spilling everything, almost euphorically. Whereupon the interrogators, carried away by their success, asked him more and more questions, which he answered readily. Then they asked him had he killed Lumumba. Yes, he said, he had. On whose instructions? "Mobutu's," he said. That part of the tape was not transcribed for Mobutu.

Who came in now, and delivered quite a speech; indeed there was none other delivered during the entire Assembly that began to match it for the enthusiasm it evoked among the delegates.

After it was over, I went home to dress for Kissinger's big dinner. I had a column to write, and though I had resolved not to write at all in my columns about the UN, I thought perhaps that something descriptive might not be out of order, so I telephoned Scali and reached him at the Waldorf. Did he mind, I asked, if I wrote something about the Mobutu speech? He replied characteristically. "Mind hell!" I wrote the words that follow.

GENERAL MOBUTU AT THE UN

It was quite a sight the other day at the United Nations General Assembly. The speaker was a chief of state. The delegates are for the most part a blasé lot, but it was in the air that General Mobutu was going to say something of some diplomatic consequence, and indeed he did, occupying an entire paragraph inside another news story in the New York *Times*. When a speech in the UN gets that much space, it is quite a speech.

As this one was. The newsmaking part of it was the decision of President Mobutu's government to discontinue diplomatic relations with Israel. He put the matter rather grandly. Israel, he said, is a friend. But Africa is a brother. "As between friends and brothers, there is no question." Tumultuous ovation from the Third World.

General Mobutu was only warming up. He was dressed with a leopard-skin U.S. Army-style overseas cap, and the motif was picked up by delegates sprinkled about the chamber. An aide to General Mobutu placed his speech on the podium, and, after he was done, retrieved it. Such menial tasks as placing one's own speech on a podium are inconsistent with the pride of the President of Zaire. Zaire is what we call the Congo nowadays, in the categorical flight from colonialism. It isn't under the circumstances exactly clear why they picked on Zaire, which happens to be a Portuguese word.

Speaking of Portugal, General Mobutu had a great deal to say on the subject, denouncing roundly Portugal's colonization of Mozambique and Angola. Portugal, he said, is a weak state without an armed force of any quality, and has managed the lowest literacy rate in Europe. The delegates went wild with delight. They did not meditate on the inexplicit counterparts of that description of Portugal. (1) If its armed services are so weak, how does it manage to control two vast areas in Africa? And (2) though it may be true that Portugal has the lowest literacy rate in Europe, it is three and one half times higher than Zaire's. Could that be because Zaire suffered a hundred years of colonialism? But Zaire's literacy rate is four times Ethiopia's, which never suffered under colonialism. All very distracting.

General Mobutu said it is very important that the African nations and African leaders not be humiliated in any way, and it was his point that much of the aid they receive is, really, humiliatingly tendered. I see his point. On one occasion, when General Mobutu was about to be assassinated—during one of those wars inside Zaire in which he needed friends much more than brothers, since his brothers were trying to kill him and his friends to save him—he got away in the nick of time by hiding in a white man's cellar, which must have ruffled his tiger hat, but saved his skin. Aid *can* be humiliating.

The General explained that much of the so-called aid to African countries is an economic swindle of sorts. Consider, he said, so-called fellowship grants to African students. The grant is made, and the student travels to America, and spends the entire sum of money in America! In other words, the economic grant is really a grant to American educational institutions, not to African students. What is confusing under the circumstances is why Zaire, having caught on to this Yankee shell game, doesn't retaliate by making huge grants to American students to study in Zaire? Study what in Zaire?

Diplomacy, of course. General Mobutu is an accomplished diplomat, as witness that he got much more applause than any other speaker thus far during the session. It is a difficult art, diplomacy. But if you master it, you can say things that are received as enthusiastically as headmasters' jokes. General Mobutu doesn't like it that he is considered a part of the Third World, because the figure "three" implies the precedence of "one" and "two," and Africa is greater than either the Western powers or for that matter Russia in any number of ways, mostly unspecified. Perhaps we could find a Portuguese term to use, and do away with the use of three?

Meanwhile, Israel will have to get along without an ambassador from Zaire. And General Mobutu's children, who attend expensive private schools in Switzerland, will presumably be instructed to bid adieu to their friends, and come home to their brothers, thus putting an end to Switzerland's economic exploitation of the children of the President of the Republic of Zaire.

Two weeks later, right in the middle of the goddamn war, Scali asked me to his office. I arrived while the CIA was briefing him and Schaufele on military developments of the past few hours—Israel was closing in and it looked as if, in a few days, Israel's victory would be complete. The CIA briefing officer having gone out, Scali pointed to Schaufele and said, "Show him."

"Do you read French?" Schaufele asked, handing me a letter.

"Yawp," I said.

The missive was from Ipoto Eyebu Bakand'Asi, the Ambassador and Permanent Representative of Zaire to the United Nations.

> Mr. Ambassador [it read]. I have just finished reading, with considered surprise, the commentary—one resists calling it something less civil—which appeared on the 11th of October 1973 in the New York *Post* under the by-line of Mr. William F. Buckley Jr., member of the American delegation to the 28th Session of the General Assembly of the United Nations.
>
> One can see that the gentleman culled from the address of President Mobutu that which he wished to cull for the purpose of giving his opinions.
>
> I desire, through you, to advise him that Zaire has taken note of his opinions.
>
> Moreover, considering the eminence of Mr. Buckley, one concludes that through him was expressed the reaction of the government of the United States to the address of President Mobutu on 4 October 1973 to the General Assembly of the United Nations.
>
> While awaiting word from Kinshasa expressing its position on this article, I wish it known that it is a deliberate and unfriendly act which will be taken into account in Zaire-American relations.

Oh dear, I said.
And then asked, "How usual is this kind of thing?"

Apparently it was quite unusual. I asked what, really, was there to say?—and told Scali nothing he proceeded to say to Kinshasa about me would disturb me in the least. Scali subsequently wrote back to stress that I had acted as a private citizen, and that President Mobutu should reflect on the fact that he had been received at the White House by President Nixon, where the identity of the views they exchanged much more closely expressed the United States position, tra-la, and he added, "I regret that the article has given offense, but you may rest assured that in writing for publication, Mr. Buckley does not represent the United States government, which values highly its traditional close and friendly relations with Zaire and deeply respects its distinguished President." Meanwhile, in Kinshasa, the American Ambassador "apologized if the article had given offense."

It was all very interesting. But of course, though it is absolutely true that my article was my own doing, it is also absolutely true that it reflected, in analysis and tone, *exactly* the true position of the American government. You cannot absorb that tone more directly than having sat listening to Mobutu's speech cheek by jowl with our two principal officials in the UN. And I know Richard Nixon well enough to know that *his* private reaction would be *exactly* my own, and for that matter, Kissinger's also. What's more, I cannot believe that what I have just said is unknown to Zaire diplomats. President Mobutu came to New York accompanied by *sixty-three* aides (including a lady-in-waiting for his wife, a maid, two valets, a radio editor, a TV editor, three cameramen, a photographer, and a lighting engineer). It is inconceivable that not one of them knows enough about America to know that American officials were sore as hell about Mobutu's speech, which was pretty outrageous and unabashedly provocative. If something is provocative, why should one be surprised if it provokes? Moreover, Mobutu thought so well of the speech he bought an entire page in the New York *Times* to publish the whole of it. He gave it the title "The Flame of Freedom" and modestly introduced it as the

"Historic speech . . . presented here in its entirety for those who wish to contemplate its infinite significance in this time of world crisis."

Incidentally, it was a fine forensic performance, laced with polemical wit, of a gallic turn. But its eloquence, like James Baldwin's, came from a sustained hostility to the white man, and to the West. Perhaps, in the case of Mobutu, this is feigned: I do not know who wrote the speech for him. But it was the harnessing bias of the speech. He dwelt—at this long historical distance from that awful period—on slave trading, and it was clear that he meant it to be understood that Western whites are still slave traders at heart. It was in the day of slavery elaborated by the West, he explained to the General Assembly, that "the whites were superior to the blacks." Things have not really changed, he suggested. He mentioned an episode I had never heard of, nor know anyone offhand who recalls it. It is an index of the extraordinary sensitivity of the breed (I mean by that, black African leaders). "In the town of Bukavu, east of Zaire, a white mercenary from Europe seriously proclaimed himself President of the Republic of Zaire. Had a black man done so in Europe, he would immediately have been taken as a hoaxer or a mental case; but, since he was a white man acting so in Africa, the colonialists mobilized the press, radio and television and placed them all at his disposal, not only to offer him publicity, but also to ridicule the Chief of State of Zaire, myself. . . . Such provocation was an intolerable insult to me which I cannot pardon." He railed against Britain for having used force to suppress the black Mau Mau in Kenya, but failing to use force against the white Englishmen of Rhodesia, leaving one helpless at the task of explaining something so obvious as the difference, in a colonial decade (the fifties), between suppressing throat-cutting Nat Turnerism and, in a post-colonial decade (the sixties), mobilizing the British Army to fight a quarter million Englishmen in the center of Africa. But Mobutu knows, and the UN loved it that he knew it, that the true motive was: racial contempt, of white for black. Again, he gave a concrete illustration, of the kind that makes one wince. "One day 2,000 black rioters who had climbed into the trees around Salisbury Airport to meet the then Prime Minister, Harold Wilson, sang an epic song, the words of which were: 'We are black. We are the orphans of Rhodesia. No one helps us. No one loves us.' The white police answered, 'Leave those damned monkeys. Let them go back to the trees they came from.'" I do not doubt that the incident took place. But to quote it as if it depicted sentiments that illuminate, let alone explain Western policy, is perverse, and Mobutu is lucky that retaliations in kind are not engaged in by—for instance—South African demagogues. It was not surprising, under the circumstances, that he should have quoted twice from the work of Franz Fanon, though that made it all the likelier that the speech was written by some local radical, or a French academic leftist, since the prejudices of Fanon have never been those of Mobutu the military man.

It is a very interesting question what is the best official reaction to such a speech. Occasionally—not often, and usually only at the expense of Cuba—we are instructed to leave the Assembly, as a gesture of disdain for the speaker or his position. That has the practical advantage of relieving us of the necessity of getting up and answering the speaker, the so-called Right of Reply. But there is very little between that and Official Enthusiasm—as witness the Mobutu speech. It is hard to understand why the State Department and USUN felt it necessary to suggest that Nixon's receiving Mobutu was an index of the warmth of our feelings for him and his presence at the United Nations. The stock argument is that we need Mobutu's vote on critical issues. Specifically, we desired him to withdraw from his co-sponsorship of the Korean Resolution. The stock reply to this should be that the erosion of American influence during the past few years suggests that we have been doing something wrong. (Look, pray, at Zaire's rating in Appendix B.) And since that erosion coincides with the erosion of UN prestige, could it be that we, every bit as much as the Mobutus, have labored to undermine the principles of the United Nations? By acquiescing in the general hypocrisy, and by sitting still, numbly, for rhetorical assaults from anyone, on any subject?

12.

Kissinger Banquet

Before going to the Metropolitan Museum for Kissinger's dinner, my wife and I went to the Waldorf, to the reception given by the Israeli delegation. The invitation was for 6 to 8 and we arrived at about 7:30 and found a huge crowd, 400 or 500 people. Considering the number of UN delegations that would either not have been invited or, if invited, would have declined to come, we wondered where they were all from. We filed quickly through the receiving line, headed by Foreign Minister Abba Eban. He greeted me most cordially and recalled that when we were last together, doing a *Firing Line* program, he had learned as he walked into the studio that Nasser had died. Tonight he seemed extraordinarily ebullient, forty-eight hours before his country was attacked and, very nearly, destroyed. As we finished the line, Pat whispered, "We can walk straight out and no one will notice," which was true. When there are so many, and you have gone through the receiving line, there is no reason to linger. It happened that that morning, a column I wrote in tribute to Jewish loyalty and perseverance had been published.

What I'd like to know is [I wrote], What do we do after the Soviet Union runs out of Jews? . . . How I wish there were some Jews in China who wished to emigrate. I have yet to hear one Congressman call for the application of any sanctions at all against China, where at least it can be said

131

that the government of Mao Tse-tung applies its repression on strict non-discriminatory grounds. I.e., everyone is discriminated against. . . . When the subject comes up of trade and credits for China, I shall raise with Senator Jackson the question of applying his reservation to China in behalf of China's Christians, but I know that the good Senator, for all that I love and admire him, will not return that telephone call. Christians are born to be martyrs, and mostly martyrs of the silent kind. Jews have had quite enough of martyrdom in this century and are resolved to fight back, and today, writing on the feast of Rosh Hashanah, I pay them tribute with all sincerity, and go so far as to say that if the Christian community today, let alone a generation ago, had displayed one one-hundredth of their tenacity and courage, the persecution of the Christians in East Europe, in Russia, and in China would have been inconceivable. I pray that every Jew in Russia will be permitted to emigrate. But I pray also that one (1) Jew will elect to remain, while pretending he wants to get out. Otherwise there will be a collapse of our foreign policy, of Congressional sanctions, and of our Army, Navy, Air Force, and probably our national anthem.

A rabbi who had seen the column grabbed me on the way out and expressed his most fervent approval of it. I thanked him, and we chatted a bit, and then I slid, head slightly down, step resolute, through the crowd, hanging on to Pat's hand, and we were off to the dinner.

It was a very grand affair, and as the saying goes, everyone was there. The host was Kissinger, and the honorees were the "UN Diplomatic Corps." Pat and I discovered that we were each in charge of a table, and that it was up to us to seat the nine people each who had been assigned to our tables. We panicked briefly, questioning rigorously the young man who gave us the list of names on whether there were matters of protocol or seniority involved. Not really, he said, though it is never a bad idea to put the portliest lady on one's right (in my case) and, in Pat's, the portliest gentleman. We went through the receiving line, and then chatted mostly with press moguls. There cannot be a grander place to stage a banquet, though I have never eaten in the Hall of Mirrors in Versailles. The food ($40 per head, I discovered, and 8 grand to the Museum) was fair. Kissinger sat with the Nelson Rockefellers and Benites. From where I sat, I could not look up without seeing the statue of Hermes, his member sticking out not exactly in the posture of a fico, but nevertheless aimed unerringly in the direction of President Benites. It was time for the toasts, and Kissinger came through with a quite extraordinarily deft and eloquent few paragraphs, leading however to the inevitable paean to the United Nations. (I wondered dizzily what would have been the reaction if, at just that moment, Hermes' member had been activated!) This time around the UN had become the "treasury of man's hopes," which was an escalation over what Kissinger had allotted to the UN ten days earlier in his address before the General Assembly. Then there was President Benites. I recalled a scene from my childhood. I was twelve, my brother Reid six, and he spoke no English, only Spanish, having been reared by a Mexican nurse. A distinguished Venezuelan came to lunch who prided herself on her English and addressed my bilingual father only in English, at great length, on most subjects, leaving Reid, who at his age was permitted the adult table only on Saturdays at noon, without any time to express himself, as was his wont, extensively, on all subjects. Taking advantage of a brief pause while the lady sipped her coffee, Reid, not suspecting that she knew Spanish, turned to my father and said, "Jesús, María, José, cómo habla esa señora!" That is to say, "Jesus, Mary, and Joseph, how that woman talks!" . . . We had to go through it all from Benites. Relaxation of tensions . . . peace . . . technology . . . brotherhood . . . human aspirations. . . . The length of it was of course doubled by the translation. It is an interesting role, the translator's. On the one hand he must be totally self-effacing, as anonymous as possible. On the other hand, he cannot transmit the speaker's rhetoric without *some* deference to the speaker's theatrical devices, tonal and linguistic. But it would hardly do for a lanky twenty-five-year-old Sunday-suited translator to sound like Martin Luther King, in translating Martin Luther King; to do so would raise eyebrows. Fortunately, Benites is not a florid elocutionist. His prose is very ornate and very meticulous, and the translator chose to relay it matter-of-factly, which was safe, but also, gnashingly soporific, so that we had to pinch ourselves to stay awake. It was finally over, and we ambled out, and I told Henry how fine I thought his toast was, and he was visibly pleased, I don't mean by my compliment, but by the whole situation. We were tilted toward a great crisis, only hours away. It was not felt that night at the Metropolitan Museum.

13.

Latin American Lunch

I have Plenary-duty and occupy the U.S. chair. Scali comes in as General Gowan, President of Nigeria, talks. He is not so well received as Mobutu. On the other hand he is relatively moderate, and he especially surprised the Chamber by not announcing the expulsion of Israel. When, after the Credentials fight, the South African Foreign Minister finally got up to speak, the chamber emptied of all but thirty-four delegates.

On to lunch. Henry Kissinger again, this time as guest of the Inter-American Union. The lunch is held in a historic mansion. Up until ten years or so ago, it had been the headquarters of the Soviet legation in New York; indeed it was from a window in that house that the defector Madame Kasenkina jumped, protesting her imminent deportation to the Soviet Union. A New York lawyer of great acumen and skill (who has been my own lawyer for a decade) got up a writ of habeas corpus, and Madame K. was spared. She had been going back at the height of one of Stalin's great crotchets, and there is little doubt that the vigilant lawyer, C. D. Williams, saved her life. And it was from the balcony facing Park Avenue that Nikita Khrushchev, to the dismay of his and our security forces, emerged repeatedly during his first visit to America, to exchange jeers and cheers with the mob outside.

I had been in the building before. Reading the paper the morning after Andrei Vishinsky died in New York, I noted

135

that his body would lie in state inside the Soviet legation at Sixty-ninth Street and Park Avenue between noon and 3 P.M. Again this was at the height of the cold war, and I felt a great curiosity to see the appointments of the residence of the Soviet representative, chief prosecutor at the Great Purge Trials of the late thirties. So I called up my brother Jim and said: Would you like to see Vishinsky dead? Jim can act on impulse, as witness that he is in the Senate, and he said sure, so we wove our way into the mourning chamber through the little crowd of Communist sympathizers and disguised FBI agents, recognizing by face only Paul Robeson and his wife as they sat solemnly in the marbled red velvet room around the catafalque with the evil Vishinsky's little body stretched out on it, along with a few mourners, in the room where now about a hundred of us sat down to lunch, at ten or so tables. On my right was the Permanent Representative from Ecuador, an amiable and intelligent man who told me that, what with Benites, a fellow Ecuadorian being President, he has to be careful how he votes in tight situations so as not to appear to tip anyone off to the sympathies of the President of the Assembly. On my left was the Ambassador from Colombia, whom I have now met two or three times. We all converse in Spanish, and I am told that it is expected that Henry Kissinger will say something of considerable importance. I did not tell them that I had heard the same thing at the African, and then the Arab lunches. I always feel a particular sympathy for the Latin American states, some of whose ministers would consider it an extraordinary event if the President of the United States would merely mention their country's name.

Kissinger's introductory little story was once again in point. He spoke of the Englishman who was puzzled by the bifurcation at Stockholm airport. One passage was marked "Swedes"; the other, "Foreigners." He approached an official and said, "I am neither a Swede nor a foreigner."

Kissinger said that "no institution or treaty arrangement is beyond reconsideration." I could not imagine exactly what he had in mind, thinking that if he was going to spring one about Panama, this would be rather soon in his career as Secretary of State. He said then what Latin American diplomats like most to hear, namely that U.S. policy toward Latin America should really be set by Latin America, and only *helped* by the United States. I feared briefly that he would forget that allergy Latin Americans have to being lumped together as though they were a single nation. But Kissinger pulled out of the dive in plenty of time, and listed here and there different nations, ascribing to them different problems, and so on. Alas, we were then toasted by Mr. Benites, though it was not as long as last night's toast. During it, the man sitting to the right of the Ecuadorian Ambassador on my right passed me a note with a startling communication. "Just a personal thought—I have no authorization to suggest it—but let me know if you're interested in becoming an Ambassador in L.A." It turned out to be Mr. Kubisch, the head of our Latin American desk in the State Department. I wrote him Monday, thanked him a lot, and told him I hoped I was doing something at least as useful as serving as Ambassador to Uruguay. He wrote back and said he didn't have Uruguay in mind, but something like Mexico. I wrote again to tender my gratitude, and to say no to an impulse which, in any case, probably would not survive the publication of this journal.

Lunch was over, and I rushed about to find a birthday present for my son, who is twenty-one today; and went off. I would be away for almost the whole of the following week, the first of the two weeks of great crisis that began when Arab troops, early Sunday morning of Yom Kippur, moved suddenly against Israel in a campaign that very nearly obliterated Israel, but which, before diplomacy finally intervened, resulted in Israel's very nearly obliterating the Egyptian war machine—for the third time since 1956. The attention now was on the Security Council.

14.

Mideast War

MONDAY

The fighting in the Mideast took the United Nations by surprise. During the first few days, when it appeared as though the Syrians, striking across the Golan Heights, would win their crucial victory, the UN was pretty much holding its breath. The Security Council met abortively, and adjourned. On Thursday, Waldheim addressed a message to the Security Council urging it to meet and to call for a cease-fire. The President of the Security Council (McIntyre, Australia) had been reluctant to convene the Council on the grounds that with the military situation in such dynamic flux, nobody would be willing to do anything resonant, let alone conclusive, and the Security Council would simply be ignored, vitiating its possible usefulness later on in the day. But after Waldheim's appeal, he felt that the pressures were such that he had to bring it together, and he did, and much steam was let out. During the first three days of the following week, as the military situation clarified, and indeed began to turn around, the Security Council dragged its heels. But on Thursday the 18th, it met again; and, on Friday, it was agreed (the United States and the Soviet Union having conferred) to call for a cease-fire the following Monday at 5:45 P.M. Greenwich Mean Time. That resolution was passed unanimously, China abstaining on the grounds that she considered the whole business nothing more than regional theater orchestrated by the two superpowers, the United States and the Soviet Union, for their strategic benefit. But no sooner was the cease-fire technically promulgated than charges and countercharges followed—that the cease-fire was being violated, by Israel, then by Egypt. Egypt then called on the Security Council to get the United States and the Soviet Union jointly to effect the cease-fire using their own military. The United States declined, and suddenly the clouds lifted, and the cease-fire seemed to come grudgingly into effect. From that moment on the great debate within the United Nations, spilling out from the Security Council to the Fifth Committee, and on to the General Assembly, was over the financing of the United Nations Emergency Force. It was a critical debate because it went beyond the economic question, attempting to accomplish political ends the Security Council had carefully skirted: trying to pin the blame, for instance, on Israel for "starting the war." One or two of the resolutions were playful exercises in economic extortion, at the expense of venerable UN minorities, like the United States and Portugal. But by the time this debate began, the war in the Mideast had ended, and the threat of a military confrontation between the United States and the Soviet Union had entirely abated, and what was left to look at was what had the UN accomplished, and how, the dust having settled, was the UN strategically affected?

When the UN runs head on into an emergency, it is almost always transacted within the Security Council. There are the exceptions—the vote to oust the Republic of China was of course an Assembly vote. But when the going gets very tough, it is the Secretary of State who is in command of the U.S. situation, and depending on who he is, and on who is the Permanent Representative in the United Nations, policy is made with varying contributions from each party, and their advisers. The public delegates are pretty much left out of things. Entirely left out as regards their advice.

In the exchanges in the Security Council during the five days beginning on October 22, it was clear how greatly the Council depended on the prior agreement of the superpowers. Sir Donald Maitland (U.K.) began by saying, "When I addressed this Council on 8 October I suggested that we had two immediate responsibilities: first, to seek the earliest possible cease-fire, and second, to treat the renewal of hostilities as a catalyst for starting a genuine diplomatic process which would lead to a settlement. In the 17 days since the present war began, this Council has been unable to find a way of discharging either of these responsibilities." Precisely. Because those responsibilities had to begin with a big power agreement, and this required a crystallization of the military situation.

Baroody, who spoke at every conceivable opportunity, notwithstanding that Saudi Arabia is not a member of the Security Council, and who announced that if he had the power to do so, he would veto the cease-fire resolution, teased the superpower representatives about their power-lessness. "Of course, Ambassador Malik of the Soviet Union does not know any more than I do what secret deal was struck between Mr. Kissinger and Mr. Brezhnev. Surely the two superpowers have come to an agreement without consulting with the members of the Council." Even so.

On the other hand, USUN being a tight ship, one hears a great deal, and of course there are the cables flowing across one's desk. These, by the way, are in several classifications. There are (a) the Unclassified cables, (b) those marked Limited Official Use, (c) those marked Confidential, (d) those marked Secret, (e) those marked Top Secret, whose distribution is specified name by name, rather than office by office. Now and then you would pick up from the cables something particularly illuminating, but far less often than one would expect. A careful reader of the Washington *Post* and the New York *Times* and *Time* and *Newsweek* and one or two of the foreign journals would be difficult to embarrass by leaning on knowledge that passed only under the eyes of the delegates reading the cables. What one does get is some idea of personal relations—what Ambassador X thinks about Foreign Minister Y; how Permanent Representative Z is spoken of at the staff meetings. Involvement at this level etches a little more keenly what is otherwise blurred. I discovered, for instance, that no one at USUN was privy to the conditions, if any, put by Henry Kissinger and Richard Nixon on the aid rushed to Israel at the peak of the war. That would have been a critical lacuna if the principal pressure for a cease-fire had actually been negotiated out of New York. In fact, of course it wasn't; it was negotiated out of Washington. But the United Nations was useful.

Here is what I have reason to believe is a reliable summary of what happened during the critical ten days:

1. For a while, the Arab military machine was working with great effect. The pressure exerted on Israel by the Syrians at the Golan Heights was very nearly crucial. Clearly the intention was to overwhelm the Heights and march across to Haifa, cutting Israel in half. When Israel succeeded finally in repelling the Syrians (who made, suddenly, unaccountably clumsy military mistakes), her attention was drawn to the invasion (if that is the right word for Egyptians swarming into Egyptian territory) in the south. At this point, United States aid was indispensable. Without it, the Israeli military would have had no choice but to cloister its ravaged military machine for the defense of Israel proper. With it, the Israelis could deploy their reserves confident that they would be replaced by a massive United States airlift. The United States came through.

2. The Israelis' counterattack proved brilliantly but not conclusively successful. They succeeded in forcing their way back across the Suez Canal, and they were headed south to cut off communications lines that fed the Egyptian contingent to the east of the Canal when the cease-fire resolution was voted by the UN Security Council. That resolution was welcomed by the Soviet Union and the Arabs for obvious reasons. And the United States wanted it because it would clearly be harder to deal with the problem of a permanent peace if Israel's successes were inordinate, and because the U.S. support for Israel had already proved damaging in our

dealings with the Arab governments and with European nations threatened by the Arabs' oil diplomacy. Accordingly, we put pressure on the Israelis to cease fire.

3. Not enough pressure. Because after a short respite the Israelis, examining the prospective advantages of marching on and consummating their victory, began to do so. It was at this point that the Russians saw the clear threat to their own interests. They could not tolerate a total Israeli success and all that this would mean in terms of an Arab sense of betrayal in the grander theater of operations, where the principal players are the United States and the Soviet Union. Accordingly, the Soviets wrote brusquely to Henry Kissinger (we have Senator Jackson's word for it on the tone of that communication), and by way of background accompaniment mobilized a few airborne units and announced that if the United States did not care to join the Soviet Union in a common enforcement of the cease-fire, why, the Soviet Union would do the job by itself.

This move scared the living bejesus out of the United States, which as we all know ordered a general military alert, and the sum total of these intricately balanced events was (this is conjecture) to cause the United States to put irresistible pressure on Israel to STOP THIS MINUTE.

4. Certain kinds of pressure Israel does understand, and in a matter of hours she complied, leaving a Soviet diplomatic corps visibly pleased with the success of its maneuver (Dino Pionzio, who attended the Security Council session, gave me a memo that included a report of the smiles on the faces of the Soviet members, a pretty reliable indication of their mood, since when they are displeased, they wear their displeasure darkly), and a United States delegation exhausted by the strains of the engagement. The tactical strain was of course the possibility of a direct military confrontation with the Soviet Union. The strategic strain was to the policy of détente. And all of this was during the worst hours of Richard Nixon's difficulties with Watergate, when he fired Archibald Cox and Elliot Richardson.

What USUN desired to accomplish it was never able to specify except as the problems took shape. It was generally agreed that Israeli intransigence on the matter of negotiating pursuant to the Jarring Resolution of November 1967 was making things harder and harder for the United States. Henry Kissinger believes preferably in motion, but, barring that, in a sense of motion. There was no sense of motion in the Mideast on our side, which has been generally pro-Israeli. Accordingly, when the war broke out, USUN had to mobilize itself to be useful as the situation evolved. It was not known at first what would be the military situation forty-eight hours later. It was not known how much U.S. aid Israel would need, how quickly or how desperately. It was not known what conditions we would attach to it. And it was not known, once the tide of battle had turned, what was Israel's strategic objective. March to Damascus? If so, then what? Destroy Egypt's army? If so, then what? What about next year? The year after? And it being at least a velleity of the United States to endear ourselves with the Arabs—for reasons altogether defensible—we needed to put a gloss on our aid to Israel, to suggest that that aid was nothing more than, *pari passu,* growing out of the situation brought on by Soviet military aid to the Arab countries. But that beyond that aid, we were looking forward to a genuine resolution—to a genuine peace.

Kissinger had spoken about the need for institutional arrangements for peace when he addressed the General Assembly. And the press greeted the role of the Security Council in that light—an approach to an enduring solution. At the moment when something had to be done, the requirements were (a) that the United States and the Soviet Union should desire roughly the same thing—a cease-fire. And (b) that China should not veto the resolution. (Britain and France possess the veto, of course. But if either country were ever to use it willfully, the probability is that the Charter would be changed in such a way as effectively to strip them of it, and that meanwhile the "Uniting for Peace" precedent would be invoked by the General Assembly to take over the action.) China will usually settle for bombast rather than simultaneously to defy the United States and the Soviet Union. And, indeed, on the occasion of one of the Security Council debates, did so extensively. At one point a recess had to be called to cool the exchange of insults between Chiao and Malik, who quite evidently dislike each other. These exchanges, as a courtesy to a predominantly English-speaking Assembly, were conducted in English, and permitted us to hear the representative of the People's Republic of China saying to the representative of the Union of Soviet Socialist Republics that he "had no *class*." (For less than such blatant lapses into mandarinism, Chinese diplomats have been felled by their Cultural Revolutions.)

But the insecurity of the Security Council itself is evident in the plaintiveness of the members representing the minor powers when they talk about the role of the UN at the peace conference on the Middle East. The Secretary-General is of course to open the conference. What then? Guinea wanted to know exactly what the Security Council is expected to do, and demanded a working relationship rather than a passive one, followed by a fait accompli. The Indians fancy themselves as the great compromisers. They are never so happy as when there is a major dispute, so that they can quickly craft a compromise resolution, at which point you see them buzzing about the chambers getting co-sponsors even as the debate rages. The Yugoslavs insisted that the Secretary-General was not to participate at all unless authorized to do so by the Security Council, and then only to communicate instructions from it. The United States talked about a "strong link" between the conference and the Security Council. In fact, if what they come up with in the Mideast suits the Soviet Union and us, that's what matters. The Security Council is symbolically useful. It would cease to be useful at all if it were neutralized by the activities of minority members. If—as the African states are beginning to insist—the Charter is revised so as to give an African state and perhaps a Latin American state a veto power, then the probability is that, in a future crisis, the crucial negotiations would be not only bilateral in substance, but also in form. The non-aligned take rhetorical satisfaction from presenting their positions in the chamber where the critical votes are cast. Observing these debates, sensible men can come to different convictions concerning their usefulness. The most popular conviction is that, through Security Council debates, people "get things out of their system." A less popular conclusion is that, thanks substantially to these public debates, the atmosphere is poisoned. One cannot survive a tense evening's debate in which, for instance, Mr. Baroody figures prominently, without wishing that the United Nations' debates were adjourned to the Union League Club, with obstreperous members barred at the door by the steward. The question of course is whether there is an impalpable impulse forward, toward reconciliation, after one of those monstrous sessions; whether the sheer fatigue of it all works us in the right direction. Optimism on this point is less easy for a Westerner. The nervous system is a much more important part of our psychic makeup, and I can (myself) imagine giving up the debate, rather than having to spend one more hour listening to drivel. There is no question about it but that iron-butted diplomats trained in oriental patience and conditioned to encephalophonic ideological indoctrination stand up better under that kind of thing than we do. John Scali, at one point in the negotiations with Malik, left the room. Not as a gesture. But in physical disgust over Malik's incumbent betrayal. I doubt Malik would have done any such thing in reversed circumstances. On the other hand, those who believe that the Communists would behave more expeditiously if they did not need to strut their stuff for the benefit of 132 non-superpowers should recall the endlessness of the private Panmunjom conferences; or, for that matter, the endlessness of Kissinger's meetings with Le Duc Tho in Paris, where there were no Baroodys present, although it is of course contended that others were doing Baroody's work, and stiffening the spine of the North Vietnamese. And this much is clearly true, that a United Nations resolution having been voted, a quasi-juridical basis for the cease-fire was born. Most of these are born to be ignored; but if the impulse is to observe them, then, perhaps indeed, they are fortified if the provenance is the only international parliament there is.

15.

Amin

WEDNESDAY

The little problems of the UN do not dissipate merely because of wars. For a while, in fact, it looked as though General Amin of Uganda was determined to take his country actively into the Mideast war. But meanwhile he announced his determination to visit New York and to deliver an address, on October 25, to the General Assembly.

General Amin, who last summer instructed Queen Elizabeth to send a warship to pick him up so that he could attend the Commonwealth Conference, set great store by his forthcoming speech. In fact, he cabled to Golda Meir instructing her about the importance of it: IN VIEW OF THE GREAT CONCERN AND STRONG VIEWS THAT I HOLD ABOUT THE MIDDLE EAST, I REQUEST THAT YOU ENABLE GENERAL DAYAN, YOUR MINISTER OF DEFENSE, GENERAL RABIN, CHIEF OF STAFF DURING THE SIX DAY WAR, AND GENERAL HOD, COMMANDER OF THE AIR FORCE DURING THE SAME TIME, AND COLONEL BAR-LEV, COMMANDER OF THE TANK UNIT WHICH CAPTURED JERUSALEM, TO BE PRESENT WHEN I AM DELIVERING MY ADDRESS TO THE GENERAL ASSEMBLY. Since the gentlemen in question were at that point fighting a very time-consuming war, it is perhaps understandable that there is no recorded response to General Amin's cable.

All of this has deeply disturbed him, one gathers, and a cable from a friendly diplomat reveals the startling news that General Amin tried out his proposed speech on him. It is apparently an extraordinary two hours in length and, we

147

learned, is substantially devoted to informing the General Assembly, the American public, and the world, about a document General Amin has just discovered—the Protocols of the Learned Elders of Zion. General Amin is apparently extremely excited about the revelations in that document, and it isn't clear from the cable whether the representative of the friendly power had the temerity to advise General Amin that the Protocols were demonstrated to be forgeries some time before General Amin was born. The prospect of General Amin, chief of state, reciting the Protocols from the podium of the central institute of New York liberal enthusiasm is—well, arresting. What will the Anti-Defamation League do?

General Amin's excitement would increase in the next few days. He announced that his intelligence service has uncovered a plot by the Israelis, the English, and the Americans, to land paratroops in Uganda and to take power away from him. Although, he assures us, he is ready to die at any time suitable to his Maker, he wished it known that his army and air force would demolish these invaders, and he has warned Kenyatta that they are not to be allowed to refuel, as has been their intention, in Kenya. Our exemplary Ambassador to Uganda, Mr. Keeley, evidently a hugely patient man, has assured Amin that we have no such plans. It is privately speculated that Amin having discovered that he is in no shape to send a military detachment to the Mideast, and that the Egyptians do not enjoy a military superiority pronounced enough to permit them to accept a force from Uganda, the whole parachute business is a diversionary maneuver, destined to distract attention from the wildness of his other promises.

Amin then canceled his trip to New York, but his pressure is intensifying. Now he has announced that American planes are being used in the Middle East, and that the pilots are chained into their cockpits, as will presently be demonstrated on Ugandan TV. He has moreover disclosed that white Americans have complained that Jews in America control 90 percent of everything, and that if Nixon speaks out against the Jews, Nixon will not last. Ambassador Keeley is becoming alarmed, particularly after Amin's statement that he will order all Americans in Uganda (there are about 250) to carry ID cards, and any who don't will be picked up as suspect members of a hostile military force.

Ambassador Keeley discussed with a colleague the possibility of walking out on the General's forthcoming UN Day speech scheduled in his own capital for October 24, but they decided against it on the grounds (a) that as a gesture of protest, it would not be understood, there being no such tradition in Uganda, and (b) the exit would therefore probably be interpreted as having been prompted by, as the cable put it, a "call of nature." This being inconsistent with the diplomatic dignity of our Ambassador, he decided against it. I am relieved to note that such decisions do not require ratification in Washington.

The UN Day speech in Kampala was without important incident, save only the revelation by General Amin to his audience that he had had a fresh communication from God at 9 A.M. which, under the circumstances, he understandably rendered also in Greenwich Mean Time (0600). The substance of it was that there should be a cease-fire in the Mideast. As a matter of fact, such a cease-fire had been voted the day before at the General Assembly. General Amin announced that he had forwarded news of his vision to the relevant people—Waldheim, Golda Meir, Arafat, Ekangaki, and the chiefs of state of various Arab republics. But USUN, now that Amin is staying home, instead of coming to New York to recite the Protocols of Zion, is serenely unconcerned. We wish Keeley every success, and note that he is quietly warning the U.S. community in Uganda. . . . The State Department, it transpires, is not so relaxed. A few days later they advise Keeley to pull out. The final cable of Mr. Keeley would not have endeared him to God's messenger in Uganda—and reminds one of the occasional uses of colonialism.

16.
Third Committee

Tomorrow, I am to make my first formal statement before the Third Committee, giving the United States' position on the celebration of the 25th Anniversary of the promulgation of the Universal Declaration of Human Rights. I went to the afternoon session to see what kind of thing is being said by the other delegates. The Swedish representative is talking at some length about the desirability of rejecting torture. He says that, however, it is "our aim not to indict any country"; and, again, "we are guided by a desire to avoid every possible controversy," a position I thought less than self-evidently sound, though in a very few hours I would understand it better. Why avoid controversy? If the point is to stimulate human rights, a corollary would be to draw attention to those places where human rights are trampled upon. But that is a kind of secular logic, characteristic of the uninitiated.

In the committees there is a Rapporteur, as they are called, who paraphrases statements, condensing them into a very few sentences which do not convey the flavor of the whole. (It is only in the General Assembly and in the Security Council that you get verbatim transcripts.) I wish I had the entire speech given by the representative of the German Democratic Republic, freshly admitted to membership in the UN. Even the very hardy, the very experienced, who had gotten their sea legs in UN effrontery long long ago, were made a little wobbly by it. The East German delegate

150

explained that in his country there is no concern whatever for human rights—because everyone has human rights. These rights are provided "by people whom Hitler ordered destroyed because of their devotion to democracy and human rights." Under socialism, he explained, "human rights are guaranteed by society." For instance, he said, Article 19 of the East German Constitution guarantees "socialist legality." It gives its citizens "the right to every freedom. It doesn't merely *proclaim* rights, it *lives* and *develops* these rights." I looked at him while he went through this. Middle age, Storm Trooper handsome, crew-cut, a trace of bravado in his voice. There was not a stir in the room, neither of approval nor of disapproval. This I found quite conventional. There is hardly ever any reaction to a delegate's statement in committee. Occasionally the chairman will thank the previous speaker for his "eloquent" statement. More often, he simply thanks him and introduces the next speaker. There is nothing that begins to suggest genuine outrage after such studied travesties as East Germany's. I learned that it was this above all that upset Patrick Moynihan when he sat in my chair two years ago.

But now I had to get to work and compose a statement.

The mechanics here are interesting.

On the one hand, there was a cable from the State Department. (There is always a cable from the State Department. It is always signed with the surname of the Secretary of State who, however, probably doesn't see 5 percent of the instructions that go out over his name.) It instructs USUN what the State Department desires said by the United States delegate in respect of a scheduled issue, problem, or resolution. That cable is received by the staff assigned to a particular committee, and a member of that staff produces a speech. I was handed the State Department cable and a draft speech. I had never before been given a draft speech, not even when I ran for mayor of New York so I took the two documents to my office and looked them over carefully. Here is the telegram, in full.

FM SECSTATE WASHDC
TO USMISSION USUN NEW YORK PRIORITY
[There followed a number of coded designations]

SUBJECT: OBSERVANCE OF 25TH ANNIVERSARY OF UNIVERSAL DECLARATION OF HUMAN RIGHTS

1. DEPT. UNDERSTANDS THAT CONSIDERATION OF SUBJECT ITEM LIKELY TO BEGIN IN THIRD COMMITTEE OCTOBER 16. USDEL STATEMENT SHOULD STRESS IMPORTANCE USG [United States government] ATTACHES TO DECLARATION AS PREEMINENT HUMAN RIGHTS DOCUMENT BASIC TO THE ACHIEVEMENT OF UN PURPOSE OF PROMOTING AND ENCOURAGING RESPECT FOR HUMAN RIGHTS. DECLARATION IS A STATEMENT OF PRINCIPLES APPROVED BY UNGA [the United Nations General Assembly] WITHOUT NEGATIVE VOTE [Russia abstained] AS A COMMON STANDARD OF ACHIEVEMENT FOR ALL PEOPLES AND ALL NATIONS. STANDARDS OF DECLARATION PROVIDE BASIS FOR MEASURING PERFORMANCE OF MEMBERS IN CARRYING OUT THEIR CHARTER PLEDGE TO ACT TO ACHIEVE RESPECT FOR AN OBSERVANCE OF HUMAN RIGHTS AND FUNDAMENTAL FREEDOMS. 2. USDEL STATEMENT SHOULD NOTE OUR BELIEF THAT SINCE ITS PROCLAMATION TWENTY-FIVE YEARS AGO, DECLARATION HAS PLAYED VALUABLE ROLE IN INFLUENCING GOVERNMENTS TO RECOGNIZE AND OBSERVE BASIC HUMAN RIGHTS. IN PAST TWENTY-FIVE YEARS REAL PROGRESS HAS BEEN ACHIEVED. BUT WE ARE FAR FROM A WORLD IN WHICH HUMAN RIGHTS ARE EVERYWHERE PROTECTED BY THE RULE OF LAW. UNFORTUNATELY, SERIOUS HUMAN RIGHTS TRANSGRESSIONS REMAIN ALL TOO PREVALENT. ACCORDINGLY, WE BELIEVE THE GA SHOULD CALL FOR RENEWED DEDICATION TO ACHIEVEMENT OF GOALS OF DECLARATION. 3. US STATEMENT SHOULD EMPHASIZE PARTICULAR SIGNIFICANCE WE ATTACH TO BASIC CIVIL AND POLITICAL RIGHTS SET FORTH IN DECLARATION. OF SPECIAL PERTINENCE IN TODAY'S WORLD ARE ARTICLE 5 (AGAINST TORTURE AND DEGRADING PUNISHMENT), ARTICLE 9 (AGAINST ARBITRARY ARREST, DETENTION OR EXILE), ARTICLE 10 (RIGHT TO FAIR TRIAL), ARTICLE 13 (THE RIGHT TO LEAVE ANY COUNTRY), ARTICLE 14 (THE RIGHT TO SEEK ASYLUM), ARTICLE 18 (FREEDOM OF THOUGHT, CONSCIENCE AND RELIGION), AND ARTICLE 19 (FREEDOM OF OPINION AND EXPRESSION AND FREEDOM OF INFORMATION AND IDEAS). STATEMENT SHOULD

NOTE IMPORTANCE WE LIKEWISE ATTACH TO ACHIEVEMENT OF
GOALS UNDER HEADING OF ECONOMIC AND SOCIAL RIGHTS, AS
SPELLED OUT IN DECLARATION. 4. STATEMENT SHOULD BE
NON-POLEMICAL IN TONE, DELIVERED AS STRAIGHTFORWARD
EXPRESSION OUR SINCERE AND TRADITIONAL SUPPORT FOR
ATTAINMENT OF GOALS OF DECLARATION THROUGHOUT THE
WORLD. THERE SHOULD BE NO REPEAT NO MENTION OF SPECIFIC
COUNTRIES OR SPECIFIC CASES INVOLVING HUMAN RIGHTS
VIOLATIONS. 5. TEXTUAL MATERIAL BEING SENT WIGGINS.
KISSINGER.

The suggested speech had been drafted by Cameron
Hume, and was tailored to the State Department cable. It is a
little long to reproduce. The following is a paraphrase:

Twenty-five years ago, the United States was in favor of
the Declaration of Human Rights. We still are. Granted,
things change. But a review of the debate twenty-five years
ago suggests that the draft written then stands up.

At this point, a comment on what I wish I could otherwise
describe than as "bureaucratic prose," but find it hard to do.
Cameron Hume, I repeat, is young, terribly intelligent, with
a fine eye for irony. I say this to stress the point that there is
no reason flowing out of a dull nature why the prose should
be so turgid. The enemy is the rhetorical sing-song of public
statements which, convention seems to require, should be
rhythmically repetitious for the sake of achieving a kind of
diplomatic orotundity.

Consider the paragraph paraphrased above in the two
sentences, *Twenty-five years ago, the United States was in favor of
the Declaration of Human Rights. We still are.*

The draft text: "Twenty-five years ago when the Third
Committee was meeting to prepare the draft of the
Declaration of Human Rights, the U.S. Government stated
clearly that this Declaration was necessary to provide a basis
for measuring performance of Member States and carrying
out the Charter pledge to achieve respect for and observance
of human rights and fundamental freedoms. We continue to

believe that the Declaration of Human Rights is a preeminent human rights document, basic to the Charter purpose of promoting and encouraging respect for human rights."

The only shock that comes to the ear is that the sentence didn't end: "for human rights and fundamental freedoms," since it is thought necessary to give both elsewhere, as it is thought necessary to "achieve respect for and observance of."

Continuing the paraphrase: *Granted, things change. But a review of the debate twenty-five years ago suggests that the draft as written then stands up.*

The draft: "Frequently, the role that constitutions and laws play in the reordering of society is changed or lessened with the passage of time. The original purpose or scope may become distorted or restricted. The hopes and aspirations of the original draftsmen and legislators may never be satisfied. However, a short review of the debate which took place in the Palais de Chaillot twenty-five years ago will indicate that the value and validity of the draft produced by the assembled delegates has been reaffirmed and strengthened by the test of time."

Constitutions and laws . . . changed or lessened . . . purpose or scope . . . distorted or restricted . . . hopes and aspirations . . . draftsmen and legislators . . . value and validity . . . reaffirmed and strengthened. One feels cheated at his not having concluded: *by the test of time and space.*

To continue the paraphrase: *The text quoted from statements in favor of the Declaration made by René Cassin for France, by Carlos Romulo for the Philippines, and Eleanor Roosevelt for the United States—*all of which quotes, begging the general pardon, were undistinguished as prose, and false as prophecy (e.g., "Mrs. Roosevelt saw with clarity the spiritual fact that the individual man must have freedom in which to develop his full stature and that the achievement of many individuals would raise the level of human dignity").

There followed an extensive accounting of the importance attached to the Declaration by Lebanon's Charles Malik, who presided over the eighty-five meetings that resulted in the final text, and a few soaring, and moving, sentences from Malik: "What we are, therefore, launching tonight is a document of the first order of importance. It can never be said, from now on, that the conscience of organized, responsible humanity has left ambiguous what inherently belongs to my own humanity. If I fail to take advantage of this responsible proclamation, it will be my fault." There is a touch here of philosophical presumption and also of historical bombast, but a certain amount of this is needed in any paradigmatic enterprise.

Then a cautionary paragraph ("Serious violations remain all too prevalent . . .").

Then a reaffirmation of the United States' devotion to human rights, in which is contained the enumeration dictated by the State Department.

Then a paragraph saying we also favor social and economic rights.

Then a concluding reference to the Decade to Combat Racism and Racial Discrimination, which is to be launched on the 25th Anniversary of the Declaration. And the closing sentence, "Twenty-five years has proved that the world cannot live in peace as long as flagrant violations of the Declaration continue, but as long as we continue to be guided in our efforts, by the goals and principles of this Declaration, we must inevitably be progressing toward a more humane society and toward promotion of human dignity." This statement is simply not true.

With the State Department's cable in front of me, I batted out a half dozen paragraphs, determined to comply *exactly* with the requirements. They follow.

Mr. Chairman, distinguished delegates:

I take the opportunity, inasmuch as I am addressing this chamber formally for the first time, to congratulate the chairman on his election as head of this important committee. I am aware that it can be a frustrating assignment, and I join my colleagues in marveling at your patience and good humor.

Mr. Chairman, on the occasion of the 25th anniversary of the promulgation of the Universal Declaration of Human Rights, what is there to say this side of the cant which I hope to spare you? I plead inexperience in the art of saying nothing with much wind, and surely if we find, on meditating the thirty Articles in the Declaration, that there ought to be thirty-one, we should consider recommending an article that declares that all men were born free of political rhetoric, but that everywhere, man is, in respect of this freedom, in chains.

My government desires to make one or two observations, some of them concrete, some ceremonial.

1. The Human Rights document is the best-known and therefore the preeminent catalogue of human rights in the world today.

2. The Declaration has been useful to several countries that have sought to devise bills of rights of their own. By consulting the UN Declaration of Human Rights, they can at least count those rights they have left out.

3. My government desires to call attention, on the 25th Anniversary of the Declaration, to a few of the enumerated rights which are conspicuously transgressed upon. To wit (Article 5) the protection against torture and degrading punishment; the protection (Article 9) against arbitrary arrest, detention, or exile; the right (Article 10) to a fair trial, and (Article 13) to leave the country; the right (Article 14) to seek asylum and (Article 18) to freedom of thought and of conscience and of religion; and (Article 19) the right of freedom of expression, information, and ideas. My government also desires to record its enthusiasm for the economic and social rights spelled out in the Declaration.

Now, Mr. President, the world is divided not between those who say they do not believe in torture and those who say that they do believe in torture. Rather it is divided between those who practice torture and those who do not practice torture. Indeed, the world is divided not between those who say they believe in human rights and those who say they do not believe in human rights, but between those

who grant human beings human rights and those who do
not grant human beings human rights. Twenty-six years ago
we could, and indeed many of our predecessors did, sit
about arguing the question what was a human right and
what was not a human right. But then the day came when
the Declaration we are here to celebrate was promulgated;
and this was done without dissenting voice. So that this
organization is committed, for instance, to the proposition
that there is a right to leave one's country. And yet we have
not heard more profuse compliments paid to the Declaration of Human Rights than by some who maintain huge
fortifications calculated to prevent the exercise of that right.

The United Nations was not designed as a military
juggernaut at the service of the Human Rights Committee
to ensure that signatories practice those rights they praise.
But Mr. President, surely it would mark the solemnity of the
occasion if, on the 25th Anniversary of the Declaration next
December 10, those nations that systematically deny the
human rights associated with the United Nations Declaration should gracefully absent themselves from this chamber
for one day?

We do not desire to be censorious, Mr. President, and
there are unquestionably times in history when the
indulgence of human rights is an encumbrance on other
policies pursued more avidly—revolution, for instance, or
counterrevolution. But that decorum which distinguishes
this chamber, and the conduct of proceedings within it,
would be, I am sure, greatly obliged if, on the day of the
great celebration, those countries whose own policies are not
congruent with the United Nations Declaration signified at
least their abstract respect for human rights by leaving the
chamber.

In closing, Mr. President, my government desires to state
its willingness to rededicate itself to human rights, and to
welcome any criticism directed at any failures within our
own country to match the high ideals of the United Nations.

Dino, who is very wise and experienced, thought the
chances were pretty good my little speech would be
authorized. Wiggins and Hume were not quite so sure—Wig-

gins thought it a little "tendentious." It was typed out and given the routine distribution, and I went home, presided over an unsuccessful money-raising function for mayoralty candidate John Marchi, went with my wife to a charity ball, and returned at midnight to find a note scribbled on my bed in the curious and hortatory Spanish of the housemaid: I was *instantly* and *without delay* to telephone Ambassador Scali in Washington *no matter how late, important.* I guessed what it was about, and decided it could very easily wait until morning.

He could not have been more kind. Look, he said, we're trying very hard for a cease-fire. We're in the middle of working out a very intricate deal between the Russians and the Arabs. Anything said by an American that smacks in any way as a defense of the Jews could throw a monkey wrench into the whole thing. My statement about freedom of emigration might rile the Arabs and the Russians. Actually, he said, he had laughed out loud at that part of the speech.

Things are hell right now, and Sadat hasn't proved as difficult as we expected, so we can't take a chance of inflaming him. Recently the State Department caught hell because the guy in charge of the African desk told Kissinger that Mobutu's speech hadn't been so bad, so Kissinger recommended to Nixon that he receive Mobutu. Then Nixon saw my column about Mobutu's speech, and hell steamed down through the ducts going in from the White House to the State Department. So if I now said something in the UN that would upset State Department policy, that would be awful. Would I therefore please amend the speech, taking out the provocative passages?

I told him I would try, but that I doubted I would succeed. He said he did not want any "disharmony" in his delegation. I told him I would certainly not cause any, that if I could not succeed in bowdlerizing the speech (I knew I couldn't), I would make an appropriate excuse about why suddenly I found I had to leave town this afternoon, and the draft speech could be delivered by an alternate. He thanked me, in his genuinely expressive way. Then five minutes later he called back. He wanted me to know, he said, that he and Tap Bennett, "i.e., the top leadership of the UN delegation," believe that what I said was in every way correct, that I said it correctly, that I had not violated in any way my commitment to the delegation in writing as I did, and that after the war in the Mideast was concluded, I would have ample opportunity to express myself vigorously on matters of human rights.

I went through the proposed motions. Robert Kitchen, the specialist in economic and social affairs, was tapped to give Hume's speech, which he did. The daily USUN roundup made the following summary: "General debate on Item 56, 25th Anniversary of Declaration of Human Rights, while generally non-polemic, led to exchange of Rights of Reply among Israel, Egypt, Iraq, and USSR over hostilities in Middle East. U.S. statement avoided specific references and sought to put anniversary in historical perspective by citing original intention of drafts of Declaration and by discussing its increased importance 25 years later. U.S. statement well received." Dino pencils in the margin: "Nonsense. No comment made other than polite noises."

17.

Mrs. Loeb Speech

Though my one proffered speech at the UN has been gently vetoed, I must today speak—outside the UN, though at a UN-oriented affair. Once a year it is United Nations Day as far as the City of New York is concerned, and Mrs. John Loeb, wife of the tycoon, is in charge. She is the New York City Commissioner on the UN, a distinguished, regal lady whom they call "Peter." The function is relatively simple. A modest buffet lunch to which all delegates are invited, followed by a speaker whose assignment it is to give a talk on "New York civics." I was conscripted for the affair a month ago.

Dino and I arrive, having stopped next door to the club where the lunch is to be held to purchase a bottle of cold white wine, fearing that we will be offered only the hard stuff or, worse, nothing. In fact, there was a white wine (inferior to ours) being passed around, and I offered to share mine with one or two, but not three, other guests. That morning, struggling with the topic—the idea is to instruct curious UN delegates about New York political issues and practices—I decided to pull out a speech I had prepared during my campaign for mayor of New York City in 1965. I thought this vaguely appropriate since the papers are full of the activities of the gentlemen running to succeed John Lindsay as mayor, and the election is exactly a week away.

The speech I brought along is in question-and-answer form. I read it over, struck out a few anachronized paragraphs, and a few others that were waspishly anti-Lindsay on the theme that Lindsay-is-not-really a Republican. Inasmuch as five years after giving that speech Lindsay left the Republican Party, I thought that to leave those parts in would on the one hand be tautological and, on the other, an invitation to the audience to admire my prescience. Otherwise, the talk concentrated on what continue to be the major issues in New York: crime, welfare, racial polarization, tax.

There were, I guess, a couple of hundred people there, half of them delegates, half a mixture of press, friends of Mrs. Loeb, and general UN-types. When I was through, I could feel the refined dismay of Peter, who is a close friend of John Lindsay and indeed his appointee. But there was nothing to be done about it, and we swung into the question period. A distinguished-looking black gentleman rose and asked, "Mr. Buckley, what are your views on the transportation bond referendum?" I replied: "To tell you the truth, I have not studied the issue, which I can divulge in good conscience because I don't have to vote on it, since I vote in Connecticut." Mrs. Loeb rose, smiling. "You see, Mr. Ambassador," she said, "in America, we don't vote where we work, we vote where we sleep." "Well," I contributed, "even that is not *exactly* correct. If I voted where I slept, I would vote in the United Nations." That jollity was not exactly a crowd-pleaser. Those who did not understand it were unappreciative. Those who did understand it were unappreciative. Come to think of it, Peter never wrote to thank me for the speech. For a long time I was sure it would prove to be the only speech I would deliver, during the 28th Session of the General Assembly, in any way connected with the UN.

I got back to the office, and there was a note. John Scali wanted to see me. He was deeply upset, and though he seldom refers to his personal problems, he confided that his doctors had told him that unless he slowed down, he would be "carried out of the UN draped in a flag." He smokes too much, he is tense, and driving, and deeply concerned. Three weeks later he would be taken out, not thank God in a casket, but under a doctor's supervision, and flown to Arizona, where he submitted to intricate heart surgery, keeping him out of action for the balance of the session, leaving Tap Bennett in command.

He was speculating, now, that the anti-Nixon fever that had been ignited by the firing of Cox and Richardson, and the explosive press conference at which Nixon and the press had howled at each other, might lead the combatants abroad to feel not only that Nixon had lost his authority, but that for factional reasons the Congress would attempt to undermine his authority as peacemaker in the Mideast. He asked my opinion whether, under the circumstances, he would be wise to spend the weekend lobbying with friends, Republicans and Democrats alike, suggesting some sort of a joint declaration to the effect that Nixon's Watergate problems would not be permitted to impair his authority as chief foreign policy maker. Scali ruminated that his hand would almost surely be stronger if he went down to Washington without advising anyone that he intended to do so, let alone ask anyone's permission. Scali has of course only two superiors. As a matter of fact, technically he has only one: the President. In practice, the UN Ambassador receives most of his orders through the Secretary of State. Scali wanted to be able to say to Democratic Senators that he had gone to them *sua sponte,* that neither Nixon nor Kissinger knew of his mission. He could then explain to these Senators, with an intimacy of detail available only to someone on the diplomatic firing line, how heavy a burden Nixon-Kissinger were in fact carrying in the delicate matter of the cease-fire and the projected negotiations. Let anything happen to suggest that Nixon was powerless, and the whole area could once again go up in smoke.

Scali reminisced a little about the different styles of different Secretaries of State. Kissinger is known for wanting to do everything himself, relying very little on institutional arrangements within the State Department. I told him that this was perhaps an aspect of Kissinger's personality; but that surely the main reason for it was the almost inevitable tension between the White House and the State Department during the five years when there were in effect two foreign policy makers, Kissinger and Rogers. Also, there is the newness of the assignment—Kissinger has been Secretary of State a mere five weeks, and he ran into a full-scale war only a fortnight after he took over. I told him that, lunching with Kissinger shortly after he became Secretary, I had asked him, "What are you going to do now that you won't have the State Department to kick around anymore?" and that Kissinger was amused. Scali's enthusiasm for his weekend mission mounts, and in a day or so he is off, and tells me over the telephone a few days later that he has been supremely successful, that he has got several dozen Senators to sponsor the right kind of resolution. Scali is a very good man.

18.

Human Rights, Analysis of Declaration and Covenants

WEDNESDAY

The vote today in the Third Committee will address itself to one of those piquant differences in parliamentary formulation on which much, technically, hangs. As usual, the Soviet Union has a stake in it. And since it looks as though the Soviet Union is going to lose this one, it will all mean, as usual, that it won't, under the circumstances, amount to very much. Though the formal point is interesting.

The general idea is to galvanize the members of the United Nations about human rights. Specifically, to urge the members of the United Nations to ratify outstanding instruments relating to human rights. More specifically, to urge these nations to ratify three instruments.

In 1948 the United Nations promulgated the Universal Declaration of Human Rights, concerning which more below. Many years later, in 1966, this Declaration was reformulated into language suitable for adoption as law by individual states. For these purposes; the Declaration was split into two parts. The first is called the International Covenant on Civil and Political Rights. The other, the International Covenant on Economic, Social and Cultural Rights. These are, by the way, virtually unreadable documents, prolix, vague, pompous—clearly the kind of document minted in the absence of Hamilton, Madison, and Jay. But that is temporarily beside the point. These Covenants were promulgated on December 16, 1966, and as of the fall of 1973, had been signed by fifty states (specifically, fifty for the one, forty-nine for the other), and ratified, which is to say translated into local law, by twenty-three states.

But there is a third document, also promulgated by the UN on December 16, 1966. It is called the Optional Protocol to the International Covenant on Civil and Political Rights. This Optional Protocol adds a single feature to everything else. It permits an individual to appeal directly to a United Nations committee, set up for that purpose, against a violation of an enumerated right, always assuming that the country in which the appellant resides has ratified the relevant Covenant, and that the plaintiff has exhausted local remedies. The Optional Protocol, as of this writing, has been ratified by nine states (for curiosity's sake: Barbados, Colombia, Costa Rica, Denmark, Ecuador, Madagascar, Norway, Sweden, and Uruguay). For obvious reasons, the Optional Protocol is not popular with the Soviet Union. And the issue is joined on what would appear at first blush as a totally insignificant question of language. Bulgaria et al. have backed a resolution enjoining member states to ratify "the said international instruments." But Costa Rica has asked that the said international instruments be named; and among the instruments, of course, is the Optional Protocol. If it is left merely as "the said international instruments," the Soviet Union can take airily the position that after all it has already ratified "the said instruments," the Soviet Union having just now (in September) ratified the first two Covenants. But if all three instruments are named, then the Soviet Union is delinquent on the one it truly cares about, which would give a Soviet citizen the (theoretical) right to appeal to a UN committee against the denial of a right by the Soviet state, foreshadowing 250 million communications to the said committee. The debate proceeds.

The sudden ratification by the Soviet Union of the two Covenants had of course a political motivation unrelated to any seizure of appreciation for human rights. The Soviet Union sought (a) to influence the Congress of the United

States, which was/is stalled on the question of whether to extend Most Favored Nation trade privileges to the Soviet Union; (b) to suggest to the world community that she is as advanced as anyone, and indeed more advanced than the United States, in its formal appreciation of human rights, since the United States has not ratified the two Covenants; and (c) to exercise the machinery of international human rights in such a way as to prepare for the possible use of it in order to harass target enemies, specifically South Africa and Portugal, and this for the purpose of attracting the admiration of the Third World, which is primarily concerned with racial discrimination and, particularly, apartheid.

The Universal Declaration, for all the paeans that are devoted to it, is a very sloppy instrument; legally, it is a swamp. (It appears in Appendix A.) This is not to say it is useless. It does in fact enumerate an ideal civil situation for the individual human being, and there is something to be said for that. Philosophical objections to the Declaration issue from the abuse of the word "right." As already mentioned, for instance (in Article 23) the right to "free choice of employment" and to "rest and leisure" (Article 24) and then to (Article 26) an "education . . . directed to the full development of the human rights and fundamental freedoms . . . promot[ing] understanding, tolerance and friendship among all nations, racial or religious groups, and . . . further[ing] the activities of the United Nations for the maintenance of peace." It is widely believed that the Universal Declaration loses its vagueness in the actual Covenants submitted to the member states for ratification. The answer is it does not. The aforesaid Article 26 of the Declaration crops up as Article 13 in the Covenant on Economic, Social and Cultural Rights, as follows:

> 1. The States Parties to the present Covenant recognize the right of everyone to education. They agree that education shall be directed to the full development of the human personality and the sense of its dignity, and shall strengthen

the respect for human rights and fundamental freedoms. They further agree that education shall enable all persons to participate effectively in a free society, promote under-standing, tolerance, and friendship among all nations and all racial, ethnic, or religious groups, and further the activities of the United Nations for the maintenance of peace.

Still, lodged within the Universal Declaration are affirmations about the relationship between the state and the individual which, as I say, everyone should cheer. So that the raw symbolism of subscription to the Declaration is not without meaning. Except insofar as it becomes wholly cynical.

The Declaration was promulgated in 1948. For a period, it ostensibly expressed a standard subscribed to even by the Soviet Union (which didn't veto it). It was in those days rhetorical hypocrisy of sorts, and as such to be sure objectionable. But when it became the solemn law of the land, it moved from verbal hypocrisy to legal travesty.

Consider. Though the Soviet Union ratified both Covenants in September, within four months Soviet state police, (a) having publicly reviled Solzhenitsyn, (b) denied him a legal residence in Moscow, (c) censored his work and denied him royalties, (d) forced their way into his apartment, (e) dragged him away without serving him with a warrant, (f) stripped him of his clothing and possessions, (g) charged him with a crime, (h) divested him of citizenship, (i) put him in an airplane, and (j) dumped him, an exile, in West Germany. In doing so, the Soviet Union violated (at least) the following strictures in the Declaration of Human Rights, ratified through the Covenant by the Soviet Union in September, which instrument of ratification was deposited with the Secretary-General of the United Nations on October 16, 1973. . . .

Article 2. *Everyone is entitled to all the rights and freedoms set forth in this Declaration, without distinction of . . . political or other opinion.*

Article 5. *No one shall be subjected to torture or to cruel, inhuman or degrading treatment or punishment.*

Article 9. *No one shall be subjected to arbitrary arrest, detention or exile.*

Article 10. *Everyone is entitled in full equality to a fair and public hearing by an independent and impartial tribunal, in the determination of his rights and obligations and of any criminal charge against him.*

Article 11 (1). *Everyone charged with a penal offense has the right to be presumed innocent until proved guilty according to law in a public trial at which he has had all the guarantees necessary for his defense.*

Article 12. *No one shall be subjected to arbitrary interference with his privacy, family, home or correspondence, nor to attacks upon his honor and reputation. Everyone has the right to the protection of the law against such interference or attacks.*

Article 13 (1). *Everyone has the right to freedom of movement and residence within the borders of each State.*

Article 13 (2). *Everyone has the right to leave any country, including his own, and to return to his country.*

Article 15 (2). *No one shall be arbitrarily deprived of his nationality nor denied the right to change his nationality.*

Article 17 (1). *Everyone has the right to own property alone as well as in association with others.*

Article 17 (2). *No one shall be arbitrarily deprived of his property.*

Article 18. *Everyone has the right to freedom of thought, conscience and religion; this right includes freedom to change his religion or belief, and freedom, either alone or in community with others and in public or private, to manifest his religion or belief in teaching, practice, worship and observance.*

Article 19. *Everyone has the right to freedom of opinion and expression; this right includes the freedom to hold opinions without interference, and to seek, receive and impart information and ideas throughout any media and regardless of frontiers.*

Article 21 (1). *Everyone has the right to take part in the government of his country, directly or through freely chosen representives.*

Article 27 (2). *Everyone has the right to the protection of the moral and material interests resulting from any scientific, literary or artistic production of which he is the author.*

Still, the Soviet Union cares about formalities, which is why, although it would never actually permit the Optional Protocol to function for the benefit of any Russian, it doesn't want to urge its adoption: whence the maneuver (unsuccessful) to back the inexplicit resolution. Over the course of its history, the United Nations has sent out eighteen covenants relating to human rights. These are enumerated in Appendix C.

19.
Protection for Diplomats

Unlike the proposed convention against terrorism, the effort to draft a convention to protect diplomats proved successful. Or at least we think it proved successful. It will not be known whether it did until we see someone from Country A who shot a diplomat in Country B punished in Country B, or returned to Country A for punishment, even if said person pleads as his motive that he was merely pursuing a struggle for national liberation. Concretely, would a citizen of, say, Mauritius, who shot the Portuguese Ambassador in Tanzania (a) be prosecuted and imprisoned in Tanzania; or (b) if sent home to Mauritius, be prosecuted and imprisoned there—or would they give him a parade?

Complicated legal documents, particularly those with ambiguities spliced into them, tend to read according as the nation in question desires. We took an official position that the Convention is plainspoken as regards the obligation of States Parties, and we will see what we will see.

It was a very long and arduous fight, and our team performed splendidly. Robert Rosenstock (whom I do not know) is reputedly a first-rater. Ron Bettauer (whom I do know, and later worked with on African art treasures) is greatly learned, patient, and bright. It was their job, primarily in the Sixth (legal) Committee, to keep the language of the proposed Convention tight enough to make it meaningful. The subject took one-third of the time of the Sixth Committee, twenty-four sessions in all.

The item (No. 90) was called "Draft Convention on the Prevention and Punishment of Crimes Against Diplomatic Agents and Other Internationally Protected Persons." Here was something made to order for the United Nations. Another way to put it is: If the machinery of the United Nations can't cope with a convention to protect diplomats, it can't really cope with anything at all. It isn't clear that they *have* coped with it, but mechanically, the thing is on its way.

We ran into two principal roadblocks. The first is the Latin American tradition of asylum. Latin American states have in almost every historical circumstance sheltered politicians whose fortunes have turned sour. Traditionally, politicians on the run—for instance, some of the principal officials of the Allende government—run into the embassy of a (preferably sympathetic) Latin American country, and squat down there where they are protected from the local police. It is not unheard of for them to stay there for years and years, though most often the local government will agree to give them safe passage to a local airport. On this one, to the extent I can penetrate the language, we gave in. I am less apologetic than I should be at being a little vague on the subject, having listened to Tap Bennett's statement, as delivered before the General Assembly on December 14 hailing the new Convention. Article 12, he explains, "states that this Convention shall not affect the application of treaties on asylum in force as between Parties to those treaties inter se." If he had left it there, the meaning would be perfectly clear. Instead, he chose to elaborate: "That is to say, even if the alleged offender is present on the territory of one Party to such a treaty and the State on the territory of which the crime has taken place is also a Party to such a treaty, if the internationally protected person attacked exercised his functions on behalf of a State not Party to such a treaty, or the alleged offender was a national of a State not Party to such a treaty, the State where the alleged offender is present may not invoke that treaty with respect to the non-Party State." Whoever wrote that sentence (Tap Bennett is too lucid to have committed it himself) must have been borrowed from Internal Revenue.

The more serious challenge to the Convention arose from African suspicion that the whole thing might stand in the way of liberation movements. The African salient struck most deeply into the heart of the Convention when, in mid-November, the African bloc, including such moderates as the Nigerians and the Ghanians, introduced an amending article which read: "No provision of these articles shall be applicable to peoples struggling against colonialism, foreign occupation, racial discrimination and apartheid in the exercise of their legitimate rights to self-determination and independence." The chairman of the Sixth Committee, a very shrewd Mexican called González Galvez, brought together representatives from critical blocs for an off-the-record session at which he persuaded them that the Convention might as well not be written at all, if it was to include so vast an escape clause. It was at one of these that Mali raised a very concrete question (I tend to feel that these matters are best understood by raising concrete questions). What, he said, if someone should take a shot at Ian Smith of Rhodesia? Well, the British and Americans pointed out with, one takes it, the satisfaction of a Philadelphia lawyer—the Convention would not apply for two simple reasons. One, Smith is not the head of any state, since no one recognizes Rhodesia (that is an observation that recalls Berkeley's epistemological inquiring into whether a tree makes any noise in falling if someone is not there to hear it fall); and the Convention applies only to acts committed against diplomats when they are abroad— and Ian Smith does not travel abroad (not true, as it happens)—which would appear to dispose of the Rhodesian problem. The argument, for reasons of mutual tact, was not pressed using John Vorster of South Africa as an example. Needless to say, it never crossed anyone's mind to ask whether a Czech patriot who shot a visiting Soviet diplomat would be protected.

The situation was finally compromised by a provision in a

resolution which "shall be published together with it [the Convention]." That provision says that " . . . the provisions of the annexed Convention cannot in any way prejudice the exercise of the legitimate right to self-determination and independence in accordance with the principles and purposes of the Charter of the United Nations and the Declaration on Friendly Relations and Cooperation among States in accordance with the Charter of the United Nations by peoples struggling against colonialism, alien domination, foreign occupation, racial discrimination and apartheid."

We struggled to detach the Resolution from the Convention. We failed. The word came in from Washington: DEPARTMENT UNDERSTANDS THAT DELEGATION'S EFFORTS TO RESIST SPECIAL PUBLICATION OF RESOLUTION ALONG WITH CONVENTION HAVE BEEN UNAVAILING. UNDER THE CIRCUMSTANCES, [THE ARRANGEMENT] IS ACCEPTABLE. KISSINGER.

We have, as I say, taken the position that the Convention is supreme over any resolution. Bennett was half debonair, half truculent, in the way he put it in his speech: "While this resolution contains some paragraphs which we would not have considered necessary, we nevertheless see no particular harm in their inclusion since they do not purport to impinge—*and of course cannot impinge*—upon the Convention." On the assumption that Bennett's optimism is well grounded, this was a solid achievement of the 28th General Assembly.

20.

Israeli Practices

WEDNESDAY

Going into the Special Political Committee to argue on the side of Israel, I felt like a member of the Light Brigade. The UN joke during the first day or so of the fighting was that Golda Meir had cabled Sadat saying, Let's make love, not war; whereupon, having weighed the alternatives, Sadat made war—the Yum Yum Kippur war, as the anti-Israelis juicily put it. If Israel had been charged with anti-Semitism, Israel would have lost, at the UN, this time around. Certainly she would lose on Resolution 291, a resolution sponsored by Afghanistan and Mauritania, endorsing a report of a Special Committee to Investigate Israeli Practices Affecting the Human Rights of the Population of the Occupied Territories. That was the tough anti-Israeli resolution (USUN 4283) finding Israel guilty of any number of violations of the recognized rights of war-occupied peoples and calling for sanctions of sorts. And then there was a second resolution, more nearly platonic in nature, Resolution 290 (USUN 4282), which merely calls on Israeli occupation authorities to abide by the provisions of the Fourth Geneva Convention in its administration of Arab territories. I arrived armed with instructions entirely unambiguous. FM SECSTATE WASHDC SUBJECT: UNGA: RESOLUTIONS ON ISRAELI PRACTICES IN OCCUPIED TERRITORIES. MISSION SHOULD VOTE IN FAVOR OF RESOLUTION TEXT IN USUN 4282 AND SHOULD VOTE AGAINST RESOLUTION TEXT IN USUN 4283. KISSINGER. On top of this, we have information that the

West European bloc would abstain on the harsh resolution rather than vote with us. That left, on Israel's side, us, and—we would see.

The Fourth Geneva Convention, passed in 1949, elaborates the approved behavior by a state administering a territory it has occupied during a war. There are any number of things you are not permitted to do. For instance, you cannot deplete the natural assets of that state. You can use the fields to grow wheat to feed the people, and you can draw water from the streams to give them drink; but you cannot, e.g., mine coal or take out oil, these being in the category of non-replenishable assets. You can build buildings for the sake of defense, but you cannot build buildings whose clear purpose is to establish something like a colonial hold over the occupied territory. You cannot pillage local architectural or archaeological treasures, you cannot interfere in any basic way with the cultural or religious practices of the occupied people, and you cannot dispossess them of their land, or move them about. All these things, it was said by a special committee constituted to investigate the question, Israel had done in the territories occupied after the 1967 war.

The investigating committee in question is staffed conspicuously, in some ways flagrantly, by anti-Israel people, and it was because of that imbalance that the United States, five years ago, declined to vote for its constitution. The Israelis, by the same token, refused to cooperate with the committee in any way, insisting that it was *parti pris* on the side of the Arabs. Under the circumstances, every year that went by, the report of the committee came in pretty much like the report of the year before. This year it was especially heated because of the war, and the consuming attention given to everything that touched on Israel.

The trouble with Israeli apologists—this is true of all their diplomats, and of not a few non-diplomats—is that they concede *nothing*. In the instant case, as an example, it was actually debated in the Knesset all year long whether a building program clearly intended to fasten down, over the very, very long haul—generations maybe—Israel's hold over the West Bank, and over parts of the Sinai, should be undertaken, with a not inconsiderable minority of Israeli legislators voting most ardently against what they denounced as moves that could not reasonably be interpreted as other than imperialist in design. But somebody like Abba Eban would rot in hell before admitting that there was the least suggestion of any truth in the assertion that the leaders of Israel had it in mind to squat down in the West Bank, and the Golan Heights, forever. (Jerusalem, yes—they would admit that they took over Jerusalem forever.)

Now in combative situations, this may be good strategy. It remains to be seen whether it will, in the end, work out well for Israel—I tend to hope so, for reasons irrelevant to this narrative. But one does request of their diplomats, for instance in private conversations, please not to proceed as though every single one of their arguments is accepted, by their allies, as the graven truth.

Israel's principal justification for the 1967 war is that it was triggered by Jordan and came in the wake of Nasser's implacable oratory about the end of the Israeli state. An Israeli minister recalled to me, in Tel Aviv in 1972, that when the United States returned Okinawa to Japan, Secretary of State Rogers announced that it was not often in world history that a victor returned to an aggressor a territory which had been used as a military offensive base, after only twenty-five years. "By those standards," the minister said, "we have twenty years more in the Sinai." A perfectly respectable argument, in my opinion; but not one that requires one to believe that, during those twenty-five years, no activity is being taken by the occupying power which is proscribed by the Fourth Geneva Convention.

Israel's Jacob Doron covered everything in his hour-long speech. (a) The investigating committee was not properly authorized; (b) its composition was biased; (c) the Geneva Convention has never been adduced to condemn any other occupying power during the twenty-seven years since it was written, suggesting that it's being used now as a bill of attainder, so to speak, against Israel; (d) Israel hasn't done any of the things it has been charged with doing; (e) if everybody is so fired up about the Geneva Convention, how come India closed off debate at the International Red Cross meeting in Teheran early this month when Israel tried to bring up the issue of POW's, which is unambiguously covered by the Geneva Convention? It was a very good piece of advocacy.

Egypt's Meguid cited the research of the Special Committee as conclusive in its probative value, and insisted that under the circumstances everything done by Israel in the occupied zone is in violation of the Geneva Convention. Jordan's Sharaf made a spirited attack, questioning in particular Israel's annexation of all of Jerusalem. Jordan cited the anti-Israel witness of Israel Shahak, described as chairman of the Israeli League for Human Rights. Shahak, who is a Jew, indeed a rabbi, and who is greatly opposed to Israeli policy, is frequently cited by Arabs while making their case against Israel. Israel's Doron has said that Shahak is a man of strange, not to say unbalanced, views, that his title is self-assumed, and that he was recently booted out of the International League for the Rights of Man for irresponsible conduct.

The next speaker was Issa Nakhleh, who is the representative of the Palestinian Arabs. The Palestinian Arabs are permitted a representative, who may speak, but who has no vote. Nakhleh speaks for eighty (80) minutes. He sits there, toward the back of the room, on the far rim of the concentric semicircles where we perch, facing the chairman. He is deeply impassioned, dangerously bitter. There is no derogation he misses. The racial illegitimacy of the present occupants of Israel . . . their war criminality . . . their disloyalty . . . Dayan's vanity . . . Jewish torture . . . Jewish excesses exceeding Nazi excesses . . . the hypocritical criticism of Hitler by the Jews . . . Israel's defiance of three Security Council and five General Assembly resolutions on Jerusalem . . . Golda's schoolteaching in

Wisconsin . . . the apparent immunity of Israel's war criminals contrasted to the punishment of Nazi war criminals. . . . "Is it because the Palestinians are `not thought of as human beings? Are we dogs?" He says that the only reason the United States continues to vote the way it does is that Congress and the United States, to a soul, are subservient to the counterfeit state of Israel—"That is what Senator Fulbright said." I thought this distortion worth contending and leaned over to ask Guy Wiggins whether we should put in for a Right of Reply. "No," he whispered. "He was worse than this at UNRWA. And anyway it's slightly infra dig, since he isn't a recognized delegate."

He concluded with a few modest proposals. (1) The United Nations should condemn the "genocidal state of Israel" and expel it from membership. (2) Constituent states should sever all diplomatic relations with Israel, as most of the African nations have done. (3) All countries should stop all aid to Israel. (4) Having recognized and affirmed the right to self-determination, we should "restore the Holy Land of Peace."

It is, of course, talk like this—never mind the historical argument—that persuades Israelis that nothing short of the end of the State of Israel is the irreducible objective of the Palestinians, and, derivatively, the Arab states.

It is truly painful. But it brings you the ferocity of Palestinian irredentism.

Needless to say, the Soviet Union had to get into the act. There is a vulgar rivalry, in the UN, between China and the Soviet Union, to win the friendship, if that is the word for it, of the Third World nations, most particularly those hostile to Israel. China accused the Soviet Union of not *really* helping the Arabs, of being a false friend. The Soviet Union, exercising its Right of Reply, shot back that words are cheap. Who gave the Arabs all their arms, all their guns, all the material things so necessary to help them in their armed struggle against the aggressor Israel? Who flew them the technical advisers and the military advisers? (The Soviet representative was happily owning up to a role in the Mideast it is given to soft-playing in other situations.) Why, if the Soviet Union wasn't a true friend, why did it receive messages of thanks from Egypt, Syria, Morocco, Algeria, and other Arab countries?

The Chinese called for a Right of Reply to the Right of Reply. Certainly, the speaker said with disgust, the Soviet Union did all these things. But for *money.* The Soviet leaders are merchants of death (that was the exact phrase). Just answer one question: Will you give the Arabs their arms free of charge? And anyway, the only reason the Soviets are interested in the Mideast, said the Chinese, is in order to expand their sphere of influence (which is exactly correct), so that their help is hardly disinterested. Finally, by allowing a lot of Jews to emigrate from the Soviet Union to Israel, the Soviet Union was in fact fortifying the Israeli military. This, by the way, is one of Baroody's favorite points—that the Soviet Union is sending soldiers to Israel to confront Soviet arms.

The Soviet Union (contrary to protocol) insisted on yet another Right of Reply, in order to reject the slanders of the Chinese and their shameful anti-Sovietism. *Why did they sit on their hands at the UN* instead of helping the Arabs work for peace by voting the resolution that brought an end to the fighting? . . . We heard that taunt, *Why did they sit on their hands at the Security Council?* a dozen times in those weeks. The Chinese, as noted, had abstained from voting the cease-fire, alleging that the whole thing was a superpower production. The Soviet Union has decided—worldwide, one suspects—to make that the theme of this season's anti-Chinese propaganda. Inevitably it suggests that the Soviet Union will have to take the toughest possible line during the negotiations, to spare itself the charge, leveled by the Chinese, of having betrayed Arab interests. . . .

When one votes other than in a routine way, it is traditional to make an "Explanation." I went back to the office across the street and wrote out the briefest Explanation I could think to write, which would suggest why the United States would vote for the one resolution, and against the other. Robert Chase, the hugely able staff officer, had given me a great deal of material on the background of our case against the investigating committee, and also a rather interesting archaeological excursion into the question who really is sovereign over Gaza and parts of Jordan; but, I feared on reading it, not much better than the kind of thing Marlon Brando's lawyer could produce in behalf of the Iroquois' claim against Detroit.

I decided to make the statement extremely short, and I wondered whether, now that there was an effective cease-fire, I would be permitted to deliver it. It follows:

> Mr. Chairman:
> My government desires to explain our motives for voting in favor of the one Resolution (290) and against the other (291).
> Manifestly, the Fourth Geneva Convention is a small step in the direction of civilizing warfare. Manifestly, there was a war in 1967 which resulted in the occupation by one set of people of land until that time occupied by another set of people. Historical arguments about who has the most convincing title to a particular territory are always interesting, and usually inconclusive. It is in our judgment as obvious that the Fourth Geneva Convention should be consulted in the Mideast as it is that it should be consulted in Eastern Europe.
> On the broader question: We are asked, in effect, to condemn the state of Israel for following practices in contravention of the Geneva Convention. Our position over the years has been that the tribunal authorized to probe the question of Israeli guilt was tainted with a partisan passion altogether understandable under the circumstances, but disqualifying when the question of justice is being weighed.
> Surely this debate, like so many others held in this chamber, illustrates the dreadful uses of human ingenuity. It is possible to construct cases of overwhelming moral

magnitude at the expense of many nations, and it is distressing to note that the awfulness of their crimes is increasingly a function of the size of the majority their accusers can summon in the United Nations. This ethic, to which we are so greatly attracted, is surely the supreme usurpation: The United Nations is not Mount Sinai, and any effort to proceed as though we could dispense justice through the juggernaut of passion, does little strategic service to the ends we seek to serve.

These ends are the restoration of dignity and freedom for oppressed people. There are very great efforts being made, as we sit here, to improve the situation in the Mideast, to drain from that area so constipated by ill-feeling and misunderstanding, the hatred that has made it the potential tinderbox of a terminal world holocaust. The serious efforts to alleviate injustices to Arabs by Jews, and to Jews by Arabs, are being made in the Security Council and, bilaterally and multilaterally, by representatives of the great powers, and the powers directly affected. To pass one more resolution at this time, to the disadvantage of one of the contending parties, when to do so refreshes that party's conviction that the world is ganging up on it, serves no purpose. Does not serve the purpose of my government, and clearly does not serve the people of the occupied territories, whose concerns should be foremost in our minds.

Dino looked at it. There was that one sentence. . . . "It is in our judgment as obvious that the Fourth Geneva Convention should be consulted in the Mideast as it is that it should be consulted in Eastern Europe." Would it survive scrutiny upstairs? We chatted for a moment. What if Tap Bennett (he was now in charge, Scali having left for Arizona), said: Okay on the statement, but please remove the sentence about Eastern Europe? I would then have two alternatives: to remove the sentence, and make the statement; or, politely, to decline to remove the sentence, and ask that a substitute delegate deliver the speech—either my own, pulped down; or another. We decided most unobtrusively to take the line—not exactly of principle: There wasn't really a principle involved. But the line, as given in the last point of my memorandum to John Scali two months ago: that I should feel free to come out in favor of human freedom even for those who suffered the lack of it because of the Soviet Union. My feeling was that that perspective is important. That Israel's argument is not entirely frivolous. If the Fourth Geneva Convention has been enacted solely to govern the activities of Israel and South Africa, and whatever Western states choose voluntarily to abide by it, then that should be known. The knowing of it—the pointing it out—is a part of our general effort, as distinguished from the effort of A/SPCL. 291. We would wait and see.

Not long. The next afternoon, Saturday, I was in the country. Schaufele called, complaining about the weather at the Yale-Harvard game. He came then to the point. "We are going to make a very low-key statement on the Israel thing. I gather you don't want to make that kind of statement?" I answered, "Well, I don't want to say *nothing*." "Well," he says, "*nothing* is pretty much what we want to say." "If you don't mind," I said, "I'll let the staff handle it then." "Okay. I don't mind at all."

It was Schaufele himself who delivered the Explanation. It had in it sentences like: "We have always been, and shall continue to be, deeply concerned about the protection of the human rights of all the peoples affected by the Middle East conflict, including the inhabitants of the Arab territories occupied by Israel. We continue to stand ready to support any approach which shows promise of relieving the suffering of any who might be victims of violations of those rights in the Middle East. . . ."

On the strong anti-Israel resolution the vote was 82 Yes (to condemn Israel), 7 No (us, Israel, and 5 Latin American countries). On the broad resolution enjoining Israel to respect the Fourth Convention the vote was 109 in favor (including us), 0 opposed, and 4 abstaining (Israel, Costa Rica, Malawi, Nicaragua).

21.
African Art

I am minding my own business, sitting at the U.S. chair in the Plenary as duty-delegate, when I am suddenly handed Item 110: Restitution of Works of Art to Countries Victims of Expropriation. Would I please (a) abstain, (b) propose an amendment to the resolution, and (c) make a speech (an Explanation) as to why the United States government (a) abstained, and (b) proposed this amendment? I am comforted by Ron Bettauer, who assures me that there will not be any debate calling on me to display my deep study of Restitution of Works of Art to Countries Victims of Expropriation.

I am proffered a prepared speech, explaining the attitude of the United States on the question. It is brisk and orderly. I revise the phrasing a little to suit me while still occupying the chair; the alterations are passed around to one of two other staff members, and no one thinks to rush it across the street for clearance: there is nothing particularly abrasive.

The resolution on which the vote is scheduled is co-sponsored by Burundi, Chad, the Congo, Guinea, Mali, Mauritania, Senegal, Uganda, Zaire, and Zambia. What it says, in a word, is that countries that have art or artifacts that originated in other countries should return them. There is, of course, no enforcement machinery. And several distinctions are neatly ignored, mostly through the instrumentality of Byelorussia, which is not anxious to stimulate an appetite for returning works of art taken by the Soviet Union from

Germany and East Europe during the war. Our problem with the resolution is its vagueness, and the procedural liberties taken in bringing it to the floor—it was never processed through a committee, and it is uncoordinated with other general moves in the indicated direction of the repatriation of art.

I do not know the origin of Resolution Rhetoric, but in the United Nations, the Elegant Variation is not only In, it is Compulsory.

All resolutions begin preferably with a present participle. But every verb introducing a clause needs, for some reason, to be different. Here is this one:

The General Assembly,

Aware of the paramount aims of the United Nations and particularly its faith in fundamental human rights, in the dignity and worth of the human person,

Recalling the Declaration on the granting of independence to colonial countries and peoples,

Considering the conclusions of the Fourth Conference of Heads of State or Government of Non-Aligned Countries, held at Algiers from 5 to 9 September 1973, and particularly paragraph 18 of the political declaration,

Noting with interest the work of the Third Congress of the International Association of Art Critics held in September 1973 at Kinshasa-N'Sele (Zaire),

Recalling the Convention on the Means of Prohibiting and Preventing the Illicit Import, Export and Transfer of Ownership of Cultural Property, adopted by the General Conference of the United Nations Educational, Scientific and Cultural Organization at its sixteenth session, on 14 November 1970,

Stressing that the cultural heritage of a people conditions the present and future flowering of its artistic values and its over-all development,

Believing that the promotion of national culture can enhance a people's ability to understand the culture and civilization of other peoples and thus can have a favorable impact on international cooperation,

Deploring the wholesale removal, virtually without payment, of objets d'art from one country to another, frequently as a result of colonial or foreign occupation,

Convinced that the restitution of such works would make good the serious damage suffered by countries as a result of such removal,

—And we are ready for the resolution, which also uses different verbs, but since they are in the active voice, they grant great relief:

1. *Affirms* that the prompt restitution to a country of its works of art, monuments, museum pieces and manuscripts by another country, without charge, is calculated to strengthen international cooperation inasmuch as it constitutes just reparation for damage done; [now that is a sneaky one]

2. *Recognizes* the special obligations in this connection of those countries which had access to such objects only as a result of colonial occupation;

3. *Calls upon* all the States concerned to prohibit the expropriation of works of art from Territories still under colonial or alien domination,

4. *Invites* the Secretary-General, in consultation with the United Nations Educational, Scientific and Cultural Organization and Member States, to submit a report to the General Assembly at its thirtieth session on the progress achieved.

It would be my historic task, as delegate to the 28th Session of the General Assembly of the United Nations, to propose an amendment, as ordered by Washington.

I strode to the podium for my maiden appearance at the Plenary.

I began by saying that nobody is more in favor of returning illicitly removed national art treasures than

President Nixon. He is for it for many reasons, of which I cited all I knew.

Under the circumstances, we deeply regretted that we are going to have to abstain on the draft resolution.` The resolution is inadequate, and it wasn't handled by normal procedures. "As it stands," I said, "it is at once vague, presumptuous, and inscrutable."

What's more, said I, we've been talking about this general subject since 1960, when UNESCO adopted the Convention on the Means of Prohibiting and Preventing the Illicit Import, Export and Transfer of Ownership of Cultural Property. So why don't we just all ratify the UNESCO Convention, I said, which takes care of all the points covered in this resolution? As for us, President Nixon sent this Convention to the Senate in 1971, the Senate has given its advice and consent to ratification, and the Executive Branch has since submitted implementing legislation to Congress—as recently as November 9, a mere month ago. Meanwhile, the United States has applied existing laws forcefully, we have enacted legislation concerning the illegal importation of pre-Columbian monuments, we've promoted the code of ethics elaborated by the International Council of Museums governing the acquisition of artifacts. And we returned to Cameroon just the other day the traditional ancestral statue discovered there.

I came now to my amendment. As it stands, the Director General of UNESCO has been ordered by the Assembly to report to the 31st Assembly on the Preservation and Further Development of Cultural Values. That's the Assembly that's supposed to cover the whole waterfront. Under the circumstances, it doesn't make sense to anticipate, by only one year, this enterprise, since the two go properly hand in hand. Accordingly—

"My delegation now proposes that operative paragraph 3 of the draft in L/717/Rev. 1 be amended by replacing 'at its Thirtieth Session with 'at its Thirty-first Session.'"

I remember a wonderful story about Victor Borge who, having at age fourteen won a national competition, found himself the piano soloist with the Copenhagen Symphony Orchestra. He was playing the Grieg A Minor Piano Concerto, in the cadenza of which there is a fairly long trill while the orchestra is silent. Young Victor, on reaching this dramatic moment, thought to himself: What an extraordinary situation! Here are 100 men with instruments sitting behind me quite silent, and 3,500 people sitting in front of me, quite silent, while I am simply moving first my second finger, then my third finger, then my second finger, back and forth between two notes. He was so carried away by the power he was exercising that he refused to release the trill, allowing it to go on and on and on until the audience was convulsed with laughter.

Walter Mitty! "*Now, Mr. President, since I'm up here in this here old podium introducing amendments, I've got a couple of other amendments I think I'd like you all to consider here, in the General Assembly, won't take long, maybe just fifteen, twenty minutes. Now to begin with. . . .*"

But I stepped down, and walked back to my desk. Ron was good enough not to tell me that my Explanation had been well received. And five days later on the very last day of the session, my amendment was rejected, 78 votes to 11, with 33 abstentions. The Europeans stuck with me, and Australia, and Canada, and Fiji.

22.

Khmer

The Khmer vote is coming to a head. Excepting possibly the Korean vote, and of course the engrossing Mideast business in the Security Council, we have probably spent more time on this one than on any other. Clearly we think it important. Tactically, because if the UN throws out the representative of Lon Nol, the effect is to undermine his government throughout the world, and at a time when it is fighting for its life against the Sihanouk insurgents, backed by Hanoi soldiers and Chinese arms. Strategically, because if we lose on this one, the UN will be tempted to decide, pretty much ad lib, in the spirit of the South African resolution, who properly represents a country. This strategic disruption could be used against the Soviet Union in the matter of its satellites, which is why we haven't felt hard Soviet pressure on this one. Sure, they have been making all the usual noises, and will vote solidly for Sihanouk. But no doubt someone in the Kremlin is considering the possibility, however remote, that an exile Polish government might one day put in for the Polish seat, pleading the Cambodia precedent.

Our diplomats around the world have been working for weeks trying to get pro-Sihanouk people to consider abstaining, and abstention-minded people to consider voting against. Every day a cable comes in on the subject from one or two foreign capitals. It is surprising how many of them speak about the felt necessity for group loyalty, and the frankness with which Foreign Ministers will admit that that is why their countries will vote against us. Cables discussing what our Ambassador said to the Foreign Minister very seldom dwell on the arguments used by the Ambassador, or those used by the Foreign Minister. Instead they tend to dwell on the relevant forces arguing for a yes-vote or a no-vote.

It began in mid-October, when the gang, by a vote of 68 yes, 24 no, and 29 abstentions, persuaded the General Assembly to write into the agenda something called "Restoration of the Lawful Rights of the Royal Government of National Union of Cambodia in the United Nations." We objected all over the place, substantively and procedurally. As regards the latter, we insisted it was an "important" question and therefore would require adoption by two-thirds of the Assembly. On the substantive points, Tap Bennett made a cogent statement, pointing out that Sihanouk had been overthrown by his own government and with due regard for the processes prescribed by the Cambodian constitution, and that if it was true, as his supporters alleged, that he "controlled ninety percent of Cambodia," why didn't he live there, instead of in Peking? Etc.

The wording of the actual resolution did not come in until November 30, but we knew pretty well what it would be. Our strategy has been, in a sense, complementary to the Soviet Union's. We want other people to take the ostensible lead in this fight. Ideally, of course, the Asians, who are most directly involved. Here we have the great advantage that with the obvious exception of the Chinese, virtually all of Cambodia's neighbors oppose any attempt by the UN at illegitimizing Lon Nol. Australia is shaky, because of the tough-left government of Gough Whitlam, but the others are solid. By the end of November, however, meeting with the Asians and head-counting very carefully around the world, we concluded that on a direct confrontation, we would lose.

We then decided to proceed as though we were arming for the big vote on the clean question, but meanwhile encouraging the Asians to take a parliamentary initiative.

Here is how it would work. The Asians would whisper it about that perhaps it was best to let the issue go over another year. A year from then it would be a lot clearer who was in command of Cambodia, who was going to win the war. But if a decision were made now, it would commit the United Nations to a kind of interference in the internal affairs of member countries which might haunt other nations in the future. Under the circumstances—and this argument was especially aimed at the fence-sitters—why not get someone to jump up in the middle of the debate and ask for adjournment of the issue until the 29th General Assembly? Under the rules of the GA, such a motion, which provides for listening to only two speakers in favor and two speakers against, takes priority over all other motions. But to go into effect, the ruling from the chair must invoke that priority. Question: Would Benites cooperate? Some people said yes, he would; others no, he would not. There is talk that he is not getting along well with Brad Morse, so it becomes, even, a question of who should approach him on it. . . .   The matter is delicately resolved.

Accordingly, Liberia got up today at the end of a very long debate, and suddenly invoked Rules of Procedure 76 and 79 (c). Uruguay and the Philippines were primed to speak for the adjournment. Fall of Senegal (who is very long-winded and resolutely anti-U.S.) and Job of Yugoslavia spoke against. (By the way, it is terribly vexing to us why the Jugs, as they are called in these parts, have been so stridently anti-U.S. this season. Not that they have ever been very helpful.) Benites came through, putting the motion to a vote. Result: 53 for adjourning the matter for one year, 50 against doing so, 21 abstentions. Norway said later that it had pushed the wrong button by mistake, that the representative had meant to abstain. Thus the winning margin was cut to 2 votes. That kind of victory is hair-raising. There was a lot of tension in the hall. The bad guys had been outwitted, though one had the feeling they weren't completely sorry. If they want to, they can kick out Lon Nol next year: the resolution now slides over automatically into the next session.

It is interesting to see how the votes went, on so narrow an issue. The Latin Americans stayed with us, except for Argentina, which abstained. (Argentina, under Peron, is being fractious.) Oh yes, and except for Guyana. France abstained, breaking an otherwise solid European front. Finland abstained, as did Saudi Arabia and Sweden. Ethiopia abstained, breaking the African monolith along with Sierra Leone, Swaziland, and Nigeria. Peru, as a half measure of goodwill, stayed away and did not vote at all. Rwanda, which had promised to vote with us, skulked off. Literally. I mean, *nobody could find Rwanda.* It's difficult enough on the map. In the UN, it can prove all but impossible. They finally found him, hiding in the Second Committee, but he refused to come into the chamber to vote, saying he had no instructions. (Not true.) The Albanians attacked the United States by name, which they wouldn't do without the okay of the Chinese; we don't like that. Zaire voted against us, notwithstanding our blandishments. Africans went strongly against us, though the issue was of remote importance to them. It suggests the endurance of an emotional anti-Americanism, the fanatical fear of colonialism, and an anxiety to please China, regarded by so many of them as a patron. The Arabs split along radical-conservative lines. Baroody, by keeping his own position (abstention) well hidden, had a negative effect on Bahrain, Yemen, and the United Arab Emirates, who might have abstained instead of voting no if they had known that Saudi Arabia planned to abstain.

The next day, Tap Bennett at the staff conference said that it was time to stimulate our bilateral contacts, and talk turkey to some of these countries. Romania, for instance, which makes a great play of its independence from the Soviet Union. We have done a whole lot for Romania, and it seems that a month doesn't go by that Ceausescu isn't toasting Nixon, or vice versa. But in the UN, they go out of their way to make trouble for us, ditto Yugoslavia. Bennett says that countries we seek to help in myriad ways ought to feel our displeasure. . . . I had a sense of *déjà vu.* A couple of years ago, Nixon gave Secretary of State Rogers instructions to bear down at the UN. Specifically, to accost individual Ambassadors in Washington, and read to them, side by side, declarations made in banquet halls about America (friendly), and declarations made in the UN (unfriendly), and ask them quite simply to account for the disparity. But, surely, that's asking people to explain paradoxes. The United Nations General Assembly is about something altogether different from bilateral relationships. Take Mobutu, for instance. He simply doesn't talk to our people, in closed sessions, the way he talks when he is strutting his stuff at the UN. There the representatives are experiencing a whole other set of satisfactions, and playing to the gallery. From time to time the United States gets upset about it. Our problem, really, is that we have no United Nations doctrine. If we took the position that the General Assembly simply didn't matter—in any decisive sense (of course it matters what people say they think about us, or what they gang up to do to try to destabilize things)—we could by a simple resolution dispose of the worst of the problem.

The President could resolve that the American representative would never again vote in the General Assembly. He would participate in discussions in the same way that the representative of the Palestinians does—speak, listen, deal maybe, but vote, never—on the grounds that voting lends parliamentary significance to the proceeding, while reality requires us to reject any such pretension, on moral and political grounds. . . . Or, going to the other extreme, we could attempt to control the General Assembly, as once we did—and for the very best of reasons, since for a couple of decades we were bankrolling the world and providing the nuclear umbrella. That ended in 1958, when we lost the vote on sending the troops into Lebanon. Probably to recapture control would require greater effort than it would be worth. And it is very hard to see how we could do it. There are too many states for whom independence is experienced only by: voting against the United States. Not inconceivably, the Soviet Union will begin one of these days to excite the same instincts. It is even ventured that at some point in the future, the Soviet Union and the United States will need to join hands to curb the General Assembly. I find that unlikely. On economic matters, yes, and a junior Soviet delegate, off guard, spoke with utter bewilderment at the thought that the Soviet Union—or the United States—should share any of its wealth with the Less Developed Countries. But, politically, that is a long way off.

How is it going for the United States, measured by the support we can count on in the General Assembly? Not so good. Many countries are situated at the way station, en route to an anti-U.S. position. It is, of course, provincial to evaluate all votes on that basis. A vote on the other side of the United States is not necessarily an anti-U.S. vote. Still, there are indices, and they are not meaningless; and one of them would take off from the behavior of the General Assembly on a cluster of issues believed, by the United States, to be important. The United States does not tend to vote its issues narrowly. Very few UN votes (for example) would center on such questions as whether American blacks in Mississippi are properly represented. I found nowhere available any tabulation tending to show the movement within the UN toward or away from the U.S. position. So I made my own, based on 14 "key" votes. By a key vote I mean one which is extra-administrative in significance, and touches on a more or less basic U.S. commitment, e.g., toward human rights, collective security, the security of foreign investments, etc. Research reveals that the gravitational pull of the United States is greatly diluted, and that—as I say—the Abstention is the form by which disassociation is, by the genteel, announced.

I list, in the appendix, the record, country by country, of association with the United States on the votes in question. The tabulation necessarily rides over subtle points. For instance, on an issue in which the United States loses by a single vote, the abstainer is more conspicuously villainous. The U.S.-Adherence Index is suggested by a few examples.

Leading the list is Portugal with +11 (out of +14 possible). Most loyal of the European bloc is the U.K. (+7), with Sweden (−3) at the other end. Venezuela with −4 is typical of Latin America. Among the sui generis countries are Israel +6; Japan, 0; and India −9. Typical Africa is Swaziland, with −8. Among the Arab states, Tunisia with −9. In the Far East, Indonesia is −10. And representative of the Communist monolith is Czechoslovakia with −11.

In short, the General Assembly is pulling away. Let those who will, say that it is pulling away in directions noble and progressive. That is another order of analysis. Suffice, for the moment, to say simply that it is pulling away from the positions that express U.S. policy.

23.

Freedom of Information

Dino called me early to say that coming up this afternoon was the debate on Freedom of Information, Item 64, and that although the United States is in favor of it, no instructions have come in from Washington to supplement the general line handed down on it in the directives distributed in Washington in September. Needless to say, we are in favor of freedom of information. But, it turns out, we are *not* in favor, at this point, of a Draft Convention on Freedom of Information, which is the second part of Item 64, the first being a Draft Declaration on Freedom of Information. We are not in favor of the latter, the State Department had explained last September, because the language is now so botched up, it is unlikely we could ever get it unscrambled. And anyway, another Convention is something of an operation, and would take a lot longer than the Declaration and, presumably, accomplish nothing more, or rather nothing less.

As of the moment, said Dino, not a single nation is inscribed to speak on the subject of the Draft Declaration, or on the Convention, with the result that the leadership of the Third Committee has scheduled not only it, but three other items to be transacted on the single afternoon. That didn't strike either of us as quite right, not much of an effort for freedom of information. So I called Tap Bennett and asked, Did he approve of my pulling an oar for freedom of information? He said all things considered, yes. I told him that I simply did not have the time (I was delivering a lecture that morning) to write out a statement, that I would have to extemporize one. "Go ahead," he said, and I faced my maiden uncensored speech before the Third Committee. I left my house wild with liberty, and read the dossier on the subject in the car.

It all began in 1948, when it was proposed that something formal be done in the direction of stimulating freedom of information. But by the time the various committees had combined their accretions, the proposed Declaration became, rather, an instrument for excusing the suppression of freedom of information, and we dropped the whole idea. In 1959, we made a more or less fresh start, drafting a respectable Declaration which, with the aid of the Philippines in particular, we pushed in the Third Committee. It bounced back and forth to the GA, which in 1968 decided to give it priority in its next (24th) session" . . . so that it may serve as an inspiration and set a standard for information media as well as governments anywhere in the world." The Declaration hitchhiked its way from session to session, never quite getting to its destination, and here we were, once again, asked to take action, preparatory to formal consideration by the General Assembly.

Now it is a lot easier to understand the general attitude toward freedom of information when one recalls that most countries in the world do not desire freedom of information. In fact, 1973 was a bad year for Freedom of Information. There were a couple of bright spots in Turkey, and in Thailand, where censorship ended. In Europe the situation was pretty much static, except that after the fresh coup in Greece, censorship was tightened. In Africa, the press is largely dominated, and even owned, by the government, and is considered an instrument of "national development." In Uganda, President Amin expelled the last foreign correspondent. South Africa has always had a remarkably free press, but this year Vorster threatened (though did not visit upon) the English-speaking press with sanctions if it continued to publish material "tending to incite racial feelings." Rhodesia allows news to come in and out uncensored, but a dozen newsmen were barred from the country. In Asia, in the war zone, there is of course censorship. (Lon Nol of Cambodia thought it prudent to declare an emergency when his palace was bombed in an attempted assassination.) The Philippines allow freedom to foreign correspondents, but nowadays control their own press, as is done, however unofficially, in Taiwan, Singapore, and Indonesia. In China, of course, there is no freedom of the press or of information of any kind. And in the Soviet Union, things are as usual, with the exception that suddenly this fall they stopped jamming foreign information programs, which they had resumed doing after the Czechoslovakian coup in 1968. The big difference in Russia was the recent contact between dissidents and the foreign press, most notably Solzhenitsyn. In the Mideast, only Lebanon and Kuwait have press freedom. In Iran, no criticism of the government is tolerated. Saudi Arabia has no official censorship, but there are pressures and sanctions keen enough so that most dispatches are sent out from Lebanon.

But what, really, was so novel about the Declaration? Article 19 of the Universal Declaration of Human Rights, to which all nations are theoretically committed, asserts:

> Everyone has the right to freedom of opinion and expression; this right includes freedom to hold opinions without interference and to seek, receive and impart information and ideas through any media and regardless of frontiers.

The stickiest article (V) of the new Declaration put it this way: "The rights and freedoms proclaimed above should be universally recognized and respected, and may in no case be exercised contrary to the purposes and principles of the United Nations. They should be subject only to such limitations as are determined by law solely for the purpose of securing due recognition and respect for the rights and freedoms of others and of meeting the just requirements of national security, public order, morality and the general welfare in a democratic society." But the Declaration didn't, really, take us all that much further than the Universal Declaration of twenty-five years ago.

Guy Wiggins was mobilized and I was inscribed to speak. The sudden flurry of interest caused eight nations suddenly to inscribe themselves. The first speaker was Baroody. Baroody's speeches come in prebuilt sections. This one was familiar; what we call, in house, *the Three S's* speech. Baroody is always the schoolteacher, and he likes the mnemonic aid, the better to instruct us. The purpose of such free speech as is allegedly exercised in the United States, he explains, is to disseminate American vulgarity. Our society likes to sell the decaying American way of life: wife swapping, miniskirts, pornography, cultural imperialism. To this end we employ *the Three S's* (I blush to render this, but see no alternative). They are: Scissors, Silence, and Static. With our *Scissors* we tailor the news to fit our perverted interests. *Silence* is for suppressing genuine news, for example the declamations of Ambassador Baroody. *Static* is to cause the friction that generates sales, a false excitement, etc. The interest the United States really has in freedom of information, he explained, is an interest born of our desire to wage the cold war. To indoctrinate, propagandize. He gave extensive historical references.

Poland spoke, explaining to us that there is no right to "misinformation." That in Poland all the information necessary to the beneficial conduct of human affairs is there, dripping all over the place. What Poland doesn't want is "interference." "These are the sovereign prerogatives of a sovereign country." He attacked Radio Free Europe as totally incompatible with the spirit of détente.

Mahmassani called on me, and I pulled together my notes. Wiggins leaned over to me and whispered, "You have noted that debate is always general, *never* directed, by name, at any individual country."

I tried to make two points I thought modest and arresting. The first was that quarrels having to do with the articles of the Declaration seemed unnecessary. Indeed, in a sense the articles themselves were unnecessary. Listen, I said, to the Preamble to the Declaration, concerning which there has been no controversy.

> . . . Whereas, everyone has the right to freedom of opinion and expression,
>
> Whereas freedom of information is essential to the respect for other human rights and fundamental freedoms,
>
> Whereas freedom of information is also fundamental to peaceful and friendly relations between peoples and nations,
>
> Whereas newspapers, periodicals, books, radio, television, films and other media of information play an important role in enabling people to acquire the knowledge of public affairs necessary for the discharge of their responsibilities. . . .

"What else do you need, other than a grammatical consummation of the sentence? Essentially what you should say after that is, Now, therefore, the General Assembly urges the nations of the world to act accordingly.

"And I don't think that anyone in this chamber is concerned to elaborate distinctions that would strike most of us as obvious. Surely most of us have been impressed with the Biblical injunction, 'You shall know the truth and the truth shall make you free.' As a matter of fact, if that were certainly the case, that would be, I suppose, a good case for *not* permitting the dissemination of the truth for those societies that above all seek inexpensive means of preventing people from enjoying human freedoms. It may very well be that knowing the truth will not make us free, but knowing the truth will at least give us an opportunity to reject the truth knowingly.

"So with due regard, Mr. Chairman, to that which certain societies can and cannot do at certain stages in the evolution of their domestic disciplines, taking into account the various priorities that necessarily permit some societies and require others to emphasize this and deemphasize the other, I do not see what is the argument against our speaking unanimously and recording ourselves as unanimously behind some of those animating principles which justify the existence of this organization. If we are here to talk to each other, it is presumably because we believe that in talking to each other we are saying things that people ought to hear. How will they hear what we have to say unless they are free to do so?"

Cold-war-wise, I note that I said: "I was not long ago in a society in which the people did not yet know that America had landed an astronaut on the moon." But I didn't say—*pace* Wiggins—"It was the People's Republic of China." I let them all guess.

And, oh dear, I found myself saying, "The gentleman from Saudi Arabia—the encephalophone from Saudi Arabia. . . ."

Sitting in the same chair, halfway across the chamber, whence he had spoken almost three months ago, when I first laid eyes on him and thought to interrupt him, was Baroody. I saw him motioning to an aide, to inscribe him for a Right of Reply.

It was lengthy.

He gave us some more on *the Three S's*. And then, he extended his hand to the assembly, asking special attention for his revelation. He told of a recent interview he had given to a reporter from the Associated Press. He had spent—I think he said hours—giving the reporter his views. (No one in the chamber doubted that.) Now listen, he said, to what the Associated Press reported; and he read a straightforward paragraph giving only a sentence or two from the treasury of his thoughts, and including a descriptive sentence to the effect that Baroody wore red suspenders. How do you like *that* for freedom of information? How do you like *that* for an exercise in *the Three S's?* "I cannot be with you here all the time," he said, reminding us that he had several more speeches to give that day in other committees. "I cannot be here all the time to remind you that there are limits to expression."

I tapped the table to exercise my own Right of Reply. I recalled, I said, the lady who soon after the Pentagon was built got lost in its maze, a common hazard in those early days, in that mammoth structure. She was suddenly whisked off to the emergency medical room, where she gave birth to a child. After she recovered, the attending physician said, "Madam, you shouldn't have come into the Pentagon in your condition." "I didn't," she said, voicing nicely, hyperbolically, the national amusement at the vastness and intricacy of the Pentagon. Neither, I said, had we convened, at the 28th General Assembly, already impregnated with Mr. Baroody's knowledge of why freedom of information is merely an excuse for suppressing Baroody's speeches. And, I said, if it is true that there are limits to expression, it is not true that Mr. Baroody has discovered them. And anyway, I said, no doubt there are members of this Assembly who envy the protections the Associated Press is in a position to pass along to *its* audience.

Baroody rose again. He knew, he said, that I was a journalist and a writer. Sometimes he respected what I said. But now, he said, he had lost all respect for me. And looking at me with eyebrows gnarled with the concentration of judgment, he said gravely, "Now I know you are nothing but a cheap politician." I thought of rising yet again to say that I was not a cheap politician, that at $130 per day I was an *expensive* politician. But there is a (widely unobserved) tradition against a Right of Reply to a Right of Reply to a Right of Reply, so we let it go, and Mahmassani, with great decorum, acknowledged the next speaker.

A week or so later the item came up before the Plenary, and I was told to prepare a statement explaining the United States' vote. Tap Bennett read it over, and asked me to modify a single sentence. He was anxious then to get all the votes he could for the upcoming vote on the prevention of harm to diplomats, and he was afraid that that one sentence might antagonize. I explained this to the staff officer sitting next to me at the Plenary as I waited to be called to the podium, my second brief appearance at the great hall. Approaching the podium, I winked at Brad Morse, but not so that Benites could see me, and read out my four paragraphs:

Mr. President,

My government wishes to record very briefly its special disappointment that the General Assembly has once again passed over an opportunity to affirm a Declaration on Freedom of Information.

It truly surpasses one's understanding why this should be so: why a Declaration on Freedom of Information should be given such stepfatherly treatment by this body.

There are a great many important subjects that have been extensively considered here and, if we may be permitted to say so, others that are not exactly hindering the motions of the stars and the planets. But freedom of information is axiomatically the business of this body. What does it matter what we do here, if word of it cannot reach the people of the world whose burdens we seek to lighten? What is the purpose of this forum, if not to plead our respective positions for the benefit of the people who are not here in this chamber to listen to us? If someone were to rise here today to propose that at the end of every session of the General Assembly, all working papers, all précis of all the statements made in the committees, all the transcripts of all the speeches delivered on this floor, should be collected, and incinerated, such a proposal would harmonize with the decision to put off our resolve to support the free flow of information. Our work is intended to be primarily educational and moral in nature. To decline to ask that the discussions held here be freely circulated is to profane the very purpose of this body, and to court that dangerous disrespect for this body which speaker after speaker has warned against.

Accordingly, Mr. President, we hope that in the next session, the highest priority will be given to endorsing the Draft Declaration on Freedom of Information.

I had written: "To decline to ask that the discussions held here be freely circulated is to profane the very purposes of this body, and to court that disrespect in which, unhappily, the United Nations is so widely held." That was the sentence Tap Bennett asked me to alter.

24.

Guinea-Bissau

TUESDAY

The issue of Portuguese Guinea came thundering down on us like a juggernaut, loosed by the Algiers Conference in September. On September 24, something called "Guinea-Bissau" declared its independence. On October 19, the African bloc proposed to the General Committee that Guinea-Bissau be placed on the agenda of the Plenary. This motion squeaked through 17 to 1 (United States), with 5 abstentions. Normally, consideration of the status of Guinea-Bissau would have come under two items already scheduled—No. 71, Question of Territories Under Portuguese Administration; and No. 7, Implementation of the Declaration on Granting Independence to Colonial Countries and Peoples. But Uhuru was in the saddle, and the UN establishment desired for it an item of its own.

Portuguese Guinea, as it was previously known and is still known in Portugal and in a few other countries, lies in Africa on the southwestern tip of the western hump. Think of it, vis-à-vis Africa, as roughly complementary to what Goa used to be, vis-à-vis India. It is a few hundred square miles of territory occupied 99 percent by natives, whose majority religion is animism, and it has been dominated by Portugal for 500 years. There are about 30,000 Portuguese troops ensuring the status quo against a rebel army of 8,000, most of them natives of the offshore Cape Verde Islands, which islands were subsumed in the resolution offered to the United Nations declaring Guinea-Bissau a sovereign country. The literacy rate is estimated at 2 to 3 percent, and the annual income per capita is about $200.

The Portuguese insist that Guinea is not a colony, not even a province, but a part of metropolitan Portugal, even as the French used to insist in respect of Algeria. The rebels have apparently made exalted claims about the amount of territory under their control, but it is nowhere contended that they control any of the population centers, and it is generally understood that they are in fact in charge of something like one-third of the countryside, which is on the order of having control, in Hong Kong, of the golf courses.

The United States has always favored, quite properly, self-determination. We have attempted, in the UN, to take the juridical position, however, that a country, in order to be sovereign, must be *de facto* independent. Indeed, the State Department referred us to a guide it has used in other situations. It is as follows:

(Contingency Guidance State 200517):

The United States Government has traditionally looked to the establishment of certain facts before it has extended recognition to a new state. These facts include the effective control over a clearly-defined territory and population; an organized governmental administration of that territory; and a capacity to act effectively to conduct foreign relations and to fulfill international obligations. In Africa these factual criteria have generally been met in the past, following a peaceful transition to independence from colonial status through an agreement between the colonial power and representatives of the people of the territory concerned. Under international law, however, even if the above factual criteria are present, a state is not obligated to recognize another entity as a state. . . . The situation in the territory concerned is not clear enough for us to conduct an initial factual appraisal. The Department will continue to follow the situation closely and assess developments there in light of our dedication to the principle of self-determination and our hope that a peaceful solution can be achieved.

Now we recognized that we were on to a lost cause here. Already, sixty governments had recognized what is more properly called the Revolutionary Government-in-Exile. In fact there are no grounds, other than racial, for supposing that this government is the genuine spokesman for the residents of Guinea, since there has never been a meaningful election. While the United States is extremely apprehensive about the precedent—the idea of going about recognizing governments-in-exile—we have decided to make our stand at the UN simply, without making heavy weather of it.

There is a domino effect here to watch out for. The first step, of course, is the recognition, by resolution, of the existence of the independent state of Guinea-Bissau. Then might come a move to give it a seat in the United Nations. This, of course, we could prevent over in the Security Council, by vetoing it. A third is a proposed invitation to the leader of the PAIGC—the African Party for Independence of Guinea and Cape Verde Islands—to address the General Assembly. The Brits (the in-house word for the United Kingdom delegation) suggested a powwow with themselves, the French, and us, each sending one delegate. At this session the situation was discussed. The Brits said they would oppose, in the Plenary, an invitation to PAIGC leader Da Luz to speak, on the grounds that it was disruptive of general procedure. They also said that they would vote in the Security Council against granting membership to Guinea-Bissau, provided both the United States and France did. This togetherness in the UN is very important. The British and in particular the French are anxious never to be isolated in any vote that might be construed as anti-African. The French are especially timid, and they gave no absolute assurances; the best we could get from them was that they would "probably" abstain on all the votes—abstaining is the great copout in the UN.

The British think that the important thing is to get a few critical countries not to recognize Guinea-Bissau. We all agreed discreetly to poll approachable delegations, seeking to maximize if possible the No vote, if not that, the Abstention vote, in the week before the item came up before the General Assembly. It was decided that it would not make sense at this point to approach members of the Security Council, most of whom are already on record. But that it would make sense to remind Waldheim of the potential danger of the forthcoming vote.

That danger is not confined to the precedent of recognizing a revolutionary government-in-exile. Conjoined to the resolution is a condemnation of Portugal as an aggressor nation against an "independent" state. If that goes through, inevitably—not this season, probably, but next —there will be a call for sanctions of various sorts, and—as with South Africa—the UN will move toward a confrontation designed to prove either that the UN has muscle, in which case we will have economic gunboatism, of the sort we have used against Rhodesia, or else that the General Assembly is a bag of wind. The United States desires neither of the two, though my guess is that the present administration would settle for the latter, if given only the choice. Several years ago Conor Cruise O'Brien, formerly a Secretariat functionary, in a well-written book about the UN supercharged however with anti-Western animus, showed how the logic of the UN suggests a military expedition sent out, presumably by the Soviet Union, to free South-West Africa (Namibia, I think we call it now). In fact this has not happened. In fact—as O'Brien said—it would put Britain and the United States on the spot if it did, inasmuch as we went along with all the initial anti-South-West Africa steps: Who says A must say B. This time around we aren't going to do that.

I didn't see the General Assembly as excited over anything this session as over the Guinea-Bissau issue. They gave—I think my calculations are correct—more time on the floor to it than to the discussion of any other issue. The reason for this wasn't that they needed to persuade faltering members, so as to produce the marginally-needed vote. They had an overwhelming majority, and everybody wanted to make a speech, to show his brethren that he was as militant as anybody else.

The line of argument was straightforward. (1) Portugal has no business in Africa. (2) The PAIGC is on the verge of conquering that part of Guinea which is not already in its hands. (3) PAIGC deserves encouragement. (4) The phony arguments of the West are purely the result of our desiring to oblige Portugal, a partner in NATO. That is why we keep sending all the arms to Portugal which are used to shoot Guinean heroes.

Our line of argument is as given already, with the additional point that NATO is a purely defensive alliance, and none of the arms given to Portugal are for the use, by Portugal, other than for the defense of itself or our NATO partners.

The British speaker made every concession possible. He began by saying, in effect, that since Britain has discovered that colonialism is wrong, so should Portugal. "My Government has frequently made clear, both in the United Nations and directly to the Portuguese Government, our strong conviction that Portugal should press ahead with all practicable speed toward the granting of self-determination in accordance with the right of, and taking into account the wishes of, the peoples of its territories in Africa. That is still our view. [It is also mine.] We call upon the Government of Portugal to follow the example of those other colonial or former colonial powers whose former dependencies in Africa and elsewhere are now sovereign independent States represented in this Assembly. . . . It pains us that Portugal, a country with which we have so many historical ties, should be pursuing policies which we regard as misguided." One assumes that sending the British fleet into Anguilla a few years ago pained, even if it did not deter, the Brits.

But on the factual point, the Ambassador continued: "As my delegation [has] pointed out in the General Committee, the Territory at present remains—as the General Assembly has previously held it to be—a non-self-governing Territory and covered by the provisions of Chapter XI of the Charter [respecting the right and wrong way to administer non-self-governing territories like the Virgin Islands]. We cannot accept, therefore, that a Government can be guilty of illegal occupation or acts of aggression in a Territory over which it is sovereign in international law. We accordingly cannot accept that the Government of Portugal can be guilty of such acts in relation to the Territory in question of the present case. I might add," he said, pointing to the future implications of the impending vote, "that when the policies and actions based on what amounts to wishful thinking take the form of legal judgments, there is a further casualty—international law, at least if that law is to have any authority as a reflection of real life. The future of the United Nations and international law—that is what our vote is about. It is not about Portuguese policies." And Mark Evans, for the United States, made similar points, and rejected scornfully the charge that the United States was sending defoliants to Portugal for use against the insurgents.

Baroody was at his impossible worst, which is when they like him best at the UN. Indeed he got a great round of applause when he was done, something that practically never happens.

"Not a single one of the NATO Powers, or those affiliated with them, has raised its voice for the independence of Guinea-Bissau. [That would suggest that the U.K. is not a NATO power.]

"Is this one world? Is this one United Nations? Are the Africans outside the pale of democracy? [Quick answers: (1) Yes. (2) No. (3) Apparently—to judge from the incidence of democracy in Africa, which is comparable to democracy in Saudi Arabia. In UN usage, as here applied, 'democracy' means rule by one or more black men, but not by a majority.] Whom do you think you are fooling, you NATO Powers? Raise your voice, if you have courage, and ask Portugal to come to its senses. [We all have see above.]

Portugal cannot continue to disregard the principle of self-determination which was spelled out first in the Covenant of the League of Nations and subsequently in the Charter of the United Nations; and later many of us elaborated that principle into a right which appears in the Universal Declaration of Human Rights. Is this principle and this right of self-determination not worth the paper and ink with which it is written? [Manifestly, it isn't. Ask East Europe.] Come out! Speak the truth! Have courage! [But not enough courage to put the finger on the Soviet Union, which presides over 100,000,000 non-Russians who are totally literate, have had an experience with self-rule, are totally abandoned by the United Nations—whose Russian overseer is sitting there enjoying Baroody's venture in moral universals.] Say that Portugal is indispensable to us; we need it; we need our bases there, the Azores—which, as one of my colleagues mentioned, were used shamefully to send arms, lethal arms, to kill people in the Middle East, American arms, Phantoms. . . .

"I am not talking to our colleagues from the United States, whom we all cherish as human beings. I am not addressing their Government, because who is Baroody, or any African or Asian member, to tell them what they shall do for the security of the world, they who have eroded their substance, upset their finances, eroded their currency, increased the burden of the taxpayer, in order to pursue a policy that might is right. [No, Baroody wouldn't dream of instructing the U.S. government, without whose exertions in the postwar years, Saudi Arabia would now be part of the Soviet Empire, and Baroody probably farmed out somewhere as a slave to teach filibustering to young Soviet bloods.]

. . . "Mr. President, you will forgive me for having treated this question first in an orthodox manner—but then in oratorical style, hoping to move the sympathy of Europeans who have suffered in two world wars because of the slogans which they sold to their peoples, to the effect that the First World War was fought to save the world for democracy, and that the Second World War was also fought for the Four Freedoms. Now, in 1973, the precious blood of our African brothers is being shed by those propagandists who fought two world wars for their own interests. . . ."(!) . . . There are no non-Portuguese fighting in Portuguese Africa, Portugal didn't fight in the Second World War, Portugal hasn't practiced democracy since 1927, Portugal doesn't preach the virtue of democracy—but passing a historical iron over a Baroody speech is like skiing across dragons' teeth. You have to stop and scale every sentence, every nuance. This is what passes for debate at the UN, though I suppose it is exhilarating for Baroody, since what passes for debate in the country he represents is, after all, nothing at all.

Oh, yes, the vote: 93 in favor of the resolution, 7 against. The 7: Brazil, Greece, Portugal, South Africa, Spain, the United Kingdom, and the United States. The Pontius Pilate vote, 30: Australia, Austria, Belgium, Bolivia, Canada, Chile, Colombia, Denmark, Dominican Republic, El Salvador, Finland, France, Guatemala, Honduras, Iceland, Ireland, Israel, Italy, Japan, Luxembourg, Netherlands, New Zealand, Nicaragua, Norway, Paraguay, Sweden, Turkey, Uruguay, Venezuela, West Germany.

We learn that the strategy of Guinea-Bissau, or whatever non-Guinean-Bissaun is now making the formal decisions, is not to appeal right away for a seat in the UN, but to ask for participation in the specialized agencies, and to edge up that way toward a showdown in the Security Council, perhaps next time around.

25.

Racial Discrimination Moves

The resolutions, as passed by the various committees, are pouring into the Plenary. From the Third Committee there are a dozen. Conspicuous among them are those that occupied most of the committee's time, and these dealt, as we expected, with all forms of racial discrimination. They were lodged in several items, but Item 53 was the most comprehensive. It called for discussion in four parts: (a) A Decade for Action to Combat Racism and Racial Discrimination; (b) Consideration of a Draft Convention on the Suppression and Punishment of the Crime of Apartheid; (c) Receiving the Report of the Committee on the Elimination of Racial Discrimination; and (d) Probing the Status of the International Convention on the Elimination of All Forms of Racial Discrimination.

On the first, we had no trouble. Margaret Young gave a moving speech about the evil of racism and racial discrimination. Our instructions were to vote for the Decade, and we did. There was a curious back-and-forth involving the British and the Russians. The British wanted to stick in a sentence encouraging an inquiry into the ways and means of promoting racial harmony. But the Soviet Union, in one of those useless exhibitions of power, gathered up the votes to strike that down, substituting additional boiler plate about apartheid. During the Decade, there will be conferences all over the world, and one big conference. The State Department told us to try to cut out those conferences that would be simply redundant, and to try to avoid the establishment of yet another committee to oversee the Decade, but Mark Evans, making his explanation at the Plenary, knew he was beaten, and the whole armada sailed through.

The second is potential dynamite. Two years ago, Guinea and the Soviet Union submitted a draft convention (on the Suppression and Punishment of the Crime of Apartheid). It was sent off to be worked over by three standing committees: the Human Rights Commission, ECOSOC itself, and the Special Political Committee on Apartheid, whose function it is to explore ways and means of changing South African policy. The Soviet Union, Guinea, and Nigeria did most of the architecture, and it came up a year ago, at which time Egypt suggested amendments. Back it went to the three committees, and now it is before the Plenary. We opposed it at the Third Committee, resignedly but doggedly, but it was passed, easily.

It is a most extraordinary document. There are outstanding, of course, any number of proscriptions of racial discrimination of any kind—in the Universal Declaration and its Covenant counterparts; in the Convention on the Elimination of All Forms of Racial Discrimination, of course. Clearly the objective of the sponsors, this time (as we had been warned at the briefing in Washington) was to come up with something that might be used substantially to harass South Africa—but not only South Africa.

The preamble rolls along saying the usual things. But then comes a paragraph as follows: "[We observe] that, in the Convention on the Non-Applicability of Statutory Limitations to War Crimes and Crimes Against Humanity, 'inhuman acts resulting from the policy of apartheid' are qualified as crimes against humanity." The architects, introducing a metaphorical use clearly unintended by the phrase "crimes against humanity"—march apartheid straight over to Nuremberg.

Article I, Section 2, of the draft Convention is straightforward: "The States Parties to this Convention declare criminal those organizations, institutions and individuals committing the crime of apartheid." A "State Party" is any state that signs and ratifies a convention. That convention comes into force when a stipulated number of states have become "Parties." It is here stipulated that only twenty states need to ratify in order to make the Convention binding upon them. So what? one says—that is not so different from multilateral diplomacy. . . . If twenty states desire to agree on something respecting the activities of those twenty states, who is to stop them?

Article II defines "the crime of apartheid." It includes (a, ii): "the infliction upon the members of a racial group or groups of serious bodily or mental harm by the infringement of their freedom or dignity or by subjecting them to torture or to cruel, inhuman or degrading treatment or punishment." Even that is not altogether extraordinary, repeating in part what is said in the Racial Discrimination Convention.

But then on the matter of enforcement.

Article III. "International criminal responsibility shall apply, irrespective of the motive involved, to individuals, members of organizations and institutions and representatives of the State, whether residing in the territory of the State in which the acts are perpetrated or in some other State, whenever they: a) Commit, participate in, directly incite or conspire in the commission of the acts mentioned in article II of this Convention; b) Directly abet, encourage or cooperate in the commission of the crime of apartheid."

And (Article IV), "The States Parties to this Convention undertake: a) To adopt any legislative or other measures necessary to suppress as well as to prevent any encouragement of the crime of apartheid and similar segregationist policies or their manifestations and to punish persons guilty of that crime; b) To adopt legislative, judicial and administrative measures to prosecute, bring to trial and punish in accordance with their jurisdiction persons responsible for, or accused of, the acts defined in article II of this Convention, whether or not such persons reside in the territory of the State in which the acts are committed or are nationals of that State or of some other State or are stateless persons."

Translated, this means: Jones, a South African traveling through—I list here only the countries that *co-sponsored* the Convention, which are fewer by far than the ninety-one that voted for it—Afghanistan, Burundi, the Congo, Cuba, Democratic Yemen, the German Democratic Republic, Ghana, Guinea, India, Mauritius, Nigeria, the Philippines, Poland, Somalia, Uganda, the Soviet Union, Tanzania, Zaire, Algeria, Czechoslovakia, Dahomey, Egypt, Gabon, Gambia, Guyana, Jamaica, Kenya, Madagascar, Mali, Mauritania, the Niger, Romania, Yugoslavia, and Zambia—could be arrested, tried for committing a crime against humanity, and stuck in prison.

And Smith, a citizen of the United States and a clerk for the Chase Manhattan Bank, which does business in South Africa, passing through any of these countries, could similarly be prosecuted—for "cooperating" with an enterprise which, by doing business in South Africa, "abetted" the commission of a crime against humanity.

Ambassador Ferguson took the floor at the Plenary, as he had done at the Third Committee. It always strikes me as theatrically unfortunate when the United States uses a Negro to plead a case that involves primarily Negro interests. Too easy. I remember Mrs. Young pleading to be given extra-racial concerns to grapple with, but sure enough she ended up talking about the Decade Against Discrimination. Now Clyde Ferguson was addressing the General Assembly on the shortcomings of the proposed Convention. It is, he said, "inconsistent with concepts basic to our legal system such as the protection of individual rights." And it is unnecessary, given the Convention on the Elimination of All Forms of Racial Discrimination and the Genocide Convention. If it were merely redundant, he said, that would be okay. "Unfortunately, however, certain provisions of this Convention could be damaging to the very structure of international law and even to the constitutional structure of the UN itself." For one thing, he argued, evil as apartheid is, it isn't a crime against humanity in the Nuremberg sense. And the Convention is therefore an assault on due process and "basic norms of fairness." "We do not . . . accept that an American citizen vacationing in a foreign country could be extradited to another foreign country and tried there for something he has said in the territory of the U.S."

But only 4 states voted against—the United States, the United Kingdom, South Africa, and Portugal. There were 26 abstentions. The abstaining vote, in such situations as these, when courage is so terribly important, is, as I have mentioned, the most commonplace moral evasion in the UN.

Clyde Ferguson, several weeks earlier, had given me to read a highly interesting, though somehow unconsummated, academic paper he had written for the American Society of International Law, called "The United Nations Human Rights Covenants: Problems of Ratification and Implementation." He was then Dean of the Law School at Howard University, and of course a civil rights advocate. In the paper, he traced the dawning idea of human rights as transcending the authority of the nation. In 1919 the Allied Powers concluded a treaty of peace, the so-called Polish Convention, under the terms of which Poland undertook to protect certain racial and religious minorities within its boundaries. What was novel was the provision that these guarantees "constitute obligations of international concern and shall be placed under the guarantee of the League of Nations." Any infraction could be brought to the attention of the Council of the League of Nations.

The Polish precedent is, of course, only symbolically interesting. For one thing, in 1919 "Poland" was hardly in a position to resist such a treaty, any more than the Southern states of the United States were in a position to resist the Fourteenth Amendment to the U.S. Constitution. Poland, of course, was easier to deal with than powers unambiguously sovereign. This is made plain by the treatment given to Japan's proposal that the League of Nations Covenant should contain provisions prohibiting discrimination on the basis of nationality, race, or religion. "This proposal," Ferguson summarized, "was rejected on the grounds that the matter of racial, national, and religious discrimination within a nation were matters of domestic jurisdiction and hence not a proper concern of an international organization whose membership consisted of sovereign nations." Ferguson quotes a "standard text on international law" which even in 1948 was saying, "There is general agreement that, by virtue of its personal and territorial supremacy, a state can treat its own nationals according to discretion." The doctrine of "humanitarian intervention," though it preceded Nuremberg, would seem to require something on the order of genocidal crimes against individuals, to levitate it to anything like an international compulsion to intervene. Still, the Polish seed can be said to have germinated, and it flowers in the instruments issued by the United Nations.

But as regards "abetting" apartheid, or racial discrimination, or racial superiority by spoken or written opinion, the UN runs into the "six fundamental human rights" which, Dean Ferguson wrote, "emerged as international human rights" after the First World War, one of them (as crystallized by one scholar) being "Free Use of Language: There were to be no restrictions placed on the free use of any language whatever by any national in private intercourse, commerce, religion, press, or other publications, or in public meetings."

On the same day that Ferguson gave his explanation at the Plenary, the report of the Committee on the Elimination of Racial Discrimination was accepted by the Plenary, on recommendation of the Third Committee. These documents are not, to say the least, widely read. It was nowhere, that I am aware, noticed that on page 9 of that report, the committee remarked that . . . "Article 4 (a) of the International Convention on the Elimination of All Forms of Racial Discrimination provides that States Parties shall declare an offense punishable by law all dissemination of ideas based on racial superiority or hatred, incitement to racial discrimination, as well as all acts of violence or incitement to such acts against any race or group of persons of another color or ethnic origin, and also the provision of any assistance to racist activities, including the financing thereof."

Now, the report, adopted with insubstantial modification by the Plenary, asks States Parties 1) to "indicate what specific penal internal legislation designed to implement the provisions of article 4 (a) and (b) has been enacted in their respective countries and to transmit to the Secretary-General in one of the official languages the texts concerned as well as such provisions of general penal law as must be taken into account when applying such specific legislation; [and] 2) Where no such specific legislation has been enacted, to inform the Committee of the manner and the extent to which the provisions of the existing penal laws, as applied by the Courts, effectively implement their obligations under article 4 (a) and (b), and to transmit to the Secretary-General in one of the official languages the texts of those provisions."

The President of the United States signed that Convention in 1966, and it was enacted, among the States Parties, in January, 1969. The Senate of the United States has yet to confirm it, and the question of how it would conform with the First Amendment is one of those that have not, as a generic question, been much argued since the days of the fight over the Bricker Amendment. Clyde Ferguson points out that the American Bar Association has reversed itself on the Bricker Amendment, and is readier to go forward in ratifying the various outstanding UN documents. Perhaps; though clearly there hasn't been much public discussion, for instance, on the question whether signing it would require the United States to forbid academic, or for that matter polemical, activities which can be held to "disseminate" "ideas based on racial superiority" or which are "incitement to racial discrimination." Ferguson cites the defense of the Illinois Group Libel Statute by Frankfurter in the Beauharnais case. But Frankfurter spoke of the Illinois legislature's right to curb "false or malicious defamation of racial and religious groups," leaving unanswered whether the operative question is racially invidious talk "false" or "malicious"—a distinction not observed by the Racial Discrimination Treaty, which would appear to say that a professor is guilty if he disseminates, let us say, crime statistics or IQ studies that appear to suggest that American Indians are socially, or intellectually, backward.*

The whole business is depressing, and when Ferguson stepped down, knowing that we had lost and lost overwhelmingly, his lawyer's mind was no doubt appeased by the knowledge that nothing of a practical consequence was likely to come from it all, at least not in America. People who linger in the United Nations appear, paradoxically, to lose something of their idealistic zest. Even the guides. The semi-official (Follett) vest-pocket handbook to the UN says, in the passage on guides, "The term of guide duty has a limit,

---

*We ran once, in *National Review*, an essay-review by a professor highly unfriendly to certain American Indian myths. Several American Indians expressed themselves as outraged, and we published their letters. One such letter, from Chief Eagle, a survivor of the Sioux, was addressed directly to the author, threatening him most direly. We published the professor's reply:

"How?
"White brother readum chicken tracks of red brother, makeum paleface heart heavy; tears of sorrow flow all over floor of teepee like great river.
"Lo, many moons ago Injun smokeum peacepipe, promise Great White Father puttum down tommyhawk, no makeum war forever no more. Now me thinkum *Injun speak with forked tongue.*
"D. Chief Eagle he says he invade white brother own hunting ground and castum lance at white brother. What kind talk this talk? Maybe D. Chief Eagle heap big silly humbug; maybe better watch out, you thinkum? White brother maybe lift up Injun hair pretty damn smart, hey? Maybe bury hatchet in D. Chief Eagle head, he come up here steal land, steal woman. Makeup damn good Injun right quick. Chrise.
"Ugh!

John Greenway
Heap Big Chief Medicine Man
Professor of Anthropology."

Is it contemplated that there would be a license for that kind of thing. Or is it suggested that polemics of such a nature would be prescribed by treaty?

which is two years and three months. It is limited because
experience has shown that when a guide keeps her job any
longer, she loses some of the enthusiasm she is otherwise able
to communicate to the United Nations visitors." In his
academic article, Clyde Ferguson had enthusiastically quoted, while recognizing it as remote, the ideal expressed by
then Justice Goldberg in February, 1965: "The time is
overdue for the adoption of a binding treaty on human
rights to implement the Declaration and for the establishment of an International Court of Human Rights to enforce
the rights guaranteed by such a treaty." Not long after he
spoke those words, Goldberg was our principal banana in the
United Nations. He did not take the initiative then, nor has
he since his retirement, to press this idea. It reminds one that
the United Nations is, or ought to be, useful as a chamber
whence ideals relating to human rights should issue; not as a
dispatching center for sheriffs to go out to enforce
compliance. This latter job it will not do in our lifetime; and
the former, it does less and less well on account of its
preoccupation with the latter, which in any case is
hypocritical in focus.

26.

Human Rights Commissioner

A tense afternoon, climaxed by the tightest parliamentary footwork I had ever seen, a quick authoritarian move by Mahmassani, a few moments of rampant confusion, and the collapse, yet again, of an idea. An idea about how the United Nations might maneuver in such a way as to enhance human rights. As ever, when human rights plays at the UN, human rights loses.

The idea is relatively simple. It is to create a new post in the United Nations, the post of a High Commissioner for Human Rights. Said Commissioner, to be elected by the General Assembly, would, in the conception of its non-casuistical sponsors, enjoy a degree of liberty. To survey the whole human rights scene, to use his good offices where they might prove helpful, to report to the Economic and Social Committee, and its Human Rights division, on the progress of human rights, and, indeed, to report directly to the General Assembly.

Now the reason this was an issue at all was the obvious one that most states within the United Nations (a) favor human rights; (b) are effectively protected within the United Nations against criticism of their neglect of, or suppression of, human rights, with the traditional exceptions: South Africa and Portugal of course; and any states which, from time to time, persecute Communist parties, or overthrow left-minded governments. (The aim of the United Nations is to make the world safe for revolution and unsafe for

221

counterrevolution.) Here was a proposal to name someone with five-year tenure who, for all that anyone knew, might actually report to the General Assembly about a deteriorated situation in one of the countries which have heretofore enjoyed immunity. Concretely, the High Commissioner might conceivably, some time after his designation, report soberly that notwithstanding the Soviet Union's ratification of the various covenants centered on the Universal Declaration of Human Rights, the Soviet Union was in fact not observing any of these rights—giving as an example, say, its treatment of Solzhenitsyn.

That's all there was to it.

The machinery of the United Nations is wonderfully instructive here, and when we received instructions from Washington to come down hard in favor of the Swedish resolution, I, as delegate in charge of the item before the Third Committee, looked into the genealogy of the proposal. On reading it, I had that sinking feeling newcomers to the UN get. I told Dino, after reading the pages and pages describing the background of the High Commissioner proposal, that I felt like the old Negro approaching the voting registrar in the pre-civil rights South and being handed to read, to prove his literacy, a passage in Greek. "It says here no nigger's going to vote today."

Not a chance.

The background (I leave out the technical details because they are totally uninteresting):

—In 1965, the General Assembly, having received the proposal for a High Commissioner, referred it to the Commission on Human Rights, with instructions to report it out in time for action in 1966.

—The Commission set up a Working Group, which ground out a resolution in 1966.

—In 1967, the General Assembly put off consideration of it for a year.

—In 1968, the General Assembly requested the Economic and Social Council to recommend the adoption of a draft resolution, and put off to 1969 its own consideration of it.

—In 1969, the Economic and Social Council recommended a draft resolution identical to the one recommended two years earlier. Amendments were of course introduced. (Amendments are always introduced.)

—In 1969, the General Assembly went on to consider it briefly, and then said it hadn't had enough time to consider it thoroughly, and put it off to 1970, marked for highest priority.

—In 1970, the General Assembly decided to defer consideration until 1971.

—In 1971, the General Assembly, "considering" (that is the word they use) that there hadn't been sufficient time, put the matter off until 1972.

—In 1972, the General Assembly, considering that there had not been sufficient time, decided to put the matter off until 1973.

1973 was us.

Now during these years, the idea was not treated perfunctorily. There was debate everywhere: in ECOSOC, in the Human Rights Commission, in the Third Committee, in the General Assembly. Dozens of amendments were introduced. Some of these were acceptable to the architects of the idea, for instance the one that suggested that the High Commissioner should be elected by the General Assembly, rather than appointed by the Secretary-General. Some were not acceptable to anyone who desired any element of authority for the High Commissioner—without which, of course, he would be merely a redundancy. One controversial clause came up again and again for discussion. The High Commissioner, the draft said, would consult with the government of any country whose human rights practices he was looking at. Would be *obliged* to consult with the government? Or would do so only *"when appropriate"*? The latter was in the original draft. Tanzania, among others, didn't like that *at all*. But of course if the High Commissioner was required to get the cooperation of a government before he could report on the doings of that government, then he would be an extremely close-mouthed High Commissioner as regards the human rights situation in any country—Tanzania, for example—that didn't want anybody talking about the state of human rights at home.

So here we were—late in the session, though the idea of a High Commissioner was, by seniority, high among the concerns of the Third Committee.

The opposition weighed in. There were three resolutions on the table. The first was backed by Costa Rica and Sweden (hereinafter the Swedish Resolution). It was straightforward, backing the High Commissioner idea with the emasculating revisions.

The second was backed by Ireland. It called for putting the matter off another year, to the 29th General Assembly.

The third was Iraq's, recommending that the whole thing be put off into the indefinite future.

The fourth was Bulgaria's and Democratic Yemen's, calling for abandoning the entire idea (hereinafter the Bulgarian Resolution).

The British representative gave a measured, gentle talk, pleading in favor of the Swedish proposal. He stressed that the UN really wasn't accomplishing very much in the field of human rights, and maybe it wouldn't accomplish very much via a High Commissioner, but surely here was a concrete idea, "an alternative approach." There was a certain resignation there, which recalled Alec Douglas-Home's collapse on *Firing Line.* "We do not think it realistic to expect the General Assembly to make a decision of substance on the High Commissioner this year." But "it would be a very serious comment on the way the United Nations approaches its responsibilities in the field of human rights if this Committee were to adopt an amendment seeking to put off to an unspecified future session any review of ways and means for improving the effective enjoyment of human rights and fundamental freedoms. Thank you, Mr. Chairman."

The opposition's arguments were well marshaled. A High Commissioner would be costly (a lousy quarter of a million dollars). It would be unmanageable, being asked to transact millions of complaints every year (there are millions of mouths to feed). It would create and heighten tensions between and within nations (correct: tensions between those who practice human rights and those who don't). It is in conflict with the work of other bodies (correct: The other bodies do nothing, and it is projected that this one would do something). It is out of style: Real human rights are the concern against racism, colonialism, and apartheid (there are human rights left over). It would conflict with the right of nations to self-determination (there were no enforcement procedures contemplated).

The Cuban representative plunged us into UN-realism by announcing that in his country, for the first time, human rights have a real meaning, and are no longer merely a poultice. East Germany said to hell with a High Commissioner, why don't we make Portugal and South Africa give up racial discrimination? The Soviet Union said it's pretty fishy, that some of the countries most enthusiastic about the High Commissioner haven't even ratified the Human Rights Covenant, the way the Soviet Union has. Nigeria wondered just what the High Commissioner would do about Mozambique, and how he would end genocide in South Africa. The Belgian representative, normally a very silent man, had clearly been working on his statement for many hours (days? weeks?) and he delivered it exhaustively, and exhaustingly. Forgive me, he concluded, if I spoke for more than ten minutes. Mahmassani, the world's most patient man, permitted himself to comment from the chair: "The distinguished representative of the government of Belgium spoke not for more than ten minutes but for more than thirty minutes." (I asked Mahmassani later why they didn't install a huge time clock to put psychic pressure on the filibusterers. He thought it would be a good idea. But I gather Baroody wouldn't like it, so that's out.)

Fifteen countries were lined up to speak. The speeches went on and on. Staff members were buzzing about, and it was clear that something was up between Iraq and Ireland. The chairman begged the speakers to observe the technical limit of ten minutes. I was inscribed to speak, and would do so extemporaneously, and so was making notes.

At this point the Irish representative announced that he and Iraq had agreed to merge their resolutions. The complicated language of amalgamation was rendered, and everyone noted carefully the proposed revisions. The gist of it was that the Human Rights Commissioner would be dropped for the 28th session, but be put down for the 30th session. Do I hear the 29th session? And then the reworked language included the perplexing phrase "alternative approaches" to enhancing human rights. Nobody quite knew what that meant, and everyone was trying to talk, and Mahmassani was being stern. He recognized Morocco, which moved that the debate be closed. Mahmassani put Morocco's motion to a vote, and it carried, 69 to 3, with 24 abstentions. The Irish draft, as amended by Iraq, was then voted on, section by section. First the operative paragraph 3, which was amended to read: "decides accordingly to include in the provisional agenda of the 30th session of the General Assembly an item entitled 'alternative approaches and ways and means within the UN system for improving the effective enjoyment of human rights and fundamental freedoms.'" That carried, but with 36 abstentions, suggesting total confusion. The Cuban delegate was in such disarray that, forgetting the technical independence he likes to flaunt, he dashed over to the Soviet desk, like a child to his mother, to ask for instructions. Visibly relieved, he returned swaggeringly to his seat. At this point, if I had had more experience and a keener wit, I would have moved for adjournment, on the grounds that we needed instructions as a result of the perplexed state of the resolution. Guy Wiggins, marvelously cool, was keeping track of the gyrations as best he could, and suggesting what was the proper vote, and passing along the word to the British and others who wished to coordinate. Then the entire Irish resolution was voted, 75 in favor, 25 abstentions. Algeria wanted a separate vote on the 30th session, reaching for something even more remote. But if you took away 30th, then 29th would be as plausible as 31st. At this point it was moved that no other draft resolutions should be considered, and Mahmassani, before anyone could see what was happening, gaveled the vote in. So that we didn't get a vote testing the strength of the Swedish Resolution. Nor did the other side get a vote testing the strength of the Bulgarian Resolution. The debate was over, and I went off with Dino to prepare the Explanation I would give the next morning. If it should actually happen that a speech by me could get through the brass unalloyed.

But before that I had promised to attend a little party. In honor of Roger Baldwin, founder and godfather of the American Civil Liberties Union, who was celebrating his ninetieth birthday. There is a lot about Roger Baldwin I have disagreed with—over the years he sometimes fused his social ideas with civil rights doctrine. There he was, in the large living room of a friend, surrounded by what seemed a mob—maybe 150 people, of every age. Old warriors from the social democratic movement in America of the thirties, young star-struck lawyers, groupies of the civil rights movement, pretty graduate students. Norman Cousins gave a little talk, witty and warm, and Baldwin rose to speak, a truly beautiful face, a virile, poised, incorruptible man: the high commissioner, in a way, of the American human rights movement. They brought in a cake with ninety candles. I was asked by the lady with the cake, would I (standing at the door—there was no way to move into the crowded room) start singing "For He's a Jolly Good Fellow"? I whispered that I had no singing voice, so she did it, and the crowd took it up. There was more devotion to human freedom in that living room than I had seen in three months with the Human Rights Committee of the United Nations.

I went back, and batted out a few paragraphs, and sent

them to Dino early in the morning. I was inscribed as third speaker. I arrived at the UN and to my astonishment was told that I was to proceed with my statement, and not a word was said about the crack with which I thought to repay myself the humiliation of listening to Cuba and East Germany talk about human rights.

I got to the chamber at 10, which was when the proceedings would begin. At 10:10 the clerk approached me. Would I mind going first, since the first two countries inscribed had not shown up? Not at all, I said. And thirty seconds later I delivered my stirring paragraphs to the chamber: more precisely, to the chairman and the Rapporteur, and to the 6 of the 100 delegates who, sensing the great drama of the occasion, had the wit to come and hear my golden words.

What did I say? Well, an introductory paragraph, and then a few paragraphs about the general confusion:

> . . . It is our understanding that the purpose of this committee is to devise a means of promoting human rights around the world. The arguments of those opposed to the creation of a High Commissioner appeared to center on the concern that said High Commissioner would interfere in the internal affairs of their countries. Our understanding was that suitable precautions against such interferences, in violation of the United Nations Charter, were built into the pending proposal. On the other hand, we cannot deny that there is a sense in which the mere espousal of human rights in an international organization is to interfere philosophically with the internal affairs of some countries. Human rights is an ideal to which we all pay lip service. Even the best intentioned among us serve that ideal asymptotically; in some societies, with such studied unsuccess as to call into question whether we can really call human rights a shared ideal. Among those who spoke yesterday in opposition to a High Commissioner for Human Rights were states who would have you believe that such is the congestion of human rights within their frontiers that it is necessary to surround themselves with great walls and oceans to prevent these

human rights from emigrating. My government registers its sorrow that all the work that in the last eight years has gone into the concept of a High Commissioner who might have proved technically useful in promoting human rights, has apparently been of no avail. We regret that the noble resolution proposed by the distinguished delegates of Sweden and Costa Rica, for which we intended enthusiastically to vote, was not submitted for action in this chamber.

Mr. Chairman, why did the United States then abstain on the proffered resolution, as amended?

—For one thing there was the lack of clarity.

It was not clear yesterday, and it is no clearer this morning—indeed my distinguished colleagues appear to be divided on the interpretation—what exactly is the meaning of the phrase "alternative approaches" as used in the third paragraph of the adopted resolution, recording that we have decided to "include in the Provision agenda of the 30th session of the General Assembly an item entitled: *Alternative approaches,* and ways and means within the United Nations system for improving the effective enjoyment of human rights and fundamental freedoms"?

—Alternative suggests a choice. As used in the adopted resolution, it could be held to mean "other than." Other than what? Other than a High Commissioner? But this committee has not rejected the idea of a High Commissioner. It can only be understood, by all members present, as having agreed to postpone action. The ambiguity, however, remains. Since the government of the United States is in favor of a High Commissioner for Human Rights, it is obvious that we could not vote for a resolution which might be interpreted as suggesting that we reject a Human Rights Commissioner as a means of promoting the cause of human rights. It is more likely, Mr. Chairman, that the majority of my distinguished colleagues intended that the phrase "alternative approaches" meant something more accurately given as "supplementary approaches." That is to say, approaches—not excluding a High Commissioner—for improving the effective enjoyment of human rights and fundamental freedoms that go beyond those approaches already institutionalized in the United Nations.

—However, Mr. Chairman, even if that ambiguity had

been clarified, my government could not in good conscience have voted to put off stimulating the pursuit of human freedoms until the 30th Session of the General Assembly. To suggest, as one of my distinguished colleagues did, that we need more "time" in order to permit our ideas to "mature" is a melancholy reflection on the priorities given to human liberty, reminding us that in the recorded history of our planet, human rights are as a grain of sand in a huge beach. It is, as several of my colleagues suggested yesterday, infinitely disappointing to the people of the world that the United Nations does not do more of a concrete nature to serve the cause of human rights. It is grotesque that the United Nations should decline formally to meditate the problem until 1975. If, as the Secretary-General said on a recent occasion, to satisfy human hunger for rights is as necessary in its way as to satisfy human hunger for bread, then we can be held to have acted as callously as the keeper of the granary who will wait two years before listening to the supplications of the hungry.

—Even so, Mr. Chairman, my government could not vote *against* any resolution that commits us to the search for means of improving the effective enjoyment of human rights and fundamental freedoms at any time, not even if the Resolution had called for turning our attention to the subject in 1985, rather than 1975.

This then the Explanation of my government, most respectfully registered.

27.

USUN Summary

At the weekly staff meeting we get an encouraging bulletin on the progress of John Scali, whose peppery presence we sorely miss. The reports from the staff are succinct, and now it is pretty well known how it is going to go on issues major and minor. For the most obvious psychological reasons, as I have said, trivial matters are given, by their advocate, the same intense treatment given to weighty matters. Each speaker has his style. I must assume, given the fluency of their recitals, that late last night, or early this morning, some of them practiced—it is after all a form of politeness, which all except extraordinarily well-disciplined speakers, should be guided by. Rosalyn Tureck, the pianist, told me that even if she has played a particular piece in recital on Monday night, and is to play it again on Tuesday night, she will rehearse it on Tuesday morning—"It's like ironing your dress," she puts it. Some of the staff, speaking to us, inject a note of excitement in their voice that makes it easy to listen to them. One or two others could be reporting on an amphibian landing on the Lower East Side, and attention will flag. Mark Evans, seated on my left, passes me a note during one recital: "I wish I could have him at my bedside instead of a sleeping pill." I remind Mark that as a good Mormon he does not have access to sleeping pills, and I scribble furiously on my note pad, the only *way* I can concentrate on what this speaker (who by the way is very smart) is saying.

How does it all look?

It is handy to think of issues we have faced as (1) Israel-related; (2) Portugal-South Africa related; (3) cold war-related; (4) economic and social; (5) human rights-related; and (6) more or less *sui generis*.

On Israel, of course, we are outvoted by thumping majorities at almost every point. The important Israel issue this year turned out to be the war. Here we held our own. We have fought incessantly, and it looks as though we will finally succeed in preventing any anti-Israel judgment about the historical responsibility for the war being attached to any of the relevant resolutions concerning the United Nations Emergency Force. We fought, again successfully—we had to use a lot of muscle here, and at one point to adumbrate our supreme sanction, pulling our economic support away altogether—to keep from assuming an outlandish share of the burden of financing that force. We compromised on the old 25 percent formula, plus 15 percent. And we won in insisting that there shouldn't be any soldiers in the peace-keeping force from any country that is "a permanent member of the Security Council." Note the generic rather than the particular classification. What we didn't want is Soviet soldiers there. But you can't say that; you need a cover category. It's like trying to invite Solzhenitsyn. We lost in our demand that the composition of the force exclude soldiers from countries with a historically anti-Israel position.

The only issue we won on as regards white-dominated territories in Africa was on the procedural point recognizing the right of the South African delegate to speak. On everything else we lost, sometimes by more than 100 votes. The word came down from Nixon-Kissinger that we were to reward Portugal for standing by us so faithfully when we needed the Azores as a staging base to help Israel during the dark hours of the war. Portugal has taken a little bit of an advantage here, having been rather unnecessarily raucous on minor points, knowing that we would have to stand by. But stand by we did.

On the cold war, we joined with the Soviet Union in a

cease-fire resolution that seems to have worked. On Korea, we are working on what they call here a "consensus," by which everyone encourages North and South Korea to proceed to settle their differences without vaporizing the United Nations Command, one of the three signatories of the Armistice (the other two: the Chinese and the North Koreans). What it boiled down to was that the other side didn't quite have the votes.

The phony Soviet proposal for a 10 percent uniform reduction in military armament, with the 10 percent going in aid to Less Developed Countries, we doused with just the cold water necessary to put it away. Bill Schaufele has devastated the Soviet Union in a speech analyzing the proposal and pointing out, among other things, that the Soviet Union made no provision for verification. We treated more kindly Mexico's proposal that a bunch of experts tell us all how to disarm, saying we'd cooperate with them, sure. And we let down gently the call for a world disarmament conference, citing the bilateral progress, if that is the word for it, we are making through SALT, and the activity of the Europeans in search of a Mutual and Balanced Force Reduction.

On the economic and social front, concerning which I have been generally inattentive, we have agreed to contribute to a working group whose aim is to come out with what they will call "A Charter of Economic Rights and Duties of States," which in turn will come forward with a "Universal Declaration of the Human Rights of Mankind to Economic Progress," which if they consult me will consist of a manifesto calling for (1) guaranteed political stability; (2) guaranteed economic freedom; (3) elimination of monopolies and cartels; (4) guaranteed maximum tax of 15 percent; and (5) guaranteed insurance against the expropriation of foreign investments. My guess is the Universal Declaration will be wordier, and less effective.

The human rights questions are, of course, the running concern of this journal.

On the *sui generis* level, there will obviously be no problem at all in convening the World Food Conference, the initiative of Henry Kissinger. And the Law of the Sea Conference has already convened, here in New York, and will reconvene in Caracas in June, 1974, for the big session. That's pretty much the way the 28th General Assembly is going.

28.

25th Anniversary Celebration

MONDAY

The celebration of the 25th Anniversary of the Universal Declaration of Human Rights is upon us. Because tonight there will be festivities in the General Assembly Hall, the Trusteeship Chamber is to be used for the ceremonies. There will be a lot of oratory, followed by the awarding of prizes to award-winning human rights recipients, a practice that began a few years ago.

The chamber is decked out with the flags of 135 members. Benites presides; Waldheim is next to him, and Mahmassani, as head of the Third Committee, is next to him. Waldheim and Brad Morse present the plaques, which are carried up by a young girl, dressed in blue, with white blouse and scarf.

One wonders whether any of the speakers will by any chance (a) say anything interesting and (b) assign the blame for the parlous state of human freedom in the world where it primarily belongs. The alternative is to talk about South Africa. It is the alternative which is primarily seized upon. But there are interesting variations. We are listening, after all, to some pretty bright people. And although one fears that President Benites will never learn, others can be seen to be reaching for fresh and liberating formulations as they say, again and again, what the UN hears, again and again.

Benites is off to a bad start. "In many parts of the world, particularly on the continent of Africa, the repulsive method of individual slavery was followed by the equally repulsive and infamous method of collective slavery which colonialism represented."

235

Why do people say things like that? The colonialization of Kenya by the British was, very simply, not "equally [as] repulsive and infamous" as the antecedent slave trading.

And again: "Basing itself on distorted religious interpretations, a State doctrine has emerged in the southern part of the African continent which in no way differs from the racism which appeared to have been crushed in the Second World War."

What utter baloney, and how egregiously offensive to survivors of Auschwitz, let alone to the memory of non-survivors of Auschwitz, to compare their lot to that of South Africans under apartheid. Benites is a lawyer, and, as a following speaker did much more specifically, he plays occasionally with the idea of actually *enforcing* human rights everywhere. How an organization which cannot muster the courage to pronounce the word "Soviet Union" in a discussion of human rights could enforce human rights in the Soviet Union is the kind of thing that produces the distinctive mistiness of UN rhetoric. But he did *say* it: "Unlike mere ethical principles which may carry neither a sanction nor an obligation, legal principles must be based on compulsion, on the ability to have them enforced in practice and to provide for sanctions in case of non-observance. That is perhaps the great task that lies ahead, and it is to be hoped that in the years following the first quarter-century, active and positive work will be done to endow the rights that have been created with a means for their effective and mandatory exercise." He went on to talk about the Decade of Action to Combat Racism and Racial Discrimination.

Waldheim struck a sober note. "It could be argued that respect for human rights has not been improved since 1948. . . . We know that the evils of racism [always the first mentioned], colonialism, deprivation of political freedoms, arbitrary arrest and discrimination of all kinds have not been eliminated." This, by UN Secretariat standards, is risqué stuff—mentioning the deprivation of political freedoms and arbitrary arrest. (To be sure, the catalogue began with racism and ended with discrimination.) He went on to enumerate the "social rights" UN-types are much more comfortable stressing. "There can be no real progress while so many of our fellow-citizens of this planet are denied the basic rights to work, to live in health, and to receive an education." That is an obvious example of the kind of difficulty one gets into when using the word "right" to signify that which is merely socially desirable. There are many places in the world where there is illiteracy, and many places where there is less than sufficient education. But I do not know of any state devoted to *repressing* literacy. Where there is widespread illiteracy it is either because of (a) endemic poverty or (b) indifference. Neither is in the category of a right denied. Waldheim then weighed in with a little boiler-plate idealism. But his sentiments are exactly correct: "While admitting failure and disappointments, we must never lose sight of the ideal. If we abandon that ideal—a world living in harmony, in which true equality exists—we will lose something in ourselves, we will have abandoned our faith, and we will have betrayed our trust." What he does not realize is that they *have* abandoned their ideal: by refusing to see it, over the heads of such delegates as surround them who are agents of states systematically and totally devoted to the suppression of human rights. It is one thing to fail to approach an ideal because of social and other realities. Another to permit that ideal to evaporate because to do otherwise is to create diplomatic and rhetorical difficulties in addressing agents of superpowers.

Protocol (which is everything) requires that if a message is received from a chief of state, it must be read out loud. Messages from chiefs of government may be distributed as press releases. One suspects that there is a little, humane bureaucrat in the United Nations who contrives to solicit messages primarily from heads of government rather than heads of state. Brad Morse had only two messages to read out. The first, from Mohammad Daoud of Afghanistan, was perfunctory. The second, from Pope Paul, was moderately ambitious. Although it suffered a little from traditional Vatican unction, it made straightforward references to God, as though He actually existed; made critical references to abortion, and juggled the metaphysical point that others would make, probably mostly because it sounds good—the point that you cannot have (a) peace and (b) denial of human rights. I suspect this is simply not true, but the argument is impressive beyond the point of merely yielding rhetorical satisfaction. That is the point Sakharov was saying when he argued in favor of the Jackson Amendment that would deny trade advantages to the Soviet Union unless the Soviet Union granted a few human rights: Détente, without human rights, cannot work, he said. And so the Pope: "Is it really possible then without grave danger for the peaceful coexistence of peoples to remain indifferent in the face of the many grave and often systematic violations of those human rights clearly proclaimed in the Declaration as universal, inviolable, and inalienable?" Even the Pope's catalogue begins nowadays with racial discrimination . . . "We cannot conceal our serious anxiety at the persistence and aggravation of situations which we bitterly deplore—situations such as racial and ethnic discriminatión; obstacles to the self-determination of peoples; the repeated violations of the sacred right to religious liberty in its various aspects and the absence of an international agreement supporting this right and specifying its consequences; the repression of the freedom to express wholesome opinions; the inhumane treatment of prisoners; the violent and systematic elimination of political opponents; other forms of violence and attacks on human life, especially on life in the womb. . . ." The Pope "reiterated" "our good wishes to your noble and eminent Assembly."

The Brazilian representative, who lives in a country where privates are black, lieutenants are mulattoes, and generals are white, spoke about "the open sore of racial discrimination" and the need to eradicate "racial prejudice and apartheid." On the economic and social rights listed in the

Declaration, the speaker was wholly realistic. "These fundamental rights . . . remain for millions of people as unattainable as the crock of gold at the end of the rainbow, and that is so because during this quarter of a century we were not able to respond adequately to the challenge that confronts this Organization: the eradication of under-development within a new system of collective economic security, which will be a basic prerequisite of social progress and, by implication, of world-wide peace and political security." There is a lot of mush in that sentence, but he seems to be saying a truth, which is that without doctors and nurses and medicines and laboratories and hospitals you do not have good health; and without a degree of material progress, you cannot have doctors and nurses and medicines and laboratories and hospitals.

Mahmassani did a nice rundown on the meaning of the Human Rights Declaration which, juxtaposed against the Brazilian reminder of the high cost of social and economic "rights," reminds one that the *basic* human rights really are *not* very costly. . . . "In theory [the Declaration] affirms that man is a free being whose inviolability is assured, and whose well-being is sacred." That much the poorest states should be able to secure, provided they are protected from external aggression. In practice, it stipulates that man is at liberty to think and to express himself as he pleases, to choose his own religion, to marry whomever he wishes, and to own his own home and property. But one slips inevitably into hyperbole. "The Declaration was made clear and unequivocal in its wording. It announced to men and women everywhere— 'These are the rights and freedoms which are yours as members of the human family. It is up to you to claim them, enjoy them, and protect them.' Moreover, it made it possible for all men and women to be fully conscious of their rights as human beings." *Why do they say these things?* Mr. Mahmassani had himself presided during this very session over a fruitless effort to enhance the freedom of information. People in most parts of the world who rise to claim their rights are never heard from again. And the notion that "all men and women" are now "fully conscious of their rights as human beings" is preposterous beyond the liberties of diplomatic rhetoric. And the usual closing thought, so pathetic in its emptiness. "Peace and security cannot prevail in today's world unless the fundamental rights and freedoms of every man are fulfilled." By and large, peace has in fact prevailed, during the past twenty-five years—marked by a systematic elimination of human rights in an area stretching from the Pacific Ocean to the Berlin Wall. Indeed—unhappy thought—it is held by some of the think-tank types that the introduction of a little human liberty in Russia *could* bring about the kind of disequilibrium that might increase, rather than reduce, the chances of war. And the great Cultural Revolution in China, in some people's understanding of it, was a social eructation aimed at crushing a few grass blades of individuality that had begun to break through the concrete.

Mr. Ramphul of Mauritius is head of the Human Rights Commission, which is the standing committee—a branch of the Economic and Social Council—charged with reporting on progress in the field of human rights. Ramphul acknowledged that there has been "no systematic approach to human rights in the United Nations and its family of organizations," that that is why there has been so much duplication, so much that has been lost, and perfunctory. He faced up directly to the extraordinary preoccupations with colonialism and apartheid. But he defended this, citing the words of President Nyerere of Tanzania who had said at another commemorative meeting of the 25th Anniversary of the UN that:

"In particular, the United Nations has to act against the forces of racialism and colonialism, for these represent the kind of tyranny and oppression which deny all hope to men, and which therefore force them to express their humanity through violence. A man can change his religion if he wishes; he can accept a different political belief—or in both cases give the appearance of doing so—if this would relieve him of intolerable circumstances. But no man can change his color or his race. And if he suffers because of it, he must either become less than a man, or he must fight. And for good or evil, mankind has been so created that many will refuse to acquiesce in their own degradation; they will destroy peace rather than suffer under it."

I do believe that this is cant. (a) Colonialism of the truly objectionable kind is nowadays practiced only in Eastern Europe and, arguably, in the Portuguese territories. (b) Every ten years or so there is a movement for liberalization in East Europe. It is promptly crushed by the Soviet Army, and organized resistance disappears. (c) Racism is practiced most systematically in South Africa. There is very little organized resistance to it, and very little blood shed in maintaining it. (d) Genocidal activity is worse than racial discrimination. There has been no genocidal activity in South Africa since the disappearance of the Hottentots in the early part of the eighteenth century. There has however been a great deal of genocidal strife in post-colonial Africa. The persecutions of the Ibos in Nigeria, of the Hutus in Burundi, of the Asians in Uganda—although they deal in slaughter by the tens of thousands—are unmentioned in any United Nations orations, and surely might have been eased under colonialism. (e) It is no less depressing to be persecuted because one's inclinations are Christian, or democratic, than because one's skin is white, yellow, or black—it is unseemly, not to say depraved, to suggest that all one need do is reject God, and freedom. (f) The historical record is very clear that Nat Turners and Mau Maus are the exception rather than the rule, that the technology of repression, whether ruthless as in the Communist world, or discreet as in South Africa, greatly outpaces the dynamic of human freedom. The reason colonialism and racism are singled out for special emphasis is that the Portuguese, the Rhodesians, and the South Africans are weak enough for United Nations orators to accost. Nigerians, Ugandese, and Tutsi are also weak, but tribal passions, which are stronger in Africa than racial passions, and far more dangerous, are not subjects concerning which well-behaved diplomats speak.

Mr. Ramphul, who is a man of subtlety, said this, however: "The pledge of the peoples of the United Nations, in the Preamble to the Charter, [is] to reaffirm faith in fundamental human rights, in the dignity and worth of the human person, in the equal rights of men and women and of nations large and small, and to point out that there is no doubt that the reference in the Charter to the dignity and worth of the human person will, in time, prove to have been the most revolutionary and momentous words ever adopted for the future of mankind." But the most significant *act* of the United Nations, in respect of these words, was the admission of the People's Republic of China to membership. Significant because the rulers of that country most consistently, most explicitly, and most categorically, *reject* any idea of fundamental human rights, of the dignity and worth of the human person. So that by stressing parliamentary universalism (and it may well have been the proper thing to do, *politically*), the United Nations diluted its philosophical commitment to a universal morality; and it is the schizophrenia of the UN, symbolized by profuse statements on human rights by the same men who welcome totalitarian governments, that results in so few people of discrimination bothering to be present in this room today to hear the gentleman talking about the revolutionary and momentous promulgation twenty-five years ago of an instrument as archly meaningless as that Declaration.

Mr. Baroody, the representative of King Faisal, deplored "those who exercise excessive power or acquire superfluous wealth [and] are too preoccupied with their own achievements and so dazzled by the adulation of the masses that they fail to pay sufficient attention to the fundamental human rights of others." He spoke of the "unstable hunger for excessive wealth" a fortnight after Saudi Arabia had tripled the price of its oil.

Easily the most adventurous address was John Humphrey's of Canada. He had been there when the Universal Declaration was promulgated, and he is for sanctions all the way. "If, as the World Court seems recently to have said, Articles 55 and 56 of the Charter bind States to respect and observe human rights and fundamental freedoms, these rights and freedoms, which the Charter does not list or define, are the rights and freedoms listed and defined in the Universal Declaration of Human Rights. That, I suggest, is a truly revolutionary development. In traditional international law and practice, human rights fell almost exclusively within the domestic jurisdiction of States. To put it very bluntly, what a State did to its own nationals was its own business and beyond the reach of international law. States, and only States, were subjects of international law. All that has changed. International law, or, as we should now call it, world law, governs the conduct and protects the rights of other entities, including the United Nations, and of individual men and women wherever they may live. That is a development which is as revolutionary as anything that has happened in history." That's right. It is certainly revolutionary. And it is taken as seriously as Waldheim would be taken if he appeared tomorrow on the podium announcing that he was Napoleon, and that the armies of the world should submit to his command. "Five years from now," said Humphrey, and one admires the zestful optimism, "the United Nations will again be celebrating an anniversary of the adoption of the Declaration. I am young enough to hope that I may have the privilege of being present at that celebration and that I will be able to say in all sincerity that the United Nations has justified the hopes that men and women everywhere continue to place in it." I am old enough to know that Mr. Humphrey will *not* be able to say any such thing five years from now.

And then the prizes were given. To six thoroughly decent people. A Mexican lady who has been President of the

Mexican Senate. An Egyptian poet, who had died a few weeks earlier. U Thant. Bishop Mozarewa of Rhodesia. And (also recently deceased) Wilfred Jenks of England, a former director of the International Labor Organization. But it was as if, in the year that Lindbergh crossed the Atlantic, the aviation trophy had been awarded to the stunt pilot at the Dutchess County Fair. The shadow of Solzhenitsyn was over that Assembly, but nobody spoke his name.

29.

Closing of Third Committee

Mahmassani is a man of taste, but also of endurance, not to say stoicism. This would be the final day of work for the Third Committee, and there were three items to be considered. Two of them were easily dispatched in the morning, and he could have gone on and got rid of the third. He didn't, for reasons I could not fathom. . . . Until the dreary afternoon session, which must have hurt him more than us.

Tributes. If he had finished it all before lunch, there wouldn't have been time for the tributes. Mahmassani is an unpretentious man, and he cannot have enjoyed what he knew he had to face, and allocated the bulk of the afternoon for. He made a brief statement of his own, giving a few statistics. The Third Committee had heard over 700 statements (exclusive of Rights of Reply and Points of Order); had met 73 times; had approved 27 resolutions. The session was highlighted, he said, by a convention on the crimes of apartheid, and resolutions on war crimes, racism, and colonialism. He thanked everyone for helping to get the work done on time. When I say he thanked everyone, I mean he thanked everyone, not excluding the chars. I assumed that someone would respond, the senior member perhaps, and that there would follow a rising ovation. No. He was thanked by the head of each regional group, and the speeches were ten to fifteen minutes in length. Even then, ambiguous regional affiliations had to be ventilated. Thus, although the Iranian had spoken in behalf of the Asians, the Philippine delegate rose to speak for the Island Asians—Singapore, Malaysia, etc. The Argentinian had spoken for the Latins. But the Guyanan rose to speak for the Caribbean nations. The Bulgarian spoke for the bloc, expressing great satisfaction with the work done by the Committee (and indeed he had good reason to be satisfied). The West German spoke for the Western European and U.S. group, but then the East German rose to agree (a cosmic first) with the West German on the matter of paying tribute. The Senegalese made a short speech expressing his devotion to the chairman, and this stimulated a half dozen more nations to pay their respects. Mahmassani obviously had a hand in the official record, where he ordered that the whole of the two hours of panegyric be described as: "After an exchange of courtesies, the Chairman declared that the Committee had completed its work for the 28th session." No reference was made to the increasingly apparent impotence of the Third Committee, which has attained the status of a simile. The other day there was a wrangle in the Sixth Committee, the legal committee, which, along with the Fifth, is taken quite seriously. The U.K. representative quipped: "Why not consider the [pending resolution] as not serious, like a Third Committee Resolution?"

30.

Closing Day—Terrorism

TUESDAY

Closing day. There were rumors that the session might be extended by one day, or even two, because of the clogged calendar. Foxy Carter, who knows all, tells me the threat is (a) habitual, and (b) idle. Its purpose is to get people to speed up a little. It is idle because airplane reservations have been made for the delegates and their wives, and plane travel being as tight as it is, approaching Christmas, the General Assembly is not likely to submit to the inconvenience of having to fight for fresh reservations. And so it will be over tonight, the end of the 28th General Assembly, and most incidentally the end of my commission.

They are droning on and on—tributes to President Benites. Sample (chosen at random) Mr. Ghorra, from Lebanon: "Mr. President, as Chairman of the Asian Group for this month, it is a singular honor for me to express to you, on its behalf and on behalf of my delegation, our congratulations on the splendid and efficient manner in which you have conducted the deliberations of the twenty-eighth session of the General Assembly. Your active and dedicated participation in the life of the United Nations over the years has earned you a special and noteworthy place in its annals. Delegations have unanimously recognized your qualities as an eminent jurist, a forthright statesman, and a devoted humanist by elevating you to the high office of President of the General Assembly. As an illustrious and noble son of Latin America, you have reflected its attachment to legality, to the primacy of human rights and values and to the cause of peace. You have. . . ."

I chat with Tap Bennett. As senior United States official representing the host country he will be the final speaker (save for a Presidential benediction). He tells me that he is going to be very severe on the matter of the failure of the UN to take any action on terrorism. That morning, terrorists killed a dozen innocent passengers in an airplane in Rome, and flew on to Athens.

I thought back to the night the Israeli athletes were captured and murdered in Munich. By chance I was dining with George Bush, at that time our permanent Ambassador to the United Nations, and he got the news from the State Department, during dinner. We spoke of the generic problem, as bulletins continued to come in every half hour or so—the terrorists were releasing the athletes; no, they weren't; there was a shoot-out; the athletes escaped; no, they hadn't escaped; they were all dead. . . . I remember remarking, as we drove home, that he had not as a matter of instinct thought about the United Nations as the probable mechanism by which to do something about international terrorism.

That fall, Secretary Waldheim had availed himself of a privilege the Secretary-General has under the charter, but which he seldom avails himself of. It is to inscribe an item on the agenda of the General Assembly in virtue of its sudden importance. That summer, a few days after Munich, he proposed that something be done about terrorism. "The world has been plagued," said Waldheim, "on an increasing scale, by acts of terrorism which have taken the lives, not only of national leaders and diplomatic envoys, but also [of] other human beings whose only offense lay in their race, religion or national origin, and even innocent bystanders." He proposed as an item for the 27th General Assembly, "measures to prevent terrorism and other forms of violence which endanger or take innocent lives, or jeopardize fundamental freedoms."

The item went, as procedures require, to the General (or Steering) Committee. Here the President of the General Assembly presides, with the seventeen Vice-Presidents, and the chairmen of the seven standing committees. Right away, they went at it. Yemen turned the thing into a forum for attacking Israel, Cuba talked about American violence in Vietnam. But the committee finally voted, two to one, to take the matter on over to the Plenary. UN-watchers, observing that vote, could have told you: It's dead. Though fifteen nations approved, those who disapproved were China, Ethiopia, Guinea, Libya, Mauritius, and Syria. Czechoslovakia and the USSR abstained.

At the General Assembly, the item seemed to be strong. Sensing this, Baroody attempted to weaken it by magnifying the item so as to make it all but meaningless. Only Baroody could have come up with the amended version of the resolution, which now reads: "Measures to Prevent Terrorism and Other Forms of Violence Which Endanger or Take Innocent Human Lives or Jeopardize Fundamental Freedoms, and Study of the Underlying Causes of Those Forms of Terrorism and Acts of Violence Which Lie in Misery, Frustration, Grievance, and Despair and Which Cause Some People to Sacrifice Human Lives, Including Their Own, in an Attempt to Effect Radical Changes." It passed, and was assigned to the Sixth Committee, which asked the Secretariat to prepare a list of existing extra-UN agreements devised to punish internationally certain offenders, so that they could have a look at them. Four instruments are listed. The 1963 Tokyo Convention deals with offenses committed on board aircraft. The 1970 Hague Convention deals with unlawful seizure of aircraft. These are in force. In 1971, a convention was negotiated in Montreal, and another negotiated in Washington involving terrorism generally, but confined to members of the Organization of American States. These were done without any reliance whatsoever upon the United Nations. It would appear fair to say, based on the current experience, that they wouldn't have got through the United Nations.

The Sixth Committee argued extensively in the fall of 1972 on the general subject, with the Western states taking the position that by all means the causes of terrorism and despair should be investigated but that there was no reason to delay a Covenant. The African states, dominated by an Arab rationale, argued, clearly as a maneuver to end the discussion, in such a way as to exculpate Palestinian terrorism. The non-aligned bloc won with an epicene resolution to establish an Ad Hoc Committee on International Terrorism to make further recommendations. George Bush called the vote "tragic," as did Ambassador Tekoah of Israel.

But of course a committee was established—the Ad Hoc Committee on Terrorism. Thirty-five states became members, and they met during this summer. A long report was born, but no conclusions reached. At the last meeting an effort was made to come forward with acceptable wording. At this point the Algerian Ambassador insisted on adding a qualifying sentence, namely: "When people engage in violent action against colonialist, racist and alien regimes as part of a struggle to retain its legitimate rights or to redress an injustice of which it is the victim, the international community, when it has recognized the validity of these objectives, cannot take repressive measures against any action which it ought, on the contrary, to encourage support, and defend."

That was it: The Ad Hoc Committee could not agree on any recommendations to submit to the 28th General Assembly. Homer Jack, who is Secretary-General of the World Conference of Religion for Peace, has published an excellent account of the whole controversy (*America,* October 20, 1973). He contests the charge that we were too unbending. "The West insisted that it compromised a great deal, and said that it was even willing to turn a blind eye on the terrorism of liberation movements with colonial, racist or alien regimes, but not if terrorism affected innocent third parties and spilled over into second countries."

It is already 8:30 and I feel sorry for Tap, who knows that people are aching to get out of there. . . . "I now call on the representative of the host country," Benites says, and Our Leader walks down to the podium. On the whole he is very cheery, and complimentary to the General Assembly, citing its good deeds. "It is, therefore, all the more tragic that, as this successful Assembly draws to a close with its record of real achievement, and on the very eve of a historic conference which we hope will open the way to a just and enduring peace in the Middle East, the world community is presented with yet another shocking display of international lawlessness—to put it bluntly, of brute insensate madness. Yesterday's murderers in Rome and in Athens are the more repellent because of their cold-blooded brutality and their purposeless waste, a waste I submit that must stun us all: wasted lives, wasted principles, wasted support, wasted sympathy. Expressions of revulsion and disapproval come from every quarter. This is a welcome advance over international reactions to earlier terrorist murders, to the massacres of Olympic athletes, to the killing of diplomats, and to other horrors of this age. But I would insist that revulsion and disappointment are not enough. The world waits for a forthright effort by this world organization to find means of safeguarding the innocent. To the shame of us all, we, the representatives of the world community, have failed to find common ground which would enable us to take measures to prevent these offenses against humankind."

And the peroration . . . "This Assembly is ending its work tonight with a sense of accomplishment, that all of us can look to the future with confidence that the momentum toward international cooperation achieved here this year will be sustained and, we hope, intensified in the year to come. . . ."

The speech was very well received.

I did not hear the closing paragraphs, which I read the next morning. I had promised to go to a harpsichord recital being given by my teacher. I knew she would miss me if I wasn't there, and that Tap would forgive me if I missed the closing remarks of President Benites, which I did not read the next morning.

Epilogue

I was undecided whether to write a concluding chapter. The obvious argument was for doing something by way of a coda. But a journal on the United Nations is not something which one concludes conclusively, particularly a journal focused as subjectively as this one. I found the few associates I consulted on the point divided. They agreed that such recommendations as I have for an improved organization are sprinkled throughout the journal, for those who care to collect them; and that as a stylistic matter, it is questionable whether it is necessary to recapitulate, or to set down these recommendations methodically.

I pondered for a while, in response to the stylistic imperative, a chapter that would begin something like this:

WEDNESDAY. *While sitting at the chair of the Plenary, attending to a few administrative details in the session following the day of the formal closing, a bulletin came in, and the place was in pandemonium. It appears that the military attached to the UN to give technical advice on world disarmament have staged a successful coup and have taken over the General Assembly, the Security Council, and the Secretariat. In due course the UN colonels will issue their instructions, but already it is disclosed that the Soviet Union will not be permitted to talk about disarming, without disarming; the Chinese may not speak about human rights without granting human rights; the Arabs will not be permitted to speak about the plight of the Less Developed Countries without foreswearing the cartelization of their oil; the Africans may not talk about racism until after subduing the leaders of Uganda, the Central African Republic, and Burundi, for a starter; and, just to prove that the colonels are not above a bill of attainder, Jamil Baroody may not speak at all, on any subject, for ninety days—after which he will be put on probation, and permitted to increase the length of his speeches by one minute per month, until he reaches the maximum of ten minutes, except that at the first mention of Zionist responsibility for World War I, he has to start all over again. The countries of East Europe must wear red uniforms when they appear on the floor and, before rising to speak, must seek explicit and public permission from the delegate of the Soviet Union. A scientific tabulation will be made, under the colonels' supervision, of the compliance of individual countries with the provisions of the Universal Declaration of Human Rights, and each country's delegate will be required to wear on his lapel his nation's ranking on that scale, which will range from 100 to 0. Any country with a ranking of less than 75 will not be permitted to speak on the subject of human rights.*

That sort of thing; and if I had the imagination of Robert Heinlein, I suppose I'd have pursued the idea. Instead I shall close by making (in some cases remaking) a few observations, some simple, some less so.

To begin with, it is not easy to prescribe simultaneously both for the United Nations and for the United States, since although it is not true that their interests, most broadly stated, must be different, their interests, insofar as they are the same, converge rather than proceed in a single line. It has become the habit of the United Nations increasingly to ignore major affronts upon the dignity of mankind while going on endlessly about relatively minor affronts, and to engross itself in economic approaches different from our own, in search of material progress.

One can with clear head and good conscience recommend that the United States abstain from voting in the General Assembly, on the grounds that so long as we do so, we confer parliamentary substance on what is after all only an illusory parliament of man. But this recommendation, made to the U.S. government, would not necessarily apply, say to Afghanistan. There is something to be said for knowing how the non-superpowers feel about a particular issue, and the General Assembly, for so long as it is not taken too seriously, is an economical way to find out what that is, assuming that we cannot find this out more easily by asking our Ambassadors in Afghanistan, or reading the Afghanistan press. Still, the point is made: that for the United States to give the impression that it will conform to such resolutions as a majority of the General Assembly can put together, on such questions as whether to recognize exile governments, or whether to pull suddenly out of South Korea troops sent there originally under UN auspices, is to contribute to a synthetic parliamentarianism which does very little more than frustrate the so-called parliament of man. Possibly there is a middle way. If one were of a mind to consider Charter reform, perhaps it might be specified that any permanent member of the Security Council would not be permitted to vote in the General Assembly. *(Quod licet Jovi non licet bovi.)* That ought to do it. Congruent reforms, for those who wish to consider them, may be inferred from a reading of this journal, and of course by anyone giving thought to the weaknesses, and strengths, of the UN.

Concerning the latter, Mr. John Scali has written me, in anticipation of seeing this journal (which as a matter of courtesy I shall not show him before publication), to say that he hoped I would also record the UN's "achievements" and comment on "its potential."

He reassures me, and, I am certain, the average reader of this book, that the "real power" of the United Nations lies not within the General Assembly, but in the Secretariat and the specialized agencies. "One might," our Ambassador aptly puts it, "in the proper company, draw a comparison with the old Sphinx of Paris, where the annual masked ball on the first floor was the center of attention, but the real business was consummated on the floors above."

He cites specific and general examples. Multilateral diplomacy is not "a substitute for bilateral diplomacy, but can be an essential complement to it." He gives as an example the Middle East cease-fire.

The United Nations is inchoately the organization that can help to give us the "institutionalized peace" Henry Kissinger spoke about in his address. And in fact, he suggests (post hoc propter hoc?), it may not be a coincidence that we have had thirty years of relative world peace, and thirty years of the UN.

The smaller nations of the world have a disproportionate voice in the General Assembly, to be sure. "This realization does not do much to temper their rhetoric, or their votes on essentially rhetorical resolutions. But on issues of substance, there remains a real margin for moderation and compromise—mostly because the UN is more important to the little states than to the big ones." Mr. Scali mentioned several votes in which, as I have noted in the journal, we received significant support from the smaller nations.

And then, finally, there are the largely non-ideological world problems, "population, law of the sea or food, for example, on which local or regional solutions simply cannot work unless they are, at a minimum, applied in a global framework. The UN is really the only institution which can provide such a framework."

All the above is more or less true, and one cannot doubt the sincerity with which these views are held by our Permanent Representative to the UN, or—I believe—by most of his predecessors.

But there is another view. It is, for instance, that of Conor Cruise O'Brien, though my paraphrase of it might not satisfy him. It is this: that, in fact, the principal action of the United Nations precisely takes place in the General Assembly. That which is important and comes out of the Security Council, or the specialized agencies, would probably be forthcoming out of ad hoc bilateral and multilateral agreements, such as those mentioned above to illustrate attempts to restrain terrorism in the Western Hemisphere. No doubt clerical, administrative, and diplomatic arrangements rooted in the United Nations make it a great deal easier for us to pursue such objectives. But that this should be so does not make it so that this is where the action is in the UN. Mr. O'Brien notes that the General Assembly is the only chamber in which the little countries can speak their minds, that they do so there, that what they do there is uniquely significant so that it can be said that the United Nations is principally *about* theater; and that theater takes place mostly in the General Assembly.

Assuming that this is so, we have something altogether different to concern ourselves with, and that is the order of moral reality. This sounds like a very grand phrase to introduce to a world that would settle for a little practical progress. But it is the only phrase grand enough to convey the importance of the survival of truth. Truth is a philosophical objective, of course. But it is also a strategic objective, because it is with reference to postulates—about metaphysical man—that the United States is organized. It is only—to give one example—by distinguishing between life in the United States and life in the Soviet Union that one generates the energy to resist the sovietization of American life. The United Nations is the most concentrated assault on moral reality in the history of free institutions, and it does not do to ignore that fact or, worse, to get used to it.

And this is a point that should not separate American conservatives from American liberals, or British or French conservatives from their democratic socialists. Mr. Daniel Patrick Moynihan, now Ambassador to India, has, throughout his extraordinary career, identified himself with American left-liberalism. When last August in New Delhi he read that the UN committee, under the prodding of Cuba, had raised doubts about the legitimacy of Puerto Rican independence, and saw the stern rebuke given the Cubans by Scali, he cabled his reflections to the Secretary of State. Mr. Moynihan's confidential cable had an extremely limited circulation, and his prescriptions are what one might call Fighting Irish. Still his words are an appropriate parable with which to conclude this journal.

I SHOULD LIKE [he cabled] . . . TO ADD A PERSONAL NOTE OF CONGRATULATIONS TO AMBASSADOR SCALI FOR HIS STATEMENT IN THE AFTERMATH OF THE AUGUST 30 VOTE ADOPTING THE TOTALITARIAN RESOLUTION, AND TO STATE MY OWN CONCERN NOT ONLY AT THE EMERGENCE OF AN ANTI-DEMOCRATIC BIAS AT THE UNITED NATIONS, BUT AT THE CURIOUS SEEMING ACCEPTANCE BY THE UNITED STATES THAT THERE IS NOTHING TO BE DONE ABOUT IT, INDEED THAT IT IS SCARCELY EVEN TO BE PROTESTED SAVE BY MEN SUCH AS SCALI WHO WILL NOT PERHAPS OBJECT TO MY DESCRIBING HIM AS SOMEONE FROM OUTSIDE THE SYSTEM.

I WAS THE "PUBLIC" MEMBER OF THE UNITED STATES DELEGATION TO THE 26TH ASSEMBLY. FROM FIRST TO LAST I WAS APPALLED AT THE EXTENT TO WHICH TOTALITARIAN NORMS AND FINLANDIZED RESPONSES HAD COME TO DOMINATE BOTH THE GENERAL ASSEMBLY AND, AS BEST I COULD LEARN, THE UN SECRETARIAT. SOME MAY RECALL THAT I TRIED TO MAKE AN ISSUE OVER THE UNITED NATIONS SOCIAL REPORT WHICH WAS ADOPTED THAT YEAR. A MATTER OF NO CONSEQUENCE, IT WAS NATURALLY ASSIGNED THE PUBLIC MEMBER TO DEAL WITH IN COMMITTEE. THE DOCUMENT WAS AN OUTRAGE. IT MEASURED THE SOCIAL WELL-BEING OF VARIOUS NATIONS IN TERMS OF ONE SINGLE DENOMINATOR: THE PRESENCE OR ABSENCE OF SOCIAL PROTEST. PRESENCE PROVED TROUBLE. ABSENCE PROVED PEACE. THIS ALL-PURPOSE SOCIAL INDICATOR ESTABLISHED, FOR EXAMPLE, THAT THE PEOPLE AND GOVERNMENT OF CZECHOSLOVAKIA LIVED IN PERFECT HARMONY, WHILST THE UNITED STATES WAS RAPIDLY APPROACHING ANARCHY AND LONG DELAYED, MUCH DESERVED—REVOLUTION. WHAT APPALLED ME WAS NOT THAT THE TOTALITARIANS WISHED TO ESTABLISH THIS DEFINITION OF WELL-BEING. NOR YET THAT THEY HAD TERRORIZED THE BUREAUCRACY INTO GOING ALONG. WHAT APPALLED ME WAS THAT THE UNITED STATES WENT ALONG. FOR TWO LONG YEARS THE DOCUMENT HAD BEEN REVIEWED AT LEISURELY CONFERENCES IN THOSE REGIONS OF EUROPE NOTED FOR THEIR SCENERY AND THEIR CUISINE. ONE PLUMP-MINDED AMERICAN OFFICIAL AFTER ANOTHER HAD SILENTLY OR ENTHUSIASTICALLY ASSENTED TO A PROLONGED SLANDER ON AMERICAN DEMOCRACY, A SUSTAINED ADVOCACY OF TOTALITARIAN

DICTATORSHIP. YOU KNOW WHY? BECAUSE WE SENT STUPID MEN AND WORSE WOMEN TO THOSE CONFERENCES. AND WHY DID WE DO THIS? BECAUSE THE HARD-NOSE COLD WARRIORS ON THE SIXTH FLOOR THINK SUCH THINGS DON'T MATTER.

WELL, THIS PUBLIC DELEGATE THOUGHT THEY DID MATTER, AND FOUND HIMSELF SPEAKING IN ALMOST PRECISELY THE SAME TERMS AS HAD AMBASSADOR SCALI. WHEN THE SOVIET LADY MAYOR OF MOSCOW (AS I RECALL HER CIVILIAN OCCUPATION) CALLED ATTENTION TO THE RISE OF TRADE UNION PROTEST AND STRIKES IN THE UNITED STATES, I ALLOWED THAT SHE HAD EVERY REASON TO THINK THIS UNUSUAL, COMING AS SHE DID FROM A NATION WHERE THE LAST TRADE UNION STRIKE OCCURRED IN 1917. AND SO WE SQUABBLED ON TO AN INDETERMINATE CONCLUSION, MUCH TO THE DISTRESS OF THE FINNISH CHAIRMAN (AND THE FINNISH AUTHOR BEHIND HER) AND, I FEAR, TO THE EMBARRASSMENT OF MY PROFESSIONAL COLLEAGUES WHO WERE WORRIED ABOUT SERIOUS MATTERS LIKE HOW MUCH AID WE SHOULD PROVIDE THE BASTARDS WHO WERE SLANDERING US.

THE MATTER IS TOO FAR DISTANT AND THE WEATHER HERE TOO DISAGREEABLE FOR ME FULLY TO RECONSTRUCT THE FURY WITH WHICH I SAT IN THE GENERAL ASSEMBLY AND LISTENED TO THE STALINIST SON OF A BITCH FROM CUBA GO ON ABOUT PUERTO RICO. BUT STILL IT WAS HIS JOB. HE IS A STALINIST. HE WORKS FOR A STALINIST. HE CAN GET KILLED IF HE MAKES A MISTAKE. WHAT DROVE ME TO DESPAIR WAS THE COMPLACENCY OF OUR PUTATIVE ALLIES IN THIS MATTER. THE HONOR OF AMERICAN DEMOCRACY WAS BEING IMPUGNED? WHAT IS HONOR? SAID OUR ALLIES. LET US TALK OF MALARIA ERADICATION, AND AID LEVELS. THERE WAS A SAYING AROUND THE KENNEDY WHITE HOUSE: DON'T GET MAD, GET EVEN. IN THE END WHAT TROUBLES ME MOST ABOUT THE PUERTO RICAN EPISODE IS THAT WE SEEM TO BE WILLING TO FORGET ABOUT A CLEAR VIOLATION OF THE CHARTER, A DIRECT LIE ABOUT THE UNITED STATES. WHAT HAS COME OVER US? FORGET ABOUT A SLANDER ON OUR HONOR? WHAT HAVE WE BECOME? ANY, REPEAT ANY, COUNTRY THAT DOES NOT SUPPORT US ON A MATTER OF THIS CONSEQUENCE NOT ONLY DAMAGES THE UNITED NATIONS, BUT MUST QUIETLY BE BROUGHT TO UNDERSTAND THAT IT HAS DAMAGED ITSELF. I LOOKED DOWN

THE LIST OF THOSE WHO GO ALONG AND THOSE WHO GO ALONG BY ABSTAINING. IN HALF OF THEM THE PRESENT REGIMES WOULD COLLAPSE WITHOUT AMERICAN SUPPORT OR AMERICAN ACQUIESCENCE. TO HELL WITH IT. SOMETHING SPECIFICALLY BAD SHOULD HAPPEN TO EACH ONE OF THEM, AND WHEN IT HAS HAPPENED THEY SHOULD BE TOLD THAT AMERICANS TAKE THE HONOR OF THEIR DEMOCRACY MOST SERIOUSLY, AND NEVER ISSUE WARNINGS TO THOSE WHO WOULD BESMIRCH THAT HONOR. WHEN THAT HAPPENS, SOMETHING EXTRAORDINARILY DISAGREEABLE HAPPENS NEXT, AND THE VICTIM IS LEFT TO FIGURE IT OUT FOR HIMSELF.

BRAVO SCALI! COJONES, MEN.

Appendix

Appendix A

UNIVERSAL DECLARATION OF HUMAN RIGHTS

Adopted and proclaimed by General Assembly resolution 217 A (III) of 10 December 1948

Preamble

Whereas recognition of the inherent dignity and of the equal and inalienable rights of all members of the human family is the foundation of freedom, justice and peace in the world,

Whereas disregard and contempt for human rights have resulted in barbarous acts which have outraged the conscience of mankind, and the advent of a world in which human beings shall enjoy freedom of speech and belief and freedom from fear and want has been proclaimed as the highest aspiration of the common people,

Whereas it is essential, if man is not to be compelled to have recourse, as a last resort, to rebellion against tyranny and oppression, that human rights should be protected by the rule of law,

Whereas it is essential to promote the development of friendly relations between nations,

Whereas the peoples of the United Nations have in the Charter reaffirmed their faith in fundamental human rights, in the dignity and worth of the human person and in the equal rights of men and women and have determined to promote social progress and better standards of life in larger freedom,

Whereas Member States have pledged themselves to achieve, in co-operation with the United Nations, the promotion of universal respect for and observance of human rights and fundamental freedoms,

Whereas a common understanding of these rights and freedoms is of the greatest importance for the full realization of this pledge,

Now, therefore,

The General Assembly

Proclaims this Universal Declaration of Human Rights as a common standard of achievement for all peoples and all nations, to the end that every individual and every organ of society, keeping this Declaration constantly in mind, shall strive by teaching and education to promote respect for these rights and freedoms and by progressive measures, national and international, to secure their universal and effective recognition and observance, both among the peoples of Member States themselves and among the peoples of territories under their jurisdiction.

Article 1
All human beings are born free and equal in dignity and rights. They are endowed with reason and conscience and should act towards one another in a spirit of brotherhood.

Article 2
Everyone is entitled to all the rights and freedoms set forth in this Declaration, without distinction of any kind, such as race, colour, sex, language, religion, political or other opinion, national or social origin, property, birth or other status.

Furthermore, no distinction shall be made on the basis of the political, jurisdictional or international status of the country or territory to which a person belongs, whether it be independent, trust, non-self-governing or under any other limitation of sovereignty.

Article 3
Everyone has the right to life, liberty and the security of person.

Article 4
No one shall be held in slavery or servitude; slavery and the slave trade shall be prohibited in all their forms.

Article 5
No one shall be subjected to torture or to cruel, inhuman or degrading treatment or punishment.

Article 6
Everyone has the right to recognition everywhere as a person before the law.

Article 7
All are equal before the law and are entitled without any discrimination to equal protection of the law. All are entitled to equal protection against any discrimination in violation of this Declaration and against any incitement to such discrimination.

Article 8
Everyone has the right to an effective remedy by the competent national tribunals for acts violating the fundamental rights granted him by the constitution or by law.

Article 9
No one shall be subjected to arbitrary arrest, detention or exile.

Article 10
Everyone is entitled in full equality to a fair and public hearing by an independent and impartial tribunal, in the determination of his rights and obligations and of any criminal charge against him.

Article 11
1. Everyone charged with a penal offence has the right to be presumed innocent until proved guilty according to law in a public trial at which he has had all the guarantees necessary for his defence.

2. No one shall be held guilty of any penal offence on account of any act or omission which did not constitute a penal offence, under national or international law, at the time when it was committed. Nor shall a heavier penalty be imposed than the one that was applicable at the time the penal offence was committed.

Article 12
No one shall be subjected to arbitrary interference with his privacy, family, home or correspondence, nor to attacks upon his honour and reputation. Everyone has the right to the protection of the law against such interference or attacks.

Article 13

1. Everyone has the right to freedom of movement and residence within the borders of each State.

2. Everyone has the right to leave any country, including his own, and to return to his country.

Article 14

1. Everyone has the right to seek and to enjoy in other countries asylum from persecution.

2. This right may not be invoked in the case of prosecutions genuinely arising from non-political crimes or from acts contrary to the purposes and principles of the United Nations.

Article 15

1. Everyone has the right to a nationality.

2. No one shall be arbitrarily deprived of his nationality nor denied the right to change his nationality.

Article 16

1. Men and women of full age, without any limitation due to race, nationality or religion, have the right to marry and to found a family. They are entitled to equal rights as to marriage, during marriage and at its dissolution.

2. Marriage shall be entered into only with the free and full consent of the intending spouses.

3. The family is the natural and fundamental group unit of society and is entitled to protection by society and the State.

Article 17

1. Everyone has the right to own property alone as well as in association with others.

2. No one shall be arbitrarily deprived of his property.

Article 18

Everyone has the right to freedom of thought, conscience and religion; this right includes freedom to change his religion or belief, and freedom, either alone or in community with others and in public or private, to manifest his religion or belief in teaching, practice, worship and observance.

Article 19

Everyone has the right to freedom of opinion and expression; this right includes freedom to hold opinions without interference and to seek, receive and impart information and ideas through any media and regardless of frontiers.

Article 20

1. Everyone has the right to freedom of peaceful assembly and association.

2. No one may be compelled to belong to an association.

Article 21

1. Everyone has the right to take part in the government of his· country, directly or through freely chosen representatives.

2. Everyone has the right of equal access to public service in his country.

3. The will of the people shall be the basis of the authority of government; this will shall be expressed in periodic and genuine elections which shall be by universal and equal suffrage and shall be held by secret vote or by equivalent free voting procedures.

Article 22

Everyone, as a member of society, has the right to social security and is entitled to realization, through national effort and international co-operation and in accordance with the organization and resources of each State, of the economic, social and cultural rights indispensable for his dignity and the free development of his personality.

Article 23

1. Everyone has the right to work, to free choice of employment, to just and favourable conditions of work and to protection against unemployment.

2. Everyone, without any discrimination, has the right to equal pay for equal work.

3. Everyone who works has the right to just and favourable remuneration ensuring for himself and his family an existence worthy of human dignity, and supplemented, if necessary, by other means of social protection.

4. Everyone has the right to form and to join trade unions for the protection of his interests.

Article 24
Everyone has the right to rest and leisure, including reasonable limitation of working hours and periodic holidays with pay.

Article 25
1. Everyone has the right to a standard of living adequate for the health and well-being of himself and of his family, including food, clothing, housing and medical care and necessary social services, and the right to security in the event of unemployment, sickness, disability, widowhood, old age or other lack of livelihood in circumstances beyond his control.

2. Motherhood and childhood are entitled to special care and assistance. All children, whether born in or out of wedlock, shall enjoy the same social protection.

Article 26
1. Everyone has the right to education. Education shall be free, at least in the elementary and fundamental stages. Elementary education shall be compulsory. Technical and professional education shall be made generally available and higher education shall be equally accessible to all on the basis of merit.

2. Education shall be directed to the full development of the human personality and to the strengthening of respect for human rights and fundamental freedoms. It shall promote understanding, tolerance and friendship among all nations, racial or religious groups, and shall further the activities of the United Nations for the maintenance of peace.

3. Parents have a prior right to choose the kind of education that shall be given to their children.

Article 27
1. Everyone has the right freely to participate in the cultural life of the community, to enjoy the arts and to share in scientific advancement and its benefits.

2. Everyone has the right to the protection of the moral and material interests resulting from any scientific, literary or artistic production of which he is the author.

Article 28

Everyone is entitled to a social and international order in which the rights and freedoms set forth in this Declaration can be fully realized.

Article 29

1. Everyone has duties to the community in which alone the free and full development of his personality is possible.

2. In the exercise of his rights and freedoms, everyone shall be subject only to such limitations as are determined by law solely for the purpose of securing due recognition and respect for the rights and freedoms of others and of meeting the just requirements of morality, public order and the general welfare in a democratic society.

3. These rights and freedoms may in no case be exercised contrary to the purposes and principles of the United Nations.

Article 30

Nothing in the Declaration may be interpreted as implying for any State, group or person any right to engage in any activity or to perform any act aimed at the destruction of any of the rights and freedoms set forth herein.

Appendix B

The following breakdown is based on an examination of votes on fourteen resolutions that divided the General Assembly. The resolutions were selected as a cross-sample, and touched on such issues as: terrorism, colonialism, the Mideast, nuclear proliferation, and the recognition of revolutionaries and governments-in-exile.

GENERAL ASSEMBLY VOTING PATTERNS

COUNTRY	VOTES CAST WITH THE US %	VOTES CAST AGAINST US %	ABSTENTIONS* %	VOTES MISSED %	NUMERICAL ‡ RATING
Portugal	79	0	21		11
South Africa	100	0	0	29	10
United Kingdom	64	15	21		7
Israel	54	8	38	7	6
France	43	7	50		5
Belgium	36	7	57		4
Italy	36	7	57		4
Luxembourg	36	7	57		4
Bolivia	55	27	18	21	3
Brazil	43	21	36		3
West Germany	29	14	57		2
Nicaragua	42	29	29		2
Canada	29	21	50		1
Denmark	29	21	50		1
Ireland	29	21	50		1
Spain	36	36	28		0
Netherlands	29	29	42		0

Japan	21	21	58		0
Uruguay	21	21	58		0
Malawi	15	15	70	7	0
Maldives	0	0	0	100	0
Costa Rica	36	43	21		−1
Dominican Republic	33	45	22	36	−1
Austria	29	35	36		−1
Norway	21	29	50		−1
Khmer Republic	40	50	10	29	−1
Paraguay	17	25	58	14	−1
Mauritius	0	100	0	93	−1
Iceland	21	36	43		−2
Greece	29	50	21		−3
Bahamas	22	56	22	36	−3
Finland	14	36	50		−3
Sweden	7	29	64		−3
Barbados	36	64	0		−4
Haiti	30	70	0	29	−4
Laos	30	70	0	29	−4
Venezuela	23	54	23	7	−4
Honduras	21	50	29		−4
Gambia	16	84	0	57	−4
New Zealand	21	58	21		−5
Australia	14	50	36		−5
El Salvador	14	50	36		−5
Colombia	15	54	31	7	−5
Fiji	23	69	8	7	−6
Gabon	20	80	0	29	−6
Panama	20	80	0	29	−6
Guatemala	14	57	29		−6
Lesotho	21	72	7		−7
Chile	17	75	8	14	−7
Bhutan	28	73	0	21	−8
Ecuador	21	79	0		−8
Ghana	21	79	0		−8
Ivory Coast	21	79	0		−8
Liberia	21	79	0		−8
Malaysia	21	79	0		−8
Mexico	21	79	0		−8
Philippines	21	79	0		−8
Singapore	21	79	0		−8
Thailand	21	79	0		−8
Jordan	17	83	0	14	−8
Upper Volta	17	83	0	14	−8
Botswana	15	77	8	7	−8
Morocco	15	77	8	7	−8
Burma	14	72	14		−8
Iran	14	72	14		−8

Turkey	14	72	14	−8
Swaziland	14	72	14	−8
Mauritania	15	85	0	7	−9
Peru	15	85	0	7	−9
Rwanda	15	85	0	7	−9
Somalia	15	85	0	7	−9
Togo	15	85	0	7	−9
Tunisia	15	85	0	7	−9
Cyprus	14	79	7		−9
Ethiopia	14	79	7		−9
India	14	79	7		−9
Kenya	14	79	7		−9
Lebanon	14	79	7		−9
Nigeria	14	79	7		−9
Sierra Leone	14	79	7		−9
Nepal	14	79	7		−9
Burundi	14	86	0		−10
Chad	14	86	0		−10
Congo	14	86	0		−10
Dahomey	14	86	0		−10
Democratic Yemen	14	86	0		−10
Egypt	14	86	0		−10
Equatorial Guinea	14	86	0		−10
Guinea	14	86	0		−10
Indonesia	14	86	0		−10
Iraq	14	86	0		−10
Libyan Arab Republic	14	86	0		−10
Mali	14	86	0		−10
Algeria	14	86	0		−10
Niger	14	86	0		−10
Romania	14	86	0		−10
Sri Lanka	14	86	0		−10
Sudan	14	86	0		−10
Uganda	14	86	0		−10
Tanzania	14	86	0		−10
Unit. Rep.				
Yemen	14	86	0		−10
Yugoslavia	14	86	0		−10
Zambia	14	86	0		−10
Jamaica	8	84	8	7	−10
Saudi Arabia	8	84	8	7	−10
Trinidad and Tobago	8	84	8	7	−10
Albania	8	92	0	14	−10
Malta	8	92	0	14	−10
China	8	92	0	7	−11
Central African Rep.	8	92	0	7	−11
Oman	8	92	0	7	−11
Senegal	8	92	0	7	−11
Syria	8	92	0	7	−11

Argentina	7	86	7	−11
Bulgaria	7	86	7	−11
Byelorussia SSR	7	86	7	−11
Cuba	7	86	7	−11
Czechoslovakia	7	86	7	−11
East Germany	7	86	7	−11
Guyana	7	86	7	−11
Hungary	7	86	7	−11
Mongolia	7	86	7	−11
Poland	7	86	7	−11
Qatar	7	86	7	−11
Ukrainian SSR	7	86	7	−11
USSR	7	86	7	−11
Kuwait	7	93	0	−12
Madagascar	7	93	0	−12
Pakistan	7	93	0	−12
Afghanistan	7	93	0	−12
Bahrain	7	93	0	−12
Cameroon	7	93	0	−12
United Arab Emirate	7	93	0	−12
Zaire	7	93	0	−12

*abstentions when the U.S. did not abstain
‡determined by assigning +1 to vote with the U.S.
                              −1 to vote against U.S.
                               0 to abstentions

Appendix C
Human Rights Instruments

1. The International Covenant on Economic, Social and Cultural Rights (not yet in force; i.e., the requisite number of countries—35—have not yet ratified it, so that it is not yet technically binding upon the signatories).

2. The International Covenant on Civil and Political Rights (not yet in force).

3. The Optional Protocol to the International Covenant on Civil and Political Rights (not yet in force).

4. The Convention on the Prevention and Punishment of the Crime of Genocide (in force since January 12, 1951).

5. The Convention on the Non-Applicability of Statutory Limitations to War Crimes and Crimes Against Humanity (in force since November 11, 1970).

6. The International Convention on the Elimination of All Forms of Racial Discrimination (in force since January 4, 1969).

7. The Convention Relating to the Status of Refugees (in force since April 22, 1954).

8. The Convention Relating to the Status of Stateless Persons (in force since June 6, 1960).

9. The Convention on the Reduction of Statelessness (not yet in force).

10. The Convention on Political Rights of Women (in force since July 7, 1954).

11. The Convention on the Nationality of Married Women (in force since August 11, 1958).

12. The Convention on Consent to Marriage, Minimum Age for Marriage and Registration of Marriages (in force since December 9, 1964).

13. The Convention on the International Right of Correction (in force since August 24, 1962).

14. The Protocol Amending the Slavery Convention—signed at Geneva on September 25, 1926 (in force since December 7, 1953).

15. The Slavery Convention of 25 December 1926 as amended (in force since July 7, 1955).

16. and 17. The Supplementary Conventions on the Abolition of Slavery, the Slave Trade, Institutions and Practises Similar to Slavery (in force since April 30, 1957).

18. The Convention for the Suppression of the Traffic in Persons and of the Exploitation of the Prostitution of Others (in force since July 25, 1951).

The United States has signed the Genocide treaty (No. 4); the Convention on the Elimination of All Forms of Racial Discrimination (No. 6); and the Marriage Convention (No. 13). We have ratified the Protocol on Refugees (No. 38); and the three slavery conventions (Nos. 15, 16, 17).

Index